AF521802

Best-Selling Albums

Best-Selling Albums

From Vinyl Records to Digital Downloads

Contributors:
Dan Auty, Chris Barrett, Justin Cawthorne, Hamish Champ, Johnny Dee, Peter Dodd, Charlotte Greig, Chris McNab, Gene Sculatti

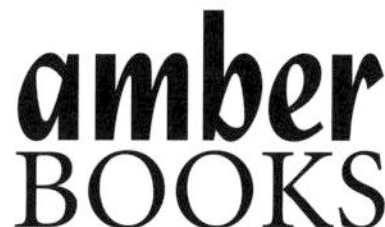

Published by
Amber Books Ltd
74–77 White Lion Street
London
N1 9PF
United Kingdom
www.amberbooks.co.uk
Appstore: itunes.com/apps/amberbooksltd
Facebook: www.facebook.com/amberbooks
Twitter: @amberbooks

ISBN: 978-1-78274-298-2

Project Editor: Michael Spilling
Additional Research: Kieron Connolly, Mark Batley, Terry Forshaw
Picture Research: Terry Forshaw
Design: Andrew Easton

Printed in China

Image credits:
The publisher would like to thank Apple Corps Ltd. for reproducing The Beatles' album covers on pages 36/37, 48/49, 50/51, 56/57, 58/59, 60/61, 64/65, 68/69, and 70/71.

Contents

Introduction

Let's face it, while we might not all admit it, everybody loves lists. And when it comes to music, lists featuring – or in many cases *not* featuring – one's favourite artists are a must-read.

Assessing each decade in turn, this book lists the top 20 selling albums from the 1960s, 70s, 80s, 90s and 2000s. For practical reasons it was decided that a shorter list of the top 10 best-selling albums would suffice for the 1950s, since the LP only appeared in truly commercial form towards the end of that decade; and five albums are featured from the 2010s, since the current decade is only half way through at the time of writing.

The ranking for the albums is based on the number of platinum and multi-platinum certifications each album received from the Recording Industry Association of America (RIAA). These awards provide one of the most effective and reliable ways to measure sales success. The figures represent minimum sales for each album – each platinum award represents sales of at least one million units – but they do provide a consistent way to rate the relative position of each decade's best-selling albums. The rankings also include UK sales figures, from the Official Chart Company and the

ABOVE: Led Zeppelin's debut album remains one of the most influential in rock history, spending 79 weeks in the UK chart and 50 in the US.

BPI (British Phonographic Industry). These figures also have the advantage of showing album sales from the date of first release right up to the present day. Compilation or greatest hits albums are not included in this list, although live albums and original soundtracks, where all of the songs have been collected together or recorded specifically for the album, are included.

Each entry is accompanied by essential information enabling the reader to make sense of the album's wider context in musical and cultural terms.

ABOVE: Six singles were released from Taylor Swift's 2010 album *Speak Now*, all of which received gold or platinum certification.

Top Sellers

Predictably, nine of the top 20 albums of the 1960s are by The Beatles, while rock giants Led Zeppelin dominate the 1970s. The 1980s feature a wide range of artists and genres, from pop-soul divas such as Whitney Houston, through to monsters of the heavy metal scene such as Metallica.

The 1990s' entries show how much country music took a hold of the US music market, thanks to Garth Brooks' creative output and Shania Twain's blend of country and pop, while the boy band pop phenomenon is represented by the group Backstreet Boys. The success of boy bands continued into the new century with the likes of *NSYNC, with the 2000s largely dominated by R&B, hip-hop and rap from artists such as Eminem and 50 Cent.

What the entries in this book provide is clear evidence of the dominance in recent years of US artists on their own turf. Whereas the 1960s and 1970s saw UK acts holding the top best-selling slots, it is American talent that held sway in the 1990s and well into the new millennium, British singer Adele's *21* being a rare exception.

ORIGINAL BROADWAY CAST
KERMIT BLOOMGARDEN
WITH
HERBERT GREENE
IN ASSOCIATION WITH FRANK PRODUCTIONS INC.
presents
THE MUSIC MAN
New Musical Comedy
STARRING ROBERT PRESTON
BOOK, MUSIC & LYRICS BY MEREDITH WILLSON
STORY BY MEREDITH WILLSON & FRANKLIN LACEY
WITH BARBARA COOK · DAVID BURNS · PERT KELTON
IGGIE WOLFINGTON · THE BUFFALO BILLS · HELEN RAYMOND · PAUL REED · EDDIE HODGES
CHOREOGRAPHY BY ONNA WHITE SETTINGS & LIGHTING BY HOWARD BAY COSTUMES BY RAOUL PENE DU BOIS
ORCHESTRATIONS BY DON WALKER DANCE ARR. BY LAURENCE ROSENTHAL PRODUCTION ASSOCIATE SYLVIA DRULIE
MUSICAL DIRECTION & VOCAL ARR. BY HERBERT GREENE
ENTIRE PRODUCTION STAGED BY MORTON DA COSTA
Capitol RECORDS
HIGH FIDELITY RECORDING

CS 8158
STEREO
FIDELITY
CBS
Lp
GUNFIGHTER
BALLADS
AND TRAIL SONGS
MARTY
ROBBINS
Big Iron ★ Cool Water ★ Billy the Kid
A Hundred and Sixty Acres ★ They're
Hanging Me Tonight ★ The Master's Call
The Strawberry Roan ★ Running Gun
El Paso ★ In the Valley ★ Utah Carol
The Little Green Valley

rom the Sound Track of the Motion Picture
Capitol RECORDS
HIGH FIDELITY RECORDING
Rodgers and Hammerstein's
Oklahoma!

PC 8163
STEREO
FIDELITY
MILES DAVIS
COLUMBIA
GUARANTEED HIGH FIDELITY
Lp
Kind of Blu
with Julian "Cannonball" Adderly
Paul Chambers
James Cobb
John Coltrane
Bill Evans
Wynton Kelly

The Best-Selling Albums of the 1950s

The album charts of the early 1950s represent the last phase of popular music before rock 'n' roll took over. Seen from one perspective, the range of this music – from Rodgers and Hammerstein to Frank Sinatra, from Mantovani to Mitch Miller – is the sound of a lost era. From another, it's a reminder of a time when popular music was in its infancy and only just developing, in terms of artists, formats and markets.

The music made for the new albums market in the 1950s was altogether different from that produced for the singles market. As far as the record companies were concerned, singles were predominantly for teenagers and children. They also catered to the tastes of less well-off adults; black music and country music were both predominantly released on singles. The album charts during the 1950s represented the tastes of the more wealthy section of the American public. This was partly based on simple economics – albums cost more than two dollars to buy, singles under a dollar – but it was also a legacy of earlier decades, in which longer classical works had needed to be released as 'albums'. As a result, the 1950s' albums chart overwhelmingly reflected the tastes of older, more conservative record buyers.

Even a cursory glance at the best-selling albums of the 1950s confirms – with the striking exceptions of Elvis Presley and Miles Davis – that this is not a list of musical innovators. Instead, it points to the fact that the top-selling music of a period is not always what is best remembered by posterity or discussed by critics. The popular image we now have of the 1950s – rock 'n' roll, jazz and James Dean – actually represents aspects of the culture that at the time were the exceptions. If you want to know why James Dean became a rebel without a cause, you just need to look at the album charts. The reason why rock 'n' roll was such a sensation becomes plain: it's because mom and pop were busy listening to Mantovani, Johnny Mathis, Ray Conniff and Tennessee Ernie Ford.

Another perennial favourite of 1950s' album buyers were the soundtracks to stage and movie musicals. The stage musical may have been coming towards the end of its golden age in the 1950s, but you'd never have thought so at the time. The popularity of the musical is certainly reflected in the list of the decade's best-selling albums, with the Broadway production of *My Fair Lady* and the movie version of *Oklahoma!* both appearing in the Top 10.

The 1950s' albums charts, then, were not the sound of teenage rebellion – they were the sound of middle America kicking back after the trauma of World War II and enjoying a new era of prosperity. The 1950s did see a number of revolutionary developments that would transform the record industry and popular culture forever: the new sounds of rock 'n' roll were starting to emerge into the mainstream and the technological advances of the era began to reveal what recorded music was capable of. But this was also a time when most album buyers prized the familiar over the radical. Rock 'n' roll may have ruled the singles charts, but for most listeners it was the enchanting show scores, the pop standards and the easy-listening favourites that truly defined the sound of the decade.

1950s
10

The Music Man

| • **Album sales:** 1,000,000 | • **Release date:** January 1958 |

The Music Man opened at the Majestic Theatre, New York, in December 1957 and ran for 1,379 performances, establishing its composer Meredith Willson as one of the leading figures of American musical theatre. The cast recording of the show became one of the biggest-selling albums of the decade, and several of the songs, including 'Seventy-Six Trombones' and 'Till There Was You' became all-time classics.

The story of *The Music Man* told of a small Iowa community who club together to create a marching band for their children. The characters and setting were drawn from Willson's own Midwestern boyhood and events take place in around 1912. The part of Harold Hill, a con man who arrives in town and is converted into a decent, law-abiding citizen, was memorably played by Robert Preston, whose songs feature rapid-fire, percussive effects. The more romantic songs were sung by Barbara Cook, who played Marian, the librarian that Hill falls in love with.

Cook's singing became one of the highlights of the album. The duet 'Till There Was You' lived on, notably with The Beatles' cover version on their 1963 album *With The Beatles*.

Number One singles: None

Grammy awards: Best original cast album (Broadway or TV)

Label: US & UK: Capitol

Recorded in: New York, USA

Personnel:
Barbara Cook
Robert Preston (d. 1987)
Eddie Hodges
Pert Kelton (d. 1968)
Herbert Greene (d. 1985)
Dick Jones
Verne Reed
Paul Reed
Buffalo Bills
Adnia Rice
Peggy Mondo (d. 1991)
Elaine Swann
Adam Hodges
Iggie Wolfington (d. 2004)
ensemble
Bob Norbert Orchestra

Producer: N/A

BROADWAY MUSICALS

The 1950s have been described as the 'golden era' of Broadway. With television only just establishing itself as a major competitor to stage productions, the 1950s saw an unprecedented output by the Broadway theatres of high quality musicals from luminaries such as Rodgers and Hammerstein, Irving Berlin, Cole Porter, and Lerner & Loewe. The popularity of Broadway musicals was aided by post-war prosperity (the American economy had not been ravaged by war in the same way as Europe) and a seeming explosion of talented actors and actresses. Furthermore, the content of musicals was much more absorbing than the saccharine productions of the 1940s. *West Side Story* (1957), for example, took as its subject gang warfare amongst the Puerto Rican community, punctuating this theme with timeless tracks by Leonard Bernstein.

▲ **BACK COVER**

1 **Overture/Rock Island (5:29)**
2 **Iowa Stubborn (1:59)**
3 **Ya Got Trouble (3:48)**
4 **Piano Lesson (1:56)**
5 **Good Night My Someone (2:46)**
6 **Seventy-Six Trombones (3:01)**
7 **Sincere (1:40)**
8 **The Sadder-But-Wiser Girl For Me (1:41)**
9 **Pick-A-Little, Take-A-Little/Goodnight (1:57)**
10 **Goodnight Ladies/Marian the Librarian (2:44)**
11 **My White Knight (3:02)**
12 **Wells Fargo Wagon (2:13)**
13 **It's You (1:25)**
14 **Shipoopi (2:11)**
15 **Lida Rose/Will I Ever Tell You? (4:17)**
16 **Gary, Indiana (1:25)**
17 **Till There Was You (2:46)**

Total album length: 44 minutes

ORIGINAL BROADWAY CAST
KERMIT BLOOMGARDEN
WITH
HERBERT GREENE
IN ASSOCIATION WITH FRANK PRODUCTIONS INC.
presents
THE MUSIC MAN
A New Musical Comedy
STARRING ROBERT PRESTON
BOOK, MUSIC & LYRICS BY MEREDITH WILLSON
STORY BY MEREDITH WILLSON & FRANKLIN LACEY
WITH BARBARA COOK · DAVID BURNS · PERT KELTON
IGGIE WOLFINGTON · THE BUFFALO BILLS · HELEN RAYMOND · PAUL REED · EDDIE HODGES
CHOREOGRAPHY BY ONNA WHITE SETTINGS & LIGHTING BY HOWARD BAY COSTUMES BY RAOUL PENE DU BOIS
ORCHESTRATIONS BY DON WALKER DANCE ARR. BY LAURENCE ROSENTHAL PRODUCTION ASSOCIATE SYLVIA DRULIE
MUSICAL DIRECTION & VOCAL ARR. BY HERBERT GREENE
ENTIRE PRODUCTION STAGED BY MORTON DA COSTA
Capitol RECORDS
HIGH FIDELITY RECORDING

Hymns

| • **Album sales:** 1,000,000 | • **Release date:** 1957 |

In the spring of 1957, Tennessee Ernie Ford was in the midst of transforming himself from a country and western singer (best known for his chart-topping single '16 Tons') into an all-round entertainer and TV presenter, known for his catchphrase 'Bless your little pea-pickin' hearts'. His TV show, *The Ford Show*, had debuted on NBC in the fall of 1956, and by the end of its first season was Number One in the ratings.

Ford had fought with TV executives to be allowed to finish each show with a spiritual number. To the producers' surprise, this turned out to be one of the most successful sections of the show. In response to huge popular demand, Ford decided to make his next album exclusively devotional in nature. Simply entitled *Hymns*, the album combined famous numbers like 'Rock Of Ages' and 'The Old Rugged Cross' with lesser-known selections such as 'In The Garden'. The material was ideally suited to Ford's powerful voice and it quickly became the biggest hit album of his career.

Hymns was the first religious album to go gold. It remained on the charts for an unprecedented 277 weeks, breaking all records and eventually selling over a million copies. In 1963, *Hymns* was honoured by Capitol as being the most successful LP ever recorded by a Capitol artist. His subsequent album *Great Gospel Songs* won a Grammy award in 1964.

Number One singles:
None

Grammy awards:
None

Recorded in:
Los Angeles, USA

Label: US: Capitol

Personnel:
Tennessee Ernie Ford (d. 1991)
Jack Fascinato (d. 1994)

Producer: N/A

TV IN THE 1950s

During the 1950s, television became a force that musicians, groups and managers could no longer ignore. In the United States, television sets began their spread during the 1930s, with 31,000 sets in the US as early as 1931. However, in the late 1940s and early 1950s, a dramatic increase in the number of broadcast companies, a (relative) cheapening of set technology, and the easy availability of loan agreements resulted in three million sets sold by 1955, and 75 per cent of US homes had a set by the following year. The typical American family would watch an average of five hours of programming each day, with light entertainment programmes – dramas, musicals, comedies and westerns – forming the bulk of content. Musicians now had a medium to project themselves visually into almost every US home.

▲ **BACK COVER**

1. **Who At My Door Is Standing (3:18)**
2. **Rock Of Ages (2:28)**
3. **Softly And Tenderly (2:43)**
4. **Sweet Hour Of Prayer (2:51)**
5. **My Task (2:15)**
6. **Let The Lower Lights Be Burning (2:02)**
7. **The Ninety And Nine (2:35)**
8. **The Old Rugged Cross (2:41)**
9. **When They Ring Those Golden Bells (3:34)**
10. **In The Garden (2:45)**
11. **Ivory Palaces (3:01)**
12. **Others (2:41)**

Total album length: 33 minutes

Tennessee Ernie Ford:
Hymns
Capitol
RECORDS
CAPITOL RECORDS
HIGH FIDELITY
RECORDING

1950s

Love Is The Thing

| • **Album sales:** 1,000,000 | • **Release date:** 1957 |

Nat 'King' Cole's *Love Is The Thing* proved a million seller for Capitol Records on its release in 1957. Among its many hit songs was 'Stardust', which had been issued in EP format earlier in the year. Composer Hoagy Carmichael said it was his favourite version of the song, reviving as it did the original introduction to the verse, and it became one of America's best-loved songs.

Throughout the album, arranger Gordon Jenkins provided a lush orchestral backdrop to Cole's understated yet carefully enunciated vocals. The result was to create a romantic mood that rendered Cole's limited vocal range irrelevant. As Cole himself put it: "I lean heavily on the lyrics. I try to tell a story with the melody as background." The combination of Jenkins' swooning strings and Cole's relaxed, urbane singing style gave a classic feel to every track on the album, including the most sentimental ballads and the most hackneyed jazz standards.

The success of *Love Is The Thing* helped to establish Cole not just as a 'sepia Sinatra', but also as the leading ballad singer of his time during a period when race was still considered by record companies to be a major obstacle to mainstream sales potential.

Number One singles: None

Grammy awards: None

Label: US & UK: Capitol

Recorded in: N/A

Personnel:
Nat 'King' Cole (d. 1965)
Gordon Jenkins (d. 1985)
and his orchestra

Producer:
N/A

AFRICAN-AMERICANS IN 1950s' MUSIC

The post-war period saw the increasing influence of African-American musicians on popular music. Jazz and swing were already established movements by the beginning of the 1950s, but the driving force of black music during the decade was 'rhythm and blues'. The rhythm and blues style was primarily an African-American creation of the 1940s – indeed, the term was coined in 1949 by Jerry Wexler (later of Atlantic Records) and was initially used to distinguish black rock and roll from that played by white musicians. The rhythm and blues influence spread out from its African-American roots to have a formative input on the music of white artists such as Elvis Presley and The Beatles. Black music provided a solid, danceable beat, and with racial segregation illegal in the US from the 1940s it could filter more freely out into the wider society.

▲ **BACK COVER**

1. **When I Fall In love (3:11)**
2. **End Of A Love Affair (3:22)**
3. **Stardust (3:15)**
4. **Stay As Sweet As You Are (2:59)**
5. **Where Can I Go Without You (2:57)**
6. **Maybe It's Because I Love You Too Much (2:50)**
7. **Love Letters (2:46)**
8. **Ain't Misbehavin' (3:17)**
9. **I Thought About Marie (3:06)**
10. **At Last (3:00)**
11. **It's All In The Game (3:07)**
12. **When Sunny Gets Blue (2:46)**
13. **Love Is The Thing (3:01)**

Total album length: 40 minutes

Capitol RECORDS
EMI
Love is the Thing
the voice of
NAT "KING" COLE
with the orchestra of
Gordon Jenkins

Heavenly

| • **Album sales:** 2,000,000 | • **Release date:** August 1959 |

Released in 1959, *Heavenly* was Johnny Mathis' tenth album in just three years and the most successful of his standard album releases – its sales were exceeded only by his 1958 *Merry Christmas* album and a later compilation of his greatest hits.

Heavenly didn't succeed by doing anything patricularly innovative, but simpy by giving the public exactly what they had come to expect from Mathis, by now an established star. That meant a selection of show tunes, some standards and a smattering of new material, all delivered in the utterly relaxed Mathis tenor.

The title track was an early composition from the writing team of Burt Bacharach and Hal David. Another successful track was the vocal version of Errol Garner's jazz classic 'Misty', to which Mathis had added new lyrics by Joe Burke. 'Misty' went on to become Johnny Mathis' first hit single in two years.

Heavenly may have been more of the same as far as critics were concerned, but with this album Mathis appeared to have got the balance just right. The public responded with great enthusiasm, and Mathis was rewarded with five weeks at Number One. It went on to spend a remarkable five-and-a-half years in the charts.

Number One singles: None

Grammy awards: None

Label: US: Columbia; UK: Embassy

Recorded in: New York, USA

Personnel:
Johnny Mathis
Glen Osser (d. 2014) orchestra

Producer:
Mitch Miller (d. 2010)

MATHIS' LATER CAREER

Johnny Mathis had one of the most durable careers in the music industry. Although his popularity peaked during the 1950s and 1960s, during which time he established himself as a solid album artist, he maintained his career into the 1970s by moving into more pop/rock-oriented numbers. The duet single 'Too Much, Too Little, Too Late' brought Mathis a Number One in 1978 (the second of his career), after which duets with major female artistes such as Dionne Warwick, Gladys Knight and Natalie Cole brought him further respectable success. Even through the 1990s, Mathis was recording, releasing and selling albums, and received a Grammy in 1992 for Best Traditional Pop Performance.

▲ **BACK COVER**

1. **Heavenly (3:23)**
2. **Hello, Young Lovers (4:18)**
3. **A Lovely Way To Spend An Evening (4:04)**
4. **A Ride On A Rainbow (4:11)**
5. **More Than You Know (4:18)**
6. **Something I Dreamed Last Night (4:32)**
7. **Misty (3:38)**
8. **Stranger In Paradise (4:06)**
9. **Moonlight Becomes You (4:06)**
10. **They Say It's Wonderful (3:33)**
11. **I'll Be Easy To Find (4:04)**
12. **That's All (3.46)**

Total album length: 48 minutes

JOHNNY MATHIS
HEAVENLY

HEAVENLY
HELLO, YOUNG LOVERS
A LOVELY WAY TO SPEND AN EVENING
A RIDE ON A RAINBOW
MORE THAN YOU KNOW
SOMETHING I DREAMED LAST NIGHT

MISTY
STRANGER IN PARADISE
MOONLIGHT BECOMES YOU
THEY SAY IT'S WONDERFUL
I'LL BE EASY TO FIND
THAT'S ALL

Gunfighter Ballads And Trail Songs

| • **Album sales:** 2,000,000 | • **Release date:** September 1959 |

Marty Robbins already had a reputation for versatility in 1959 – he had recorded straight country, smooth pop, novelty songs and even some gentle rock 'n' roll – but when he cut his classic album of Western songs he surprised everyone. The cowboy song had had its heyday years before when the likes of Gene Autry had ruled the airwaves, and was generally seen as hopelessly out of date.

Robbins nursed a secret passion for this music, however, and had quietly composed a whole set of cowboy songs of his own. One afternoon in Nashville he went into the studio and recorded them all, aided and abetted by his back-up singers (later stars in their own right) brothers Jim and Tompall Glaser. The result was that this side project became by far the biggest-selling album of Robbins' career. Its phenomenal success began with the release of the single 'El Paso' which, despite being four-and-a-half minutes in length, was an immediate hit, reaching Number One on both pop and country charts.

The album soon followed suit and went on to become the definitive cowboy album – the aural equivalent of the classic TV series of the era, *Bonanza* or *Gunsmoke*. Robbins won a Grammy for Best Country and Western Performance for 'El Paso' in 1960.

Number One singles:
US: El Paso

Grammy Awards:
Best country & western performance – El Paso

Label: US: Columbia; UK: CBS

Recorded in: Nashville, USA

Personnel:
Marty Robbins (d. 1982)
Thomas Grady Martin (d. 2001)
Jack H. Prett
Bob Moore
Louis Dunn
Jim Glaser
Tompall Glaser (d. 2013)

Producer:
Don Law

THE 1950s' TV WESTERN

As television became a more culturally entrenched phenomenon in the 1950s, programme producers sought dependable formulas to entertain the new mass audience. The Western genre was ideal, combining strong men, beautiful women, action and often song. Movie theatre Westerns initially declined in number owing to competitive programming on TV from shows such as *The Cisco Kid* (1950–56), *The Lone Ranger* (1949–57) and *The Roy Rodgers Show* (1951–57). However, Hollywood fought back with intelligent, character-study movies such as *The Gunfighter* (1950), starring Gregory Peck, and Fred Zinneman's *High Noon* (1952), and also with epic wide-screen spectaculars including William Wyler's *The Big Country* (1958) and the updated Western *Bad Day at Black Rock*, with Spencer Tracey as the famous one-armed hero.

▲ **BACK COVER**

1. **Big Iron (3:58)**
2. **Cool Water (3:11)**
3. **Billy The Kid (2:21)**
4. **A Hundred And Sixty Acres (1:42)**
5. **They're Hanging Me Tonight (3:06)**
6. **The Strawberry Roan (3:25)**
7. **El Paso (4:21)**
8. **In The Valley (1:51)**
9. **The Master's Call (3:07)**
10. **Running Gun (2:12)**
11. **Down In The Little Green Valley (2:30)**
12. **Utah Carol (3:15)**

Total album length: 35 minutes

CS 8158 STEREO FIDELITY

CBS
GUARANTEED HIGH FIDELITY

GUNFIGHTER BALLADS
AND TRAIL SONGS

MARTY ROBBINS

Big Iron ★ Cool Water ★ Billy the Kid
A Hundred and Sixty Acres ★ They're Hanging Me Tonight ★ The Master's Call
The Strawberry Roan ★ Running Gun
El Paso ★ In the Valley ★ Utah Carol
The Little Green Valley

PHOTO: DON CRAVENS OF BLACK STAR

Merry Christmas

| • **Album sales:** 2,000,000 | • **Release date:** 1958 |

Over a 50-year career in the music business, Johnny Mathis has recorded an extraordinary nine Christmas albums, but this, his first venture into seasonal recording, remains the best loved. At the time of the recording Mathis was 23 and the hottest young crooner in the business. He'd just made his film debut, appearing as a nightclub singer, and a Christmas album was an obvious next move for Mathis.

For the album he was paired up with the legendary arranger Percy Faith and his orchestra. The material they chose was mostly of the tried and tested variety: Bing Crosby's 'White Christmas' is here, as is Nat 'King' Cole's signature 'Christmas Song'. However, Mathis managed to find a signature tune of his own as well with the opening 'Winter Wonderland'.

The result was an album that has continually sold for more than 40 years, to the point where for many Americans it's an integral part of the Christmas experience. As Oprah Winfrey has said 'If you don't have Johnny Mathis, you don't have Christmas', while Mathis himself jokes that, "The only thing I'm not so fond of at Christmas is hearing myself so much."

RELIGION IN THE 1950s

The enduring appeal of Christmas albums is set against the ambiguous trends of post-World War II Christianity in the Western world. In the United States, church attendance was set at around 50 per cent of the population, slightly less in European countries, and this was the high water mark of 20th century formal Christianity. Christianity was still the bedrock of social and governmental values in the United States, and the country has sustained its church attendance to the present day. In Europe, however, the domestic traumas of World War II precipitated several 'death of God' theologies that picked up on a disillusionment with orthodox Christianity. In many UK cities, for example, church attendance dropped to 10 per cent of urban population by the 1960s, and has never recovered.

Number One singles: None

Grammy awards: None

Label: US: Columbia/CBS; UK: Fontana

Recorded in: N/A

Personnel:
Johnny Mathis
The Percy Faith Orchestra

Producer:
Percy Faith (d. 1976)

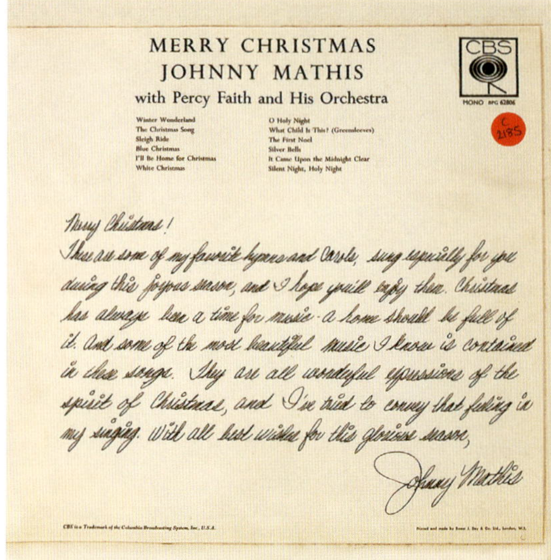

▲ **BACK COVER**

1. **Winter Wonderland (3:18)**
2. **Christmas Song (4:18)**
3. **Sleigh Ride (3:01)**
4. **Blue Christmas (3:02)**
5. **I'll Be Home For Christmas (4:06)**
6. **White Christmas (2:32)**
7. **O Holy Night (4:36)**
8. **What Child Is This? (4:00)**
9. **First Noel (3:50)**
10. **Silver Bells (3:34)**
11. **It Came Upon A Midnight Clear (3:11)**
12. **Silent Night (3:55)**

Total album length: 44 minutes

1950s

Oklahoma!

| • **Album sales:** 2,000,000 | • **Release date:** August 1955 |

Oklahoma! the movie arrived 12 years after the opening of the Broadway show. Based on *Green Grow The Lilacs*, the public were still entranced by Rodgers and Hammerstein's first work together and what became a landmark musical. The accompanying soundtrack to the movie sold 2,000,000 copies.

Composer Richard Rodgers and lyricist Oscar Hammerstein had a remarkable degree of control over the film version, ensuring that Hollywood remained faithful to the original work. Only two of the original songs ('Lonely Room' and 'It's a Scandal! It's a Outrage!') were missing from the two-and-a-half-hour movie, and Jay Blackton continued to conduct. The orchestrations of arranger Robert Russell Bennett were recorded in stereo (as opposed to the mono recording of the Broadway cast album), giving the lush musical arrangements a breadth and depth that has continued to impress listeners. Complementing the sweeping orchestrations were the voices of the cast, all of them chosen as much for their vocal talent as for their box-office pull as movie stars. Gordon MacRae took the male lead role, while 20-year-old Shirley Jones played the female lead. Gloria Grahame took the role of Ado Annie. Their confident singing added warmth, intimacy and character to the lavish production.

Number One singles: None

Grammy awards: None

Label: US & UK: MCA/Capitol

Recorded in: N/A

Personnel:
Shirley Jones
Gordon MacRae (d. 1986)
Gloria Grahame (d. 1981)
Rod Steiger (d. 2002)
Charlotte Greenwood (d. 1977)
Gene Nelson (d. 1996)
James Whitmore (d. 2009)
Jay Blackton (d. 1994)
Robert Russell Bennett (d. 1981)

Producer:
Ron O'Brien

RODGERS AND HAMMERSTEIN

The surnames of Richard Rodgers and Oscar Hammerstein came to be synonymous with the stage and film musicals of the 1950s. The two men began collaborating on musical productions in 1940, Rodgers having previously worked with Lorenz Hart. Rodgers and Hammerstein's first musical was the blockbuster *Oklahoma!* in 1943. The musical was ground-breaking because it had a substantial plot and characterization, rather than being simply a vehicle for enjoyable songs. This formula enabled the two men to set the pace for musicals over the next decade, with stage productions including *Carousel* (1945), *South Pacific* (1949), *The King and I* (1951) and *The Sound of Music* (1959). The partnership ended with Hammerstein's death from cancer in 1959.

▲ **BACK COVER**

1 **Overture (4:52)**
2 **Oh, What A Beautiful Morning (2:36)**
3 **The Surrey With The Fringe On Top (4:53)**
4 **Kansas City (2:36)**
5 **I Cain't Say No (3:10)**
6 **Many A New Day (3:09)**
7 **People Will Say We're In Love (4:21)**
8 **Pore Jud Is Daid (4:16)**
9 **Out Of My Dreams (2:25)**
10 **The Farmer And The Cowman (2:58)**
11 **All Er Nothin' (2:59)**
12 **Oklahoma! (3:18)**

Total album length: 42 minutes

From the Sound Track of the Motion Picture
Capitol
RECORDS
CAPITOL RECORDS
HIGH FIDELITY
RECORDING
Rodgers and Hammerstein's
Oklahoma!
COPYRIGHT 1955, CAPITOL RECORDS, INC.

My Fair Lady

I • **Album sales:** 3,000,000 I • **Release date:** March 1956 I

This recording of Lerner and Loewe's *My Fair Lady* was performed by the original stage cast, and on its release in 1956 topped the Billboard charts for 292 weeks – a record that has yet to be broken.

The stage musical had been a huge success, running for 2,700 performances. It was considered superior to the average Broadway show: based on George Bernard Shaw's *Pygmalion*, Alan Jay Lerner's lyrics retained much of Shaw's wit and sparkle, while Frederick Loewe's songs ranged from the romantic ('I Could Have Danced All Night' and 'On The Street Where You Live') to the humorous ('The Rain In Spain' and 'Get Me To The Church On Time'). Few musicals can boast as many classic numbers. The original cast featured 22-year-old Julie Andrews (Eliza Doolittle) on top vocal form, Rex Harrison (Henry Higgins) perfecting his urbane 'talk-singing' style, and Stanley Holloway (Alfred P. Doolittle) adding a touch of English music-hall comedy to the proceedings.

Not surprisingly, Broadway fans consider this original mono recording of the stage musical to be fresher than the technically polished recording of the 1964 film, in which Audrey Hepburn played Eliza, with vocals dubbed on by Marni Nixon.

MUSICAL SUPERSTARS

Musicals dominated the turntables, stages and film screens of the 1950s. The 1950s' music charts were frequently topped by show tunes, and the genre made superstars out of figures such as Gene Kelly, Rex Harrison, Yul Brynner, Ethel Merman and Mary Martin. The last two figures from that list performed in a revue concert broadcast live on television from Broadway's Central Theater on 15 June 1953, the occasion being the fiftieth anniversary of the Ford Motor Company. Such was the pull of the event that it was watched by 60 million Americans, and the recordings of Merman and Martin's duets sold 100,000 copies in two days.

Number One singles:
None

Grammy awards: None

Label: US: Columbia;
UK: Philips

Recorded in: London, UK

Personnel:
Julie Andrews
Rex Harrison (d. 1990)
Stanley Holloway (d. 1982)
Gordon Dilworth (d. 1991)
John Michael King (d. 2008)
Philippa Bevans (d. 1968)

Producer:
Goddard Lieberson (d. 1977)

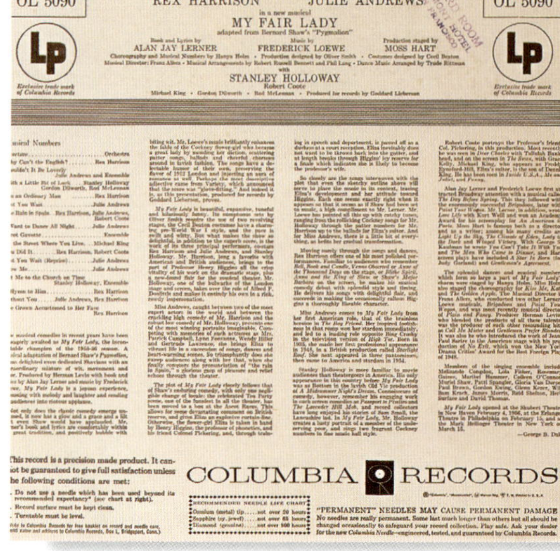

▲ **BACK COVER**

1. **Overture (2:59)**
2. **Why Can't The English (2:40)**
3. **Wouldn't It Be Loverly (3:55)**
4. **With A Little Bit Of Luck (3:55)**
5. **I'm An Ordinary Man (4:38)**
6. **Just You Wait (2:41)**
7. **The Rain In Spain (2:39)**
8. **I Could Have Danced All Night (3:28)**
9. **Ascot Gavotte (3:13)**
10. **On the Street Where You Live (2:56)**
11. **You Did It (4:25)**
12. **Show Me (2:10)**
13. **Get Me To The Church On Time (2:42)**
14. **A Hymn To Him (3:28)**
15. **Without You (2:01)**
16. **I've Grown Accustomed To Her Face (5:14)**

Total album length: 53 minutes

OL 5090

COLUMBIA MASTERWORKS

A HIGH FIDELITY RECORDING

LP

Herman Levin presents

REX HARRISON JULIE ANDREWS MY FAIR LADY

adapted from Bernard Shaw's "Pygmalion"

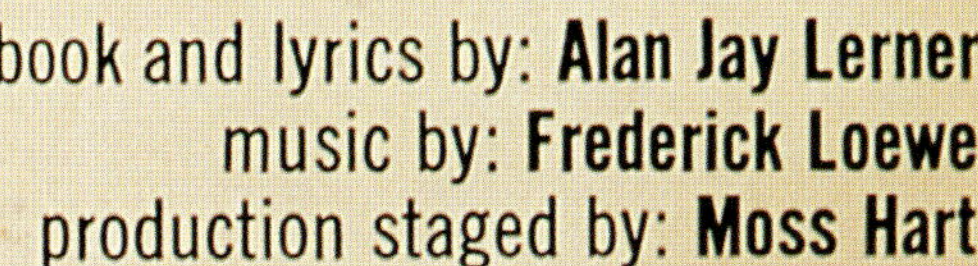

choreography and musical numbers by: **Hanya Holm**
production designed by: **Oliver Smith**
costumes designed by: **Cecil Beaton**

musical director/Franz Allers
orchestrations/Robert Russell Bennett
dance music arrangements/Trude Rittman
lighting/Feder

with **Stanley Holloway**
Robert Coote
Michael King/Rod McLennan

produced for records by Goddard Lieberson

1950s
2

Kind Of Blue

| • **Album sales:** 5,000,000 | • **Release date:** August 1959 |

Recorded in just two days, *Kind Of Blue* is not only the best-selling jazz album of all time, but also one of the most influential. It's likely to be the only jazz album that many rock fans have in their collection, and more than 50 years after its release, its reflective, sparse style is still considered modern.

The recording of *Kind Of Blue* was sandwiched in between two of Davis' big band projects: *Porgy And Bess* (which won a Grammy award for Best Soundtrack) and *Sketches Of Spain*. For *Kind Of Blue*, Davis assembled a small combo featuring pianist Bill Evans, whose input here is almost as great as that of Davis himself, and legendary saxophonists John Coltrane and 'Cannonball' Adderley, who improvise superbly around the haunting modal themes and the crack rhythm section of Chambers and Cobb. The sessions were unrehearsed and spontaneous; Jimmy Cobb later remarked that the resulting recording was "made in heaven".

On release, the album sold respectably for a modern jazz record, but didn't enter the mainstream charts. However, with each passing year its reputation grew, to the extent that it now sells at least 5,000 copies a week in the US, and has sold more than 5,000,000 copies.

Number One singles: None

Grammy awards: None

Label: US: Columbia; UK: Fontana

Recorded in: Columbia 30th Street Studio, New York City, USA

Personnel:
Miles Davis (d. 1991)
John Coltrane (d. 1967)
Julian 'Cannonball' Adderley (d. 1975)
Bill Evans (d. 1980)
Paul Chambers (d. 1969)
Jimmy Cobb
Wynton Kelly (d. 1971)

Producer:
Irving Townsend (d. 1981)

JAZZ IN THE 1950s

The 1950s were a troubled time for world jazz. Rock 'n' roll became the dominant force in popular music, and jazz's commercial appeal fell away almost entirely. As many of the big jazz bands broke up, the smaller groups created idiosyncratic new jazz forms, such as the improvisational West Coast 'cool school', led by figures such as Gerry Mulligan and Dave Brubeck, and the blues- and gospel-oriented 'hard bop' of Art Blakey, Miles Davis and Horace Silver. Other jazz musicians, including Charles Mingus and Jimmy Giuffre, explored 'third stream', an experimental fusion of jazz and classical music that had only a small following.

▲ **BACK COVER**

1. **So What (9:25)**
2. **Freddie Freeloader (9:49)**
3. **Blue In Green (5:37)**
4. **All Blues (11:35)**
5. **Flamenco Sketches (9:25)**

Total album length: 45 minutes

Sleeve artwork by Joy Maisel

Elvis' Christmas Album

| • **Album sales:** 16,000,000 | • **Release date:** October 1957 |

Recorded in 1957, Elvis' first album of Christmas songs helped to establish him as the king of light entertainment as well as rock 'n' roll. Despite causing uproar on its release (Irving Berlin, the composer of 'White Christmas' led a campaign to stop Elvis' version being played on radio), the album hit Number One on the Billboard chart and continued to sell in large numbers each Christmas until 1962. Since then, it has become a Christmas classic, and is now the best-selling album of the 1950s.

The album, along with other material, was recorded in three days (5–7 September) at Radio Recorders in Hollywood. It contained a mixture of hymns, gospel tunes and secular Christmas songs, all of which Presley handled with characteristic panache. During the sessions, songwriters Leiber and Stoller wrote the opening track 'Santa Claus Is Back In Town', which became one of the collection's highlights.

On its release in October, media pundits, churchmen and music industry figures – knowing nothing of Presley's southern gospel roots – denounced it as an attempt by the young rock 'n' roll rebel to profane Christianity. The public felt differently, however, and the album's obviously heartfelt religious spirit helped confirm Presley's status as an all-American folk hero.

Number One singles: None

Grammy awards: None

Label: US & UK: RCA

Recorded in: Hollywood, USA

Personnel:
Elvis Presley (d. 1977)
Scotty Moore
Bill Black (d. 1965)
DJ Fontana
The Jordanaires
Millie Kirkham (d. 2014)

Producer:
Steve Sholes (d. 1968)

THE ELVIS CONTROVERSY

Elvis is now so integral to the history of mainstream rock 'n' roll that it is hard to imagine the controversy his act initially created. He was provocative both musically and physically, being a white man playing music indebted to African-American culture, and having an electrifying style of dance which earned him the nickname 'Elvis the Pelvis'. His abdominal gyrations on the Milton Berle TV show in 1956 – particularly to the track 'Hound Dog' – elicited huge audiences, but also accusations of lewdness. Ed Sullivan, then America's most influential chat show host, said he would never have Elvis on his show, but relented three times owing to Elvis' enormous popularity. On Elvis' final performance on the show in January 1957, the cameras filmed Elvis only from the waist up to avoid any scandal, but this simply added to the snowballing publicity around the young performer.

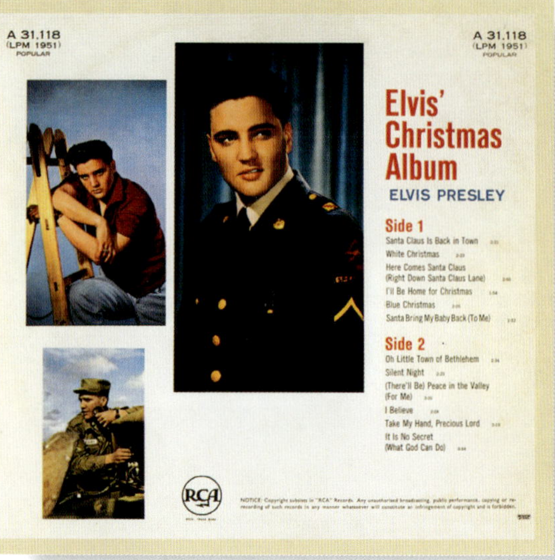

▲ **BACK COVER**

1 **Santa Claus Is Back In Town (2:12)**
2 **White Christmas (2:44)**
3 **Here Comes Santa Claus (Right Down Santa Claus Lane) (1:56)**
4 **I'll Be Home For Christmas (1:55)**
5 **Blue Christmas (2:08)**
6 **Santa Bring My Baby Back (To Me) (1:52)**
7 **Oh Little Town Of Bethlehem (2:37)**
8 **Silent Night (2:25)**
9 **Peace In The Valley (3:22)**
10 **I Believe (2:05)**
11 **Take My Hand, Precious Lord (3:21)**
12 **It Is No Secret (What God Can Do) (3:52)**

Total album length: 30 minutes

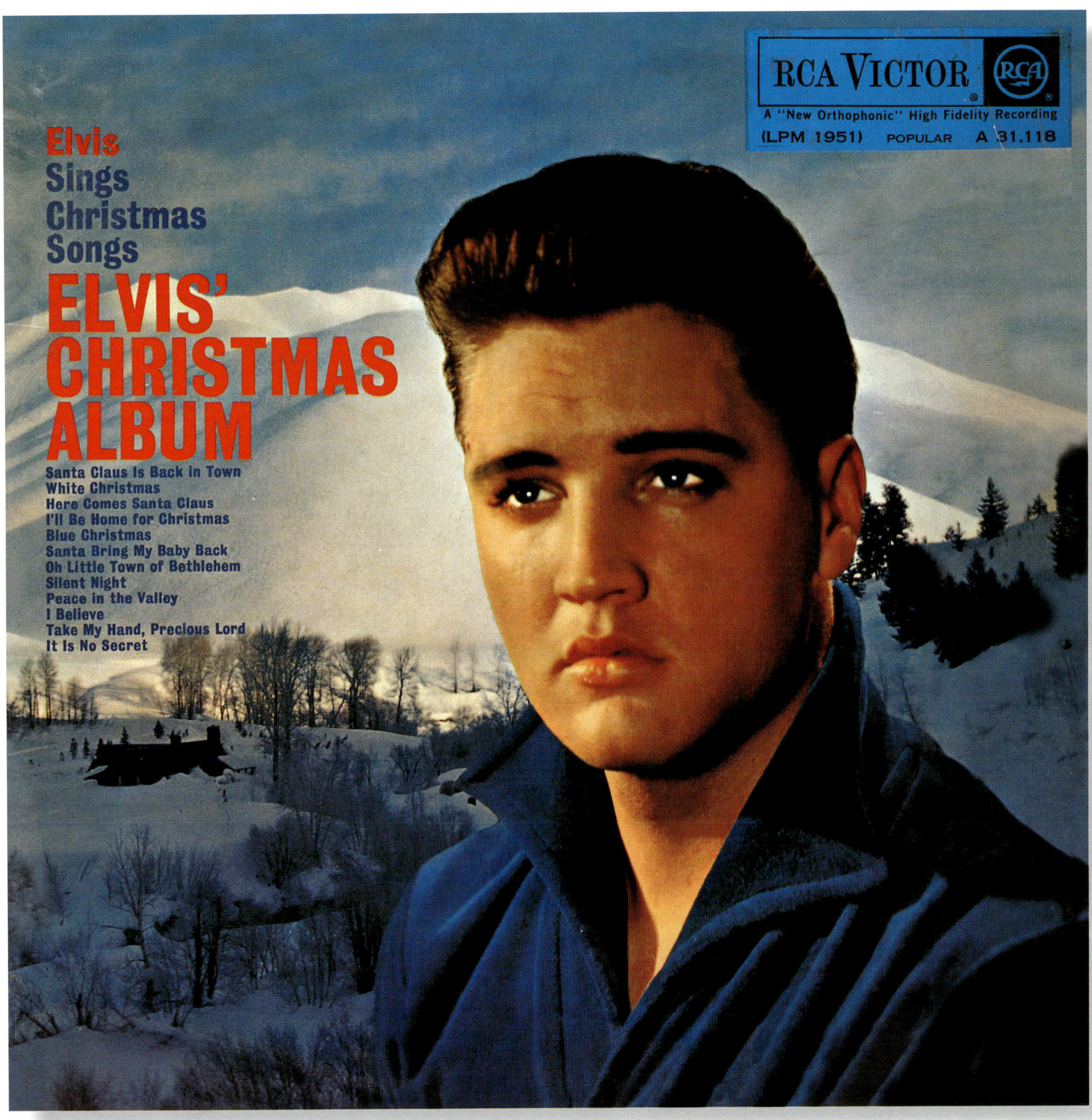
RCA VICTOR
A "New Orthophonic" High Fidelity Recording
(LPM 1951) POPULAR A 31.118
Elvis
Sings
Christmas
Songs
ELVIS' CHRISTMAS ALBUM
Santa Claus Is Back in Town
White Christmas
Here Comes Santa Claus
I'll Be Home for Christmas
Blue Christmas
Santa Bring My Baby Back
Oh Little Town of Bethlehem
Silent Night
Peace in the Valley
I Believe
Take My Hand, Precious Lord
It Is No Secret

STEREO
Iron Butterfly
In-A-Gadda-Da-Vida
33-250

ARE YOU EXPERIENCED
ARE YOU EXPERIENCED

CROSBY, STILLS & NASH

STEREO
Led Zeppelin
II
40 037
(SD 8236)

The Best-Selling Albums of the 1960s

It's tempting to declare that the long-playing record came of age in the 1960s. In truth, the 1960s was when the format began acting much younger than its years. Throughout the 1950s, the 12-inch album had been adult record-buyers' more expansive, expensive format of choice. Younger consumers, especially rock 'n' roll consuming teenagers, had to be content with the cheaper, more restrictive seven-inch single. Thirty minutes of content vs. three minutes of thrills.

All that had changed by the mid- to late-1960s. By the time album sales overtook singles in America in 1967, the LP's principal purchasers were teenagers, and the prevailing repertoire was pop and rock – not the soundtracks, Broadway show scores and easy-listening favourites of the 1950s. Indeed, rock band recordings from the last third of the 1960s account for more than half of the decade's best-sellers. This dramatic turn of events owed much to The Beatles, whose arrival supercharged both the business engine and the aural aesthetic of popular music. Armed with new resources and inspiration, late-1960s' musicians embarked on artistic ventures undreamed of only a few years before. These albums contained much highly innovative music, and the freedom from prior restraints generated such musical milestones as Jimi Hendrix's *Are You Experienced* and Van Morrison's *Moondance*.

The massive commercial success of rock led to the development of whole new subgenres, each sparking its own hugely popular works. Led Zeppelin helped create the heavy metal genre, and bands such as Blood, Sweat & Tears and Chicago experimented with brass-assisted rock.

So great was the young public's appetite for the new music that a fresh radio format, FM, emerged to expose the wealth of releases that could not be accommodated by AM Top 40 stations with their restrictions on record length and subject matter. Further fallout from the rock-album era was an increased attention to packaging, which can be seen on the rich diversity of designs featured in the Top 20. Another expression of this trend could be seen in the development of the promotional music video – The Monkees' musical success was a consequence of their frequent appearances on television.

Later 1960s' non-rock artists benefitted greatly from the expanded album-buying market, especially if they had some connection to the rock audience. Johnny Cash's *At Folsom Prison* and *At San Quentin* are a case in point. The singer's iconoclastic stance and irreverent material drew fans from the college crowd as much as it did older country fans, which helped boost sales of *Folsom* past the three million mark.

The new album format provided pop musicians with a whole new palette with which to work. In 1959, the Recording Industry Association of America (RIAA) reported total phonograph-record sales of $603 million. By 1969, these sales had reached almost $1.6 billion. The sales figures for the decade suggest that in the 1960s the public's musical expectations were being met, regularly and richly. And the fact that so many of the albums of the 1960s continue to be bought today – in many cases by members of generations unborn at the time of the records' initial release – says even more than the statistics.

1960s
20

Blood, Sweat & Tears

| • **Album sales:** 3,000,000 | • **Release date:** August 1969 |

"They ousted me from the band I had envisioned, regrouped with a singer of their choice, and made millions of dollars." That's how Blood, Sweat & Tears founder Al Kooper recounted the genesis of this Number One album in his autobiography 'Backstage Passes'.

Blood, Sweat & Tears, recorded under the aegis of producer James William Guercio, was the reconstituted band's second long-player. The original group's more adventurous debut album, *Child Is Father To The Man*, was among the first rock-with-horns experiments, but had lacked the commercial punch of *Blood, Sweat & Tears*.

Three top five singles came from the album, 'You've Made Me So Very Happy', was the first gold single, peaking at Number Two. The next single, 'More and More/Spinning Wheel' also peaked at Number Two and went gold. Finally, released in September of 1969, the third gold single from the album, 'And When I Die', also made Number Two by November. It was the first time since the RIAA started certifying gold records that an album had spawned three gold singles. The album reached Number One in the US charts, staying there for seven weeks. It went double platinum by the end of 1969, and stayed in the Top 40 for 66 weeks.

Number One singles: None

Grammy awards: Album of the Year; Best contemporary instrumental performance

Label: US: Columbia; UK: CBS

Recorded in: N/A

Personnel:
David Clayton-Thomas
Steve Katz
Chuck Winfield
Jerry Hyman
Fred Lipsius
Dick Halligan
Jim Fielder
Bobby Colomby
Lew Soloff (d. 2015)

Producer:
James William Guercio

ALBUM AWARDS

In 1958, the Recording Industry Association of America (RIAA) began a gold award programme for any album with sales of 500,000 copies. The gold award stood on its own until 1976, when it was considered that other grades of award should be added to reflect the massive sales of some industry artists. In that year the platinum award was introduced for sales of one million albums, and a decade later the multi-platinum award would be given for sales of two million albums. Most recently, the RIAA introduced the diamond award in 1999. To receive this award, an artist or group has to sell over 10 million copies of an album.

▲ **BACK COVER**

1. **Variations On A Theme By Eric Satie (1st & 2nd Movements) (2:35)**
2. **Smiling Phases (5:11)**
3. **Sometimes In Winter (3:09)**
4. **More And More (3:04)**
5. **And When I Die (4:06)**
6. **God Bless The Child (5:55)**
7. **Spinning Wheel (4:08)**
8. **You've Made Me So Very Happy (4:19)**
9. **Blues (Part 2) (11:44)**
10. **Variations On A Theme By Eric Satie (reprise) (1:49)**

Total album length: 44 minutes

Sleeve artwork by Timothy Quay

1960s
19

Sounds Of Silence

| • **Album sales:** 3,100,000 | • **Release date:** March 1966 |

Simon & Garfunkel's 'The Sound of Silence' and the Byrds' 'Mr. Tambourine Man' were the twin defining moments of folk-rock, even if the former enjoyed a less than organic origin.

While Paul Simon visited England in 1965, in New York the duo's producer added amplified backing to the acoustic track, which had been issued on their previous album. Released as a single, the electrified version topped the Hot 100 for two weeks, obliging Simon & Garfunkel to quickly assemble an album to accompany it. The title song had been released previously on the album *Wednesday Morning, 3 A.M.*, and would also appear on the soundtrack to the 1967 movie *The Graduate*.

Consisting almost entirely of Simon originals, *Sounds Of Silence* introduced the pop public to the songwriter's considerable talent. The outline of his maturing style is first sketched in the narrative vignettes 'A Most Peculiar Man' and 'Somewhere They Can't Find Me', the imagistic 'Leaves That Are Green' and the more directly personal 'I Am A Rock'. Of the two non-originals, 'Richard Cory' is an adaptation of an Edward Arlington Robinson poem, and the instrumental 'Angie' is a cover of a tune by British guitarist Davey Graham.

'I Am A Rock' was Simon & Garfunkel's third top five hit, released as a single following their second, 'Homeward Bound', from 1966's *Parsley, Sage, Rosemary and Thyme*. That set, like *Sounds Of Silence*, was produced by Bob Johnston.

Number One singles: US: The Sound Of Silence (UK: unreleased)

Grammy awards: None

Label: US: Columbia; UK: CBS

Recorded in: Nashville and Los Angeles, USA

Personnel:
Art Garfunkel
Paul Simon

Producer:
Bob Johnston

THE GRADUATE

***The Graduate* was one of the most successful movies of the 1960s in terms of critical acclaim, and has become representative of the creative sensitivity so prevalent during the decade. Starring Dustin Hoffman, Anne Bancroft and Katharine Ross, the film tells the tale of college graduate Benjamin (Hoffman) who is seduced by the wife of his father's boss – Mrs Robinson, played by Anne Bancroft – while also falling in love with Robinson's daughter, Elaine (Ross). Enhanced by superlative tracks from Simon & Garfunkel, the film won Mike Nichols the Best Director Oscar and a Golden Globe for Best Picture.**

▲ **BACK COVER**

1 **The Sound Of Silence (3:03)**
2 **Leaves That Are Green (2:20)**
3 **Blessed (3:13)**
4 **Kathy's Song (3:17)**
5 **Somewhere They Can't Find Me (2:34)**
6 **Angie (2:13)**
7 **Homeward Bound (2:30)**
8 **Richard Cory (2:54)**
9 **A Most Peculiar Man (2:29)**
10 **April Come She Will (1:48)**
11 **We've Got A Groovy Thing Goin' (1:56)**
12 **I Am A Rock (2:49)**

Total album length: 29 minutes

32020
CBS
SIMON & GARFUNKEL
SOUNDS OF SILENCE
including 'Homeward Bound'

1960s

1960s
18

Help!

• Album sales: 3,600,000 | **• Release date:** July 1965

Help! was the soundtrack to The Beatles' second movie and was the band's sixth Number One album in the US, a position it held for nine weeks. In the UK, a vastly different configuration of the record substituted additional Beatles' tracks for Ken Thorne's movie-score selections and also topped the chart.

The US version of *Help!* contains the seven Beatles tracks that actually appear in the film, but they're all first-rate. Among them are two Number One hits, the somewhat folk-rockish title cut and the highly imaginative 'Ticket to Ride'. More conventional Lennon–McCartney fare includes 'The Night Before' and 'Another Girl', and Lennon's faux-Dylan 'You've Got To Hide Your Love Away'. George Harrison's contribution, 'I Need You', provides a refreshing change of pace.

Help! premiered in New York in August 1965, just as The Beatles commenced their third US tour. The same month, the soundtrack album wrested the UK's top slot from 'Mr. Tambourine Man', the debut by The Beatles-inspired Byrds.

Number One singles: US & UK: Help!; Ticket To Ride

Grammy awards: None

Label: US: Capitol; UK: Parlophone

Recorded in: London, UK

Personnel:
John Lennon (d. 1980)
Paul McCartney
George Harrison (d. 2001)
Ringo Starr
George Martin
John Scott
Various other personnel

Producers:
George Martin
Dave Dexter, Jr (d. 1990)

FAN PROBLEMS

Fan hysteria directed towards pop groups reached previously unseen dimensions during the 1960s. Girls would scream themselves to exhaustion or simply faint at the mere sight of their idols, while concert hall security became a serious headache through overcrowding and crushes. The US youth magazine *Hit Parader* published an article on the phenomenon, wondering: 'The girls who flip over the current breed of pop singers seem to be much wilder than those who swooned over Sinatra or even the ones who ripped Elvis Presley's clothing to shredded souvenirs. If this is the way audiences are blowing their cool over The Rolling Stones in 1965, how will the next generation of fans react?' A darker side crept into the concert experience at The Rolling Stones' Altamont gig in 1969, in which one man was beaten to death by Hell's Angels security, and three other people died in accidents. After the peace and love of Woodstock, it was a dark end to the decade.

▲ BACK COVER

US:

1 Help! (2:35)
2 The Night Before (2:33)
3 From Me to You Fantasy (Instrumental) (2:03)
4 You've Got to Hide Your Love Away (2:08)
5 I Need You (2:28)
6 In the Tyrol (Instrumental) (2:21)
7 Another Girl (2:02)
8 Another Hard Day's Night (Instrumental) (2:28)
9 Ticket to Ride (3:03)
10 Bitter End (2:20)
11 You're Gonna Lose That Girl (2:18)
12 Chase (Instrumental) (2:24)

Total album length: 29 minutes

UK:

1 Help! (2:30)
2 The Night Before (2:37)
3 You've Got To Hide Your Love Away (2:11)
4 I Need You (2:32)
5 Another Girl (2:08)
6 You're Gonna Lose That Girl (2:20)
7 Ticket To Ride (3:13)
8 Act Naturally (2:33)
9 It's Only Love (1:59)
10 You Like Me Too Much (2:38)
11 Tell Me What You See (2:40)
12 I've Just Seen A Face (2:07)
13 Yesterday (2:08)
14 Dizzy Miss Lizzy (5:54)

Total album length: 38 minutes

1960s

1960s
17

Moondance

| • **Album sales:** 3,600,000 | • **Release date:** December 1969 |

Though preceded by 1967's bomb *Blowin' Your Mind* and 1968's critically esteemed *Astral Weeks, Moondance* was George Ivan Morrison's (popularly known as Van Morrison) first commercially successful album. As focused and accessible as *Astral Weeks* was expansive and demanding, *Moondance* is one of the seminal sets of the 1960s.

On it, Morrison lays out the style that has served him ever since: bluesy melodies, punchy reed and brass accents, and intensely personal visions delivered in a compelling, soulful manner. The lilting, jazz-like title cut remains his signature song, recorded by dozens of artists over four decades, though 'Crazy Love' has also enjoyed its share of cover versions. The use of vocal support from church-trained female singers, on 'Brand New Day' and 'Crazy Love', reflects the pop-gospel arranging style popular with many rock artists of the early 1970s period.

Of the up-tempo tracks, the brisk 'Come Running' was issued as a single peaking at Number 39. *Moondance* peaked at Number 29 on Billboard's pop albums chart. Nonetheless, the lasting impact made by the album was more aesthetic than commercial.

Number One singles: None

Grammy awards: None

Label: US & UK: Warners

Recorded in: London, UK

Personnel:
Van Morrison
Cissy Houston
Collin Tilton
David Shaw
Emily Houston
Gary Mallaber
Guy Masson
Jack Schroer (d. 1995)
Jackie Verdell (d. 2002)
Jeff Labes
John Klingberg
John Platania
Judy Clay (d. 2001)

Producer:
Van Morrison

SOUNDTRACK TO VIETNAM

The Vietnam War (1963–75) was the most vilified political and military expedition of the 1960s. Its political aims and the tactics employed by the US military were the opposite of everything the counter-culture movement stood for. Accordingly, musicians of the 1960s created hundreds of tracks opposing the war, including Bob Dylan's 'All Along The Watchtower', Don McClean's 'The Grave', Jimi Hendrix's 'Machine Gun', Malvina Reynolds' 'What Have They Done to the Rain?' and Edwin Starr's 'War'. The music had a powerful effect in coalescing public antipathy towards the war into common anthems, and rarely since has music had such an important political effect.

▲ **BACK COVER**

1 **And It Stoned Me (4:30)**
2 **Moondance (4:35)**
3 **Crazy Love (2:34)**
4 **Into The Mystic (3:25)**
5 **Caravan (4:57)**
6 **Come Running (2:30)**
7 **These Dreams Of You (3:50)**
8 **Brand New Day (5:09)**
9 **Everyone (3:31)**
10 **Glad Tidings (3:13)**

Total album length: 38 minutes

1960s

Sleeve artwork by Bob Cato and Eliot Landy

1960s
16

At Folsom Prison

| • **Album sales:** 4,000,000 | • **Release date:** January 1968 |

This recording of a concert at a California penitentiary in front of 2,000 convicted felons initiated Cash's ascent to icon status. Cash had already been a rockabilly star, notched country hits and occasionally crossed over into Top 40 territory. But something about *At Folsom Prison* – the song selection, energized performances and spirited audience reaction – resonated universally with the public. The album sold four million copies.

Folsom's repertoire is rich in the themes and attitudes audiences have long loved in Cash's music. The title track is joined in its joyous defiance by 'Cocaine Blues' and the condemned-man saga '25 Minutes To Go'.

At Folsom Prison made Cash fans of country enthusiasts, folk purists, college students and conservatives, staying on Billboard's album chart for more than two years. The title-track single gave Cash a Top 40 pop hit and his eighth Number One country hit.

Number One singles: None

Grammy awards: Best album notes; Best male country vocal performance; Best country and western performance duet, trio or group

Label: US: Columbia; UK: CBS

Recorded in: California, USA

Personnel:
Johnny Cash (d. 2003)
Al Casey (d. 2006)
June Carter Cash (d. 2003)
Luther Perkins (d. 1968)
Marshall Grant (d. 2011)
W.S. Holland
The Carter Family
The Statler Brothers

Producer:
Bob Johnston

1960s SOCIAL PROBLEMS

While the 1960s are presented as an era of peace and love, in reality there was an equal expansion in crime, violence, social disorder and drug problems. The 1964 US presidential election was largely fought over public concerns with crime and disorder, although many of these 'crimes' were the endemic riots manifesting during civil rights protests. However, in general terms, crimes against property and person multiplied fourfold in the United States in the 1960s when compared with the 1950s, and similar problems were experienced across Europe. Increased drug use was one cause of the problem, but gross inequality was another. A full 40 per cent of African-Americans, for example, lived below the federal poverty line, and President Johnson's National Advisory Commission on Civil Disorders concluded a report by saying that 'chronic poverty is a breeder of chronic chaos'.

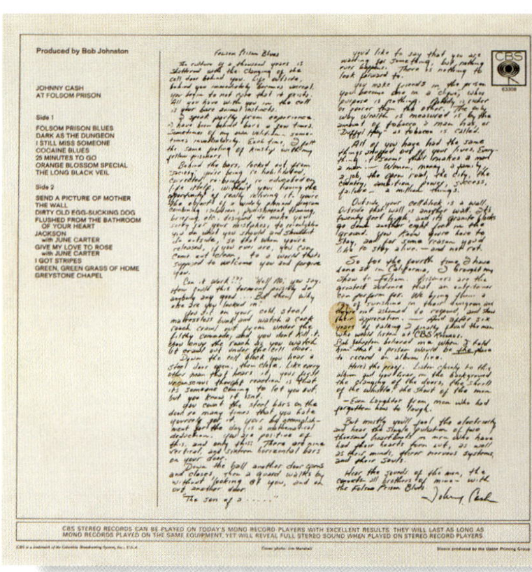

▲ **BACK COVER**

1 **Folsom Prison Blues (2:42)**
2 **Dark As A Dungeon (3:04)**
3 **I Still Miss Someone (1:37)**
4 **Cocaine Blues (3:01)**
5 **25 Minutes To Go (3:31)**
6 **Orange Blossom Special (3:00)**
7 **The Long Black Veil (3:57)**
8 **Send A Picture Of Mother (2:10)**
9 **The Wall (1:36)**
10 **Dirty Old Egg Sucking Dog (1:30)**
11 **Flushed From The Bathroom Of Your Heart (2:17)**
12 **Jackson (3:12)**
13 **Give My Love To Rose (2:40)**
14 **I Got Stripes (1:57)**
15 **Green Green Grass Of Home (2:29)**
16 **Greystone Chapel (6:02)**

Total album length: 45 minutes

Sleeve artwork by Jim Marshall

1960s
15

In-A-Gadda-Da-Vida

| • **Album sales:** 4,200,000 | • **Release date:** July 1968 |

British outfits like Deep Purple and Black Sabbath are generally credited with inventing heavy metal, but California psychedelic rockers like Blue Cheer ('Summertime Blues') and Iron Butterfly can stake an equally valid claim.

Relentless, minor-key bass riffs, gnarled guitar and funereal organ are the essence of the 17-minute 'In-A-Gadda-Da-Vida', the centrepiece of San Diego-based Iron Butterfly's second album, recorded at Goldstar Studios in Hollywood. The tune began life as a ballroom crowd-pleaser, became an FM-rock favourite and was edited down to a three-minute single, where it helped push its parent album to a 140-week stay on the Billboard chart, 81 weeks on the Top 10.

The remainder of *In-A-Gadda-Da-Vida* is comprised of five shorter, more pop-ish group originals. A soul riff and a solo inspired by The Doors' 'Light My Fire' somewhat distinguishes 'Most Anything You Want', while 'Flowers and Beads' employs airy harmonies to give off a slight Rascals flavour.

Iron Butterfly were awarded the recording industry's first platinum album, and continued to chart albums through to 1975. The band's metal/stoner-rock credentials are underscored by the fact that *In-A-Gadda-Da-Vida* was Atlantic Records' best-seller until the 1969 arrival of Led Zeppelin – and by a certain resemblance in the two bands' names.

Number One singles: None

Grammy awards: None

Label: US: Atco; UK: Atlantic

Recorded in: Hollywood, USA

Personnel:
Doug Ingle
Erik Braun (d. 2003)
Lee Dorman (d. 2012)
Ron Bushy

Producer:
Don Casale
Jim Hilton

HEAVY METAL

At the sharpest, blackest edge of the counter-culture movement were the emerging phenomena of hard rock and heavy metal. Heavy metal (a term taken from William Burroughs' 1962 novel *The Soft Machine*) actually emerged from blues music, with bands such as Blue Cheer using high-power amps and distorted guitars to turn the blues riffs into something much harder. The 'electric blues' bands soon proliferated, from Jimi Hendrix's inspired riffs to the adrenalin-fuelled sounds of The Who. By the end of the 1960s, heavy rock/metal was emerging from these elements as a genre in its own right, with purer rock sounds from the hands of King Crimson, Deep Purple, Black Sabbath and Led Zeppelin. Bands such as Black Sabbath also embraced a nihilistic philosophy imbued with horror and social collapse, embracing the dark side of music for which metal would become known.

▲ **BACK COVER**

1. **Most Anything You Want (3:44)**
2. **Flowers And Beads (3:09)**
3. **My Mirage (4:55)**
4. **Termination (2:53)**
5. **Are You Happy (4:29)**
6. **In-A-Gadda-Da-Vida (17:05)**

Total album length: 36 minutes

Sleeve artwork by Loring Eutemey, Michael Ochs and Stephen Paley

1960s
14

Crosby, Stills & Nash

| • **Album sales:** 4,300,000 | • **Release date:** June 1969 |

Crosby, Stills & Nash, known by the initials CSN, were one of the most anticipated rock music debuts of the late 1960s. The public defections of the band's members (David Crosby, Stephen Stills and Graham Nash) from established bands (The Byrds, Buffalo Springfield and The Hollies) were a first, introducing the notion of rock musicians as free agents and creating a brief vogue in 'supergroups'. They were one of the few American bands that even came close to rivalling The Beatles in the late 1960s.

Although Nash's incessantly tuneful travelogue 'Marrakesh Express' and Stills' paean to Judy Collins, 'Suite: Judy Blue Eyes', were Top 30 hits, the hippie harmonists initially found their home in the counter-culture: FM-rock radio and the festival circuit (the group performed at the Woodstock festival). There is no doubt that Crosby, Stills & Nash's quiet, heavily acoustic songs provided a welcome tonic for audiences overdosed on hard rock and the incessant political turmoil of the period. In 1969, the album sold two million copies, and the group won a Grammy for the year's best new artist.

The trio added Neil Young, Stills' Buffalo Springfield bandmate, to its lineup for 1970's *Deja Vu*. Solo careers have occupied all four principals since the early 1970s, but they have re-formed, in various configurations, for occasional touring and recording.

Number One singles: None

Grammy awards: Best new artist of the year

Label: US & UK: Atlantic

Recorded in: N/A

Personnel:
David Crosby
Stephen Stills
Graham Nash
Dallas Taylor (d. 2015)

Producer:
Bill Halverson

WOODSTOCK

The 1969 Woodstock festival encapsulated the 1960s counter-culture in one event. Originally the music and arts festival was planned to be held in Woodstock, Ulster County, New York, but town opposition demanded a relocation. It was eventually held at a 600-acre dairy farm owned by Max Yasgur in Bethel, New York, on 15–17 August, but retained the name Woodstock. The planned 50,000 crowd swelled to 400,000, who flooded the countryside to listen to bands ranging from Joe Cocker and the Grateful Dead to Janis Joplin and Jimi Hendrix. No violence was reported from the festival, only copious amounts of drug-taking, love-making and music-loving.

▲ **BACK COVER**

1. **Suite: Judy Blue Eyes (7:25)**
2. **Marrakesh Express (2:39)**
3. **Guinnevere (4:40)**
4. **You Don't Have To Cry (2:45)**
5. **Pre-Road Downs (3:01)**
6. **Wooden Ships (5:29)**
7. **Lady Of The Island (2:39)**
8. **Helplessly Hoping (2:41)**
9. **Long Time Gone (4:17)**
10. **49 Bye-Byes (5:16)**

Total album length: 40 minutes

Sleeve artwork by Gary Burden and Henry Diltz

1960s
13

Are You Experienced

| • **Album sales:** 4,500,000 | • **Release date:** May 1967 |

In a pop-music year rich in debuts and breakthrough recordings, Hendrix's arrival stood out. By the time *Are You Experienced* was released in the US, the expatriate singer-guitarist had notched three Top 10 singles in the UK ('Hey Joe', 'Purple Haze' and 'The Wind Cries Mary') and stolen the show at California's Monterey Pop Festival. However, this hit-single success was not duplicated in the US. With little Top 40 airplay, Hendrix and company promoted their debut with a national tour, and with the enthusiastic aid of the newly emerging 'underground' FM rock stations, many of which began playing the import version of *Are You Experienced.*

Simply put, the album introduces one of rock music's seminal artists. Blues is the basis for such songs as 'Foxy Lady' and 'Fire', but Hendrix's compositions and performances stretch the root form into something utterly original and unprecedented.

Hendrix revolutionized the way amplified guitar was played, and not just with his way with bruising blues licks. Tracks such as 'May This Be Love' and 'The Wind Cries Mary' display as much beauty and sensitivity as the rockers exhibit raw power. Hendrix likewise proves himself an impressive vocalist, as he animates the album's songs of love, lust, interstellar travel and drug disorientation.

Number One singles: None

Grammy awards: None

Label: US: Reprise; UK: Track

Recorded in: London, UK

Personnel:
Jimi Hendrix (d. 1970)
Noel Redding (d. 2003)
Mitch Mitchell (d. 2008)

Producer:
Chas Chandler (d. 1996)

THE DRUG SCENE

Use of drugs rocketed during the 1960s, from the mildest marijuana to the hardest heroin. Marijuana in particular was appropriated by the psychedelia movement, and in the US, where only 1.8 per cent of young people had tried the drug in 1965, a decade later that figure stood at around 20 per cent. However, it was LSD in particular that caught the hippie imagination. The late Dr Timothy Leary of Harvard University advocated the spiritual, mind-expanding positives of the drug following tests involving students – for which he was fired from Harvard in 1963 along with his co-experimenter Dr Richard Alpert. Drug use was also mythologized in the literature of the time, such as Tom Wolfe's 1968 hippie exploration *The Electric Kool-Aid Acid Test*.

▲ **BACK COVER**

UK:
1 Foxy Lady (3:19)
2 Manic Depression (3:42)
3 Red House (3:44)
4 Can You See Me (2:33)
5 Love Or Confusion (3:12)
6 I Don't Live Today (3:55)
7 May This Be Love (3:11)
8 Fire (2:45)
9 Third Stone From The Sun (6:44)
10 Remember (2:48)
11 Are You Experienced? (4:14)

US:
1 Purple Haze (2:46)
2 Manic Depression (3:42)
3 Hey Joe (3:23)
4 Love Or Confusion (3:15)
5 May This Be Love (3:14)
6 I Don't Live Today (3:55)
7 The Wind Cries May (3:21)
8 Fire (2:45)
9 Third Stone From The Sun (6:40)
10 Foxy Lady (3:15)
11 Are You Experienced? (3:55)

Total album length: 40 minutes

Sleeve artwork by Bruce Flemming and Karl Ferris

1960s
12

A Hard Day's Night

| • **Album sales:** 4,500,000 | • **Release date:** July 1964 |

Though The Beatles are present on only about two thirds of its tracks, the soundtrack to the band's first motion picture – a fictionalized day in the life of the band – gave them their second US Number One album and topped the charts in the UK. The film received two Academy Award nominations, for Best Original Screenplay and Best Adapted Musical Score.

While the British edition of *A Hard Day's Night* was comprised exclusively of 13 Beatles' tracks, the US version included George Martin's four instrumental selections from the film, including 1964's mid-charting single 'This Boy (Ringo's Theme)', and The Beatles' cuts.

Some of the group's finest pop rock 'n' roll is on display here. The invigorating 'Tell Me Why', the title track and 'Can't Buy Me Love' arrange joyous marriages of power and melody. The latter two tracks were US and UK Number One singles.

The Beatles' February 1964 performance on *The Ed Sullivan Show* remains one of the highest-rated television programmes of all time, with around 73 million people tuning in.

Number One singles: US & UK: A Hard Day's Night; Can't Buy Me Love

Grammy awards: Best performance by a vocal group

Label: US: Capitol; UK: Parlophone

Recorded in: London, UK; Paris, France

Personnel:
John Lennon (d. 1980)
Paul McCartney
George Harrison (d. 2001)
Ringo Starr
George Martin
Various other personnel

Producer:
George Martin

1960s' CINEMA

The cinema industry found the 1960s a turbulent decade with TV, radio music, records and live pop performances all competing for the public's time, money and enthusiasm. In the US, 1963 saw film production drop to its lowest point in half a decade, with only 121 films released, and in the following year imported films (mostly from the UK) outnumbered indigenous productions by 361 to 141. Made-for-TV movies had the biggest impact upon cinema-going, although the creation of the first 'multiplex' cinemas, beginning in Kansas City in 1963, drew some volumes back. There were movie successes, such as *The Longest Day* (1963) and *The Sound of Music* (1965), but many disasters, including the four-hour $44 million epic *Cleopatra* from 20th Century Fox, and the big movie houses haemorrhaged stars, cash and property to make ends meet.

▲ **BACK COVER**

US:
1 A Hard Day's Night (2:28)
2 Tell Me Why (2:04)
3 I'll Cry Instead (1:47)
4 I Should Have Known Better (instrumental) (2:16)
5 I'm Happy Just to Dance WIth You (1:59)
6 And I Love Her (Instrumental) (2:29)
7 I Should Have Known Better (2:42)
8 If I Fell (2:16)
9 And I Love Her (2:27)
10 This Boy (Instrumental) (3:06)
11 Can't Buy Me Love (2:15)
12 A Hard Day's Night (Instrumental) (2:00)

Total album length: 29 minutes

UK:
1 A Hard Day's Night (2:33)
2 I Should Have Known Better (2:44)
3 If I Fell (2:22)
4 I'm Happy Just to Dance WIth You (1:59)
5 And I Love Her (2:29)
6 Tell Me Why (2:10)
7 Can't Buy Me Love (2:12)
8 Any Time at All (2:13)
9 I'll Cry Instead (1:47)
10 Things We Said Today (2:38)
11 When I Get Home (2:18)
12 You Can't Do That (2:37)
13 I'll Be Back (2:20)

Total album length: 30 minutes

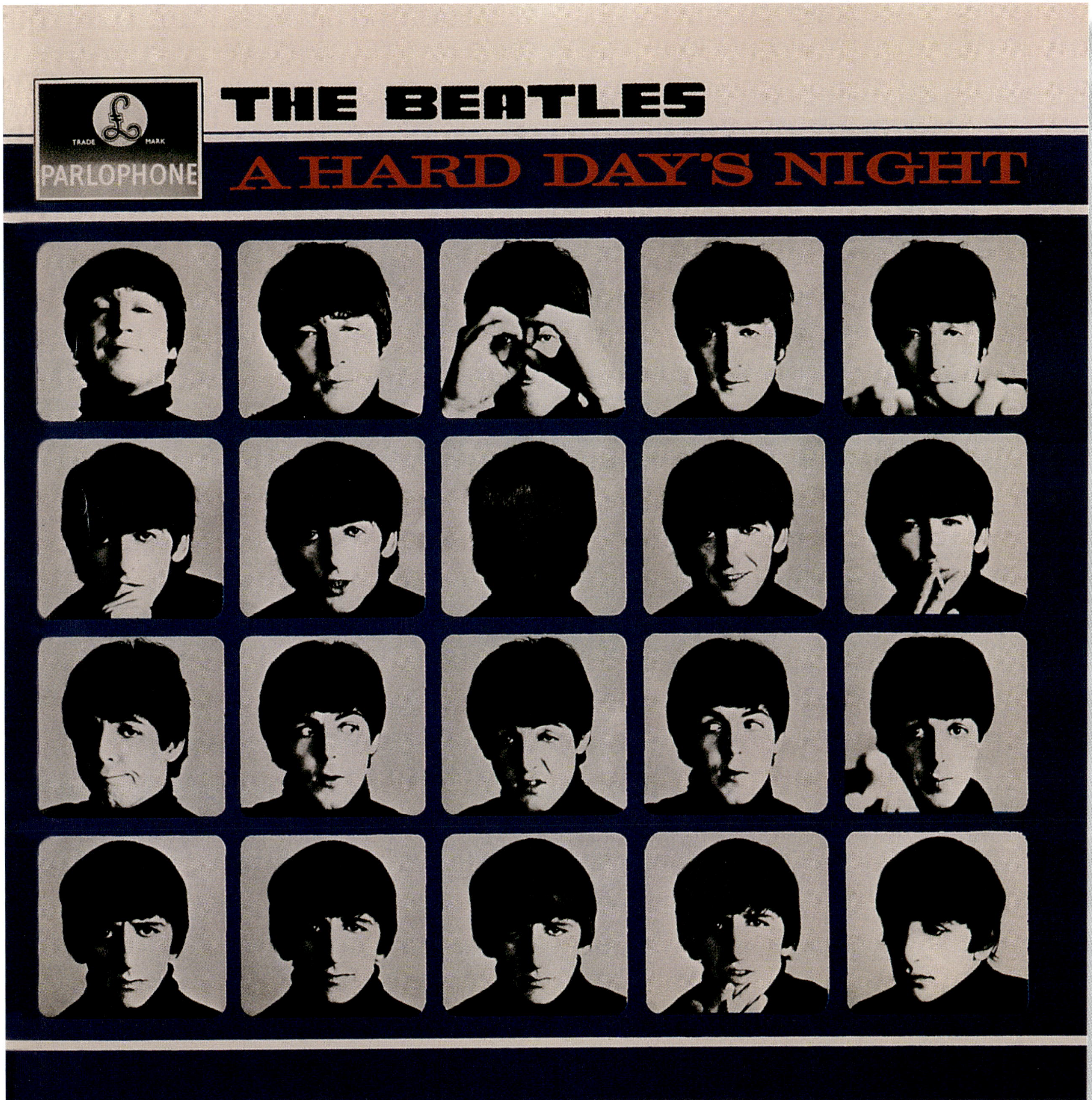

THE BEATLES

A HARD DAY'S NIGHT

1960s
11

Meet The Beatles!

| • **Album sales:** 5,000,000 | • **Release date:** January 1964 |

The 1960s' most significant debut still retains much of its initial appeal, both in terms of the sheer originality of its songs and The Beatles invigorating performances. *Meet The Beatles!*, unlike the UK album *With The Beatles* from which it was adapted, is comprised solely of Beatles compositions (excepting 'Till There Was You').

Their first major-label US album, it became America's best-selling LP of all time within a week of its release. In April, The Beatles occupied the top five positions on the US singles chart. *Meet The Beatles!* gave the band their first gold album and their first gold single, 'I Want To Hold Your Hand', on the same day. Obvious highlights are the two sides of the Lennon–McCartney single that introduced America to the group, the clap-happy 'I Want To Hold Your Hand' and the pulsing 'I Saw Her Standing There'. There's little decline in quality thereafter, as track after sterling track establishes The Beatles' talent and charms.

Meet The Beatles! reveals the group's genius at absorbing and synthesizing varying styles into music that is uniquely its own. Thus, the poppy 'All My Loving' uses country elements while the girl-group sounds of The Shirelles inform 'All I've Got To Do'. The album features the first George Harrison composition, 'Don't Bother Me'.

Number One singles: US & UK: I Want To Hold Your Hand

Grammy awards: None

Label: US: Capitol

Recorded in: London, UK

Personnel:
John Lennon (d. 1980)
Paul McCartney
George Harrison (d. 2001)
Ringo Starr
George Martin

Producer:
George Martin

THE BRITISH INVASION

While the Beatles were the battering ram that opened up the United States to the 'British invasion', they were not the only element of British culture to enter the States in the 1960s. The Beatles took the US market by storm from 1964, after which *Life* magazine ran an article which observed: "First England fell, victim of a million girlish screams. Then last week, Paris surrendered. Now the US must brace itself." The Fab Four were quickly followed into North America by bands such as The Kinks, The Rolling Stones, The Animals and The Dave Clark Five. Following the wave of British beat bands came the British rock bands of the late 1960s and early 1970s, including Led Zeppelin, The Who, Deep Purple and Black Sabbath. In their wake all these bands dragged British fashion and mannerisms after them.

▲ **BACK COVER**

1. **I Want To Hold Your Hand (2:24)**
2. **I Saw Her Standing There (2:50)**
3. **This Boy (2:11)**
4. **It Won't Be Long (2:11)**
5. **All I've Got To Do (2:05)**
6. **All My Loving (2:04)**
7. **Don't Bother Me (2:28)**
8. **Little Child (1:46)**
9. **Till There Was You (2:12)**
10. **Hold Me Tight (2:30)**
11. **I Wanna Be Your Man (1:59)**
12. **Not A Second Time (2:03)**

Total album length: 27 minutes

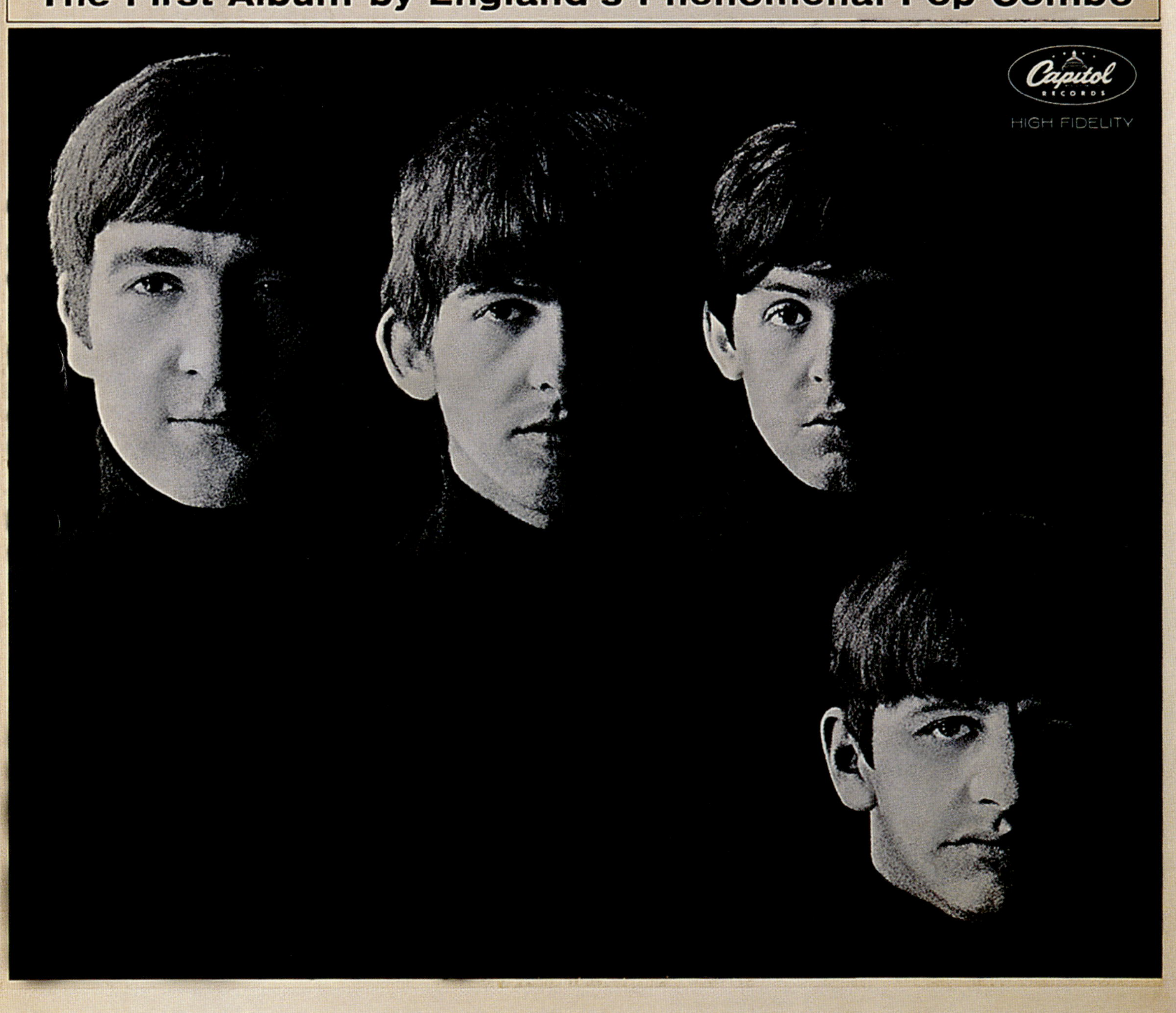
MEET THE BEATLES!
The First Album by England's Phenomenal Pop Combo
Capitol
RECORDS
HIGH FIDELITY

1960s
10

More Of The Monkees

| • **Album sales:** 5,000,000 | • **Release date:** April 1967 |

Like their debut, the second set by The Monkees was a top-ranking album in the US (for 18 weeks); it also went to Number One in the UK charts. Though the group's role remains limited to singing, *More Of The Monkees* is a measurably better record, thanks in part to Neil Diamond, whose composition 'I'm A Believer' was the group's second Number One single. Another Diamond song, and one of the album's obvious high points, is 'Look Out (Here Comes Tomorrow)'. The track rests squarely in the rock 'n' roll camp, as does Boyce and Hart's 1960s' garage-rock classic '(I'm Not Your) Steppin' Stone'. The tune gets a ferocious treatment from Dolenz, who reveals himself to be one of the period's most underrated vocalists.

Within weeks of the album's release, Mike Nesmith lobbied, successfully, with *The Monkees* TV-show producer Bob Rafelson for the group to be allowed to play, as well as sing, on forthcoming records. The TV series *The Monkees* won the Emmy for Best Comedy 1966.

Number One singles: US & UK: I'm A Believer

Grammy awards: None

Label: US: Colgems; UK: RCA Victor

Recorded in: Los Angeles, USA

Personnel:
Mike Nesmith
Micky Dolenz
Peter Tork
Davy Jones (d. 2012)
Artie Butler
Bill Lewis
Don Randi
Gary Coleman (d. 2010)
Hal Blaine
Neil Sedaka
Norm Jeffries
Various other personnel

Producers:
Tommy Boyce (d. 1994)
Neil Sedaka
Michael Nesmith
Jack Keller (d. 2005)
Gerry Goffin (d. 2014)
Carole Bayer Sager
Carole King
Bobby Hart

1960s TELEVISION

The 1960s were a formative decade for television. Colour television had its advent, entering the United States in 1965 and the United Kingdom two years later. The new medium, and the revolutionary ideas of the decade, led programmers to be more experimental with content, apart from the family-friendly light entertainment shows which still pervaded the schedules. Major series that had their debut in the 1960s included *Star Trek, The Saint, The Persuaders, Batman* and *Dragnet*, while hallucinatory programmes like *The Prisoner*, starring Patrick McGoohan, were of limited commercial success, but generated enormous cult followings that last to this day. Music shows also abounded, with the UK's *Top of the Pops* becoming a major showcase for new and existing talent.

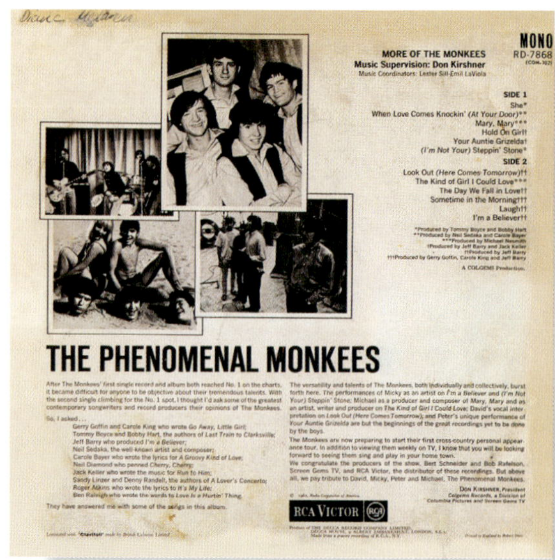

▲ **BACK COVER**

1. **When Love Comes Knockin' (At Your Door) (1:49)**
2. **Mary, Mary (2:16)**
3. **Hold On Girl (2:29)**
4. **Your Auntie Grizelda (2:30)**
5. **(I'm Not Your) Steppin' Stone (2:25)**
6. **Look Out (Here Comes Tomorrow) (2:16)**
7. **The Kind Of Girl I Could Love (1:53)**
8. **The Day We Fell In Love (2:26)**
9. **Sometime In The Morning (2:30)**
10. **Laugh (2:30)**
11. **I'm A Believer (2:50)**

Total album length: 26 minutes

mono RD-7868
MORE OF THE
Monkees
RCA VICTOR
RCA

1960s
9

The Monkees

| • **Album sales:** 5,000,000 | • **Release date:** January 1967 |

The Monkees' debut was the first of four consecutive US Number Ones for the group, and also topped the UK charts. Assembled by television producers Bob Rafelson and Bert Schneider to portray a Beatles-type pop band in a new series, the quartet recorded (vocals only) between rehearsals for the weekly show.

While subsequent albums would improve on its quality, largely due to the group's increased participation, *The Monkees* remains an appealing mix of pop songs and performances. Mickey Dolenz delivers a rousing lead on the brisk 'Last Train To Clarksville', a US Number One single and one of several tunes written by veteran hitmakers Tommy Boyce and Bobby Hart, while Davy Jones handles the ballad 'I Wanna Be Free'. Mike Nesmith, the member with the most extensive musical background, sings lead on his own country-flavoured compositions, 'Papa Gene's Blues' and 'Sweet Young Thing' (co-written with the legendary Gerry Goffin/Carole King team).

Though critics disparaged The Monkees as the 'Pre-Fab Four', the TV series was a hit. The symbiotic relationship between the show and the records' radio play enabled The Monkees to hold down the top-selling album slot for 13 weeks.

Number One singles: US: Last Train To Clarksville (UK: unreleased)

Grammy awards: None

Label: US: Colgems; UK: RCA Victor

Recorded in: Hollywood, USA

Personnel:
Davy Jones (d. 2012)
Mickey Dolenz
Mike Nesmith
Peter Tork
Various other musicians

Producers:
Tommy Boyce (d. 1994)
Bobby Hart
Jack Keller
Mike Nesmith

CREATING THE MONKEES

The idea for the group The Monkees was derived from the Beatles' film *A Hard Day's Night* (1964), and producers Bob Rafelson and Bert Schneider auditioned actors/musicians to make a television series derivative. The four chosen – Davy Jones, Mickey Dolenz, Mike Nesmith and Peter Tork – had their public debut in *The Monkees* show in September 1966, the show subsequently running for two series and making enormous stars out of its young protagonists. There was initial controversy about the fact that the four men did not play the instruments on the first and second albums. Such is true, yet all had been jobbing musicians prior to The Monkees and session musicians were used purely so that the group could focus on a hectic filming schedule. However, the group played live and after the release of *More of the Monkees* they fired music impresario Don Kirschner, previously in charge of the show's tunes, and took greater control of the musical output.

▲ **BACK COVER**

1. **(Theme From) The Monkees (2:21)**
2. **Saturday's Child (2:45)**
3. **I Wanna Be Free (2:27)**
4. **Tomorrow's Gonna Be Another Day (2:39)**
5. **Papa Gene's Blues (2:00)**
6. **Take A Giant Step (2:31)**
7. **Last Train To Clarksville (2:47)**
8. **This Just Doesn't Seem To Be My Day (2:09)**
9. **Let's Dance On (2:32)**
10. **I'll Be True To You (2:49)**
11. **Sweet Young Thing (1:58)**
12. **Gonna Buy Me A Dog (2:44)**

Total album length: 30 minutes

1960s

mono RD-7844
RCA VICTOR
RCA
the MONKEES
(theme from) THE MONKEES/Saturday's Child
I Wanna Be Free/Tomorrow's Gonna Be Another Day
Papa Gene's Blues/Take a Giant Step
Last Train to Clarksville/This Just Doesn't Seem to Be My Day
Let's Dance On/I'll Be True to You
Sweet Young Thing/Gonna Buy Me a Dog

1960s
8

Revolver

| • **Album sales:** 5,300,000 | • **Release date:** August 1966 |

Regarded widely as one of the greatest pop albums of all time, *Revolver* represents The Beatles' coming of age as songwriters and musicians. Yet another step in the band's continuing effort to go beyond the confines of standard pop-song fodder, *Revolver* is loaded with an eclectic array of subject matter, including Harrison's caustic indictment of an unfair tax system ('Taxman'), McCartney's haunting portrait of a lonely spinster ('Eleanor Rigby') and Lennon's tape-looped rumination 'Tomorrow Never Knows'. Meanwhile 'Here, There And Everywhere' remains one of the band's most affecting love songs. The Beatles also began to explore fully the possibilities of the recording studio on *Revolver*, bringing the material to sonic life with innovative electronic wizardry.

Revolver shot to the top of the charts and stayed there for six weeks, spurred by the double-sided hit single that paired 'Yellow Submarine' (Number Two) with 'Eleanor Rigby' (Number 11). The album also garnered two Grammy Awards: McCartney won for Best Contemporary (R&R) Solo Vocal Performance (for 'Eleanor Rigby'), and Klaus Voormann won for Best Album Cover, Graphic Arts.

Number One singles:
None

Grammy awards:
Paul McCartney, Best contemporary (R&R) solo vocal performance – 'Eleanor Rigby'; Klaus Voormann, Best album cover, graphic arts

Label: US: Capitol; UK: Parlophone

Recorded in: London, UK

Personnel:
John Lennon (d. 1980)
Paul McCartney
George Harrison (d. 2001)
Ringo Starr
George Martin
Anvil Bhagwat
Alan Civil
Various other personnel

Producer:
George Martin

RECORDING TECHNOLOGY

The most important shift in listener enjoyment during the 1960s was the move away from monophonic to stereophonic recordings. Practical stereophonic recordings had been achieved back in the 1930s at Bell Laboratories (they were formed by cutting one track onto each wall of the record grooves), but the technology was prohibitively expensive for a mass market. However, in 1958 stereophonic long-playing (LP) records using Bell's principles were made viable by the major recording companies. At the turn of the 1960s, most people owned only monophonic equipment, but steadily the new high-quality sound caught on, until by the late 1960s, the large record companies no longer produced monophonic records. The Beatles were at the forefront of recording technology and were the first mainstream artists to employ tape-loops and backward recordings on their records.

▲ BACK COVER

1 Taxman (2:39)
2 Eleanor Rigby (2:07)
3 I'm Only Sleeping (3:01)
4 Love You To (3:01)
5 Here, There And Everywhere (2:25)
6 Yellow Submarine (2:40)
7 She Said She Said (2:37)
8 Good Day Sunshine (2:09)
9 And Your Bird Can Sing (2:01)
10 For No One (2:01)
11 Doctor Robert (2:15)
12 I Want To Tell You (2:29)
13 Got To Get You Into My Life (2:30)
14 Tomorrow Never Knows (2:57)

Total album length: 35 minutes

REVOLVER

1960s
7

Magical Mystery Tour

| • **Album sales:** 6,600,000 | • **Release date:** December 1967 |

In 1967, another chart-topping Beatles' album seemed par for the course. The soundtrack to the group's British television special (the first to air worldwide) was, sequentially, the follow-up to *Sgt. Pepper*, issued that summer. While *Magical Mystery Tour* might suffer in cut-by-cut comparison to this acknowledged masterpiece, it's nonetheless a compelling set, due mainly to the presence of all six sides of the Beatles' most recent – and highly adventurous – singles. These include the sublime 'Penny Lane' (Number One in the US and Number Two in the UK), 'All You Need Is Love' (Number One on both sides of the Atlantic) and 'Hello Goodbye'.

In addition to these tracks and the album's psychedelic title cut, the program features 'The Fool On The Hill', notable for one of McCartney's most moving vocals, the wordless 'Flying' and Harrison's eerie, fog-bound 'Blue Jay Way'. McCartney's 'Your Mother Should Know' harks back to such music-hall salutes as *Sgt. Pepper's* 'When I'm Sixty-Four'.

In the UK, *Magical Mystery Tour* was issued as a double EP (extended-play single). While the soundtrack, in both its US and UK forms, was an artistic and commercial success, The Beatles' TV special took a beating from critics, who found it plotless and confusing.

Number One singles:
US & UK: All You Need Is Love; Hello Goodbye;
US: Penny Lane

Grammy awards: None

Label: US: Capitol;
UK: Parlophone

Recorded in: London, UK

Personnel:
John Lennon (d. 1980)
Paul McCartney
George Harrison (d. 2001)
Ringo Starr
George Martin
David Mason (d. 2011)
The Mike Sammes Singers
Various other personnel

Producer:
George Martin

PSYCHEDELIA

The psychedelic movement originated with the California hippies, and spread outwards to become a pillar of the 1960s counter-culture by the beginning of the 1970s. Psychedelia is often identified with drug use, particularly of LSD and other mind-altering substances. Drug use was certainly fundamental to the psychedelic 'philosophy', but psychedelia was also a movement of fashion and graphics. Artists such as Wes Wilson, Michael English and Nigel Weymouth created surreal poster and album art using vivid swirls of day-glo colours, with the classic recurrent motifs of flowers and rainbows, and this style also spread into the loose hippie clothing characteristic of psychedelia's followers. Bands of the psychedelic movement included The Grateful Dead and Jefferson Airplane.

▲ **BACK COVER**

1. **Magical Mystery Tour (2:51)**
2. **Fool On The Hill (3:00)**
3. **Flying (2:16)**
4. **Blue Jay Way (3:56)**
5. **Your Mother Should Know (2:29)**
6. **I Am The Walrus (4:37)**
7. **Hello Goodbye (3:31)**
8. **Strawberry Fields Forever (4:10)**
9. **Penny Lane (3:03)**
10. **Baby You're A Rich Man (3:03)**
11. **All You Need Is Love (3:48)**

Total album length: 37 minutes

Magical Mystery Tour
The Fool On The Hill Flying Blue Jay Way
Your Mother Should Know I Am The Walrus
BEATLES
MAGICAL MYSTERY TOUR
Includes 24-page full color picture book
Hello Goodbye Strawberry Fields Forever
Penny Lane Baby You're A Rich Man
All You Need Is Love

1960s
6

Rubber Soul

| • **Album sales:** 7,000,000 | • **Release date:** December 1965 |

Two years of unbridled Beatlemania had afforded the Fab Four considerable career clout. On *Rubber Soul,* the group's 1965 yuletide offering, they began to display that confidence, stretching out musically – not even bothering to put their name on the album's cover.

Gone were the echo-drenched, electrified big-beat performances and teen love anthems of previous years, replaced with a more mature, acoustic-guitar-driven sound and introspective lyrical slant. Highlights include Lennon's 'Norwegian Wood (This Bird Has Flown)', a thinly veiled reference to an extra-marital affair, with sitar by George Harrison; 'In My Life', a poignant memory-lane trip; and 'I'm Looking Through You', McCartney's swipe at then-current girlfriend, British actress Jane Asher. Paul's faux-French ballad 'Michelle' garnered Lennon and McCartney a Grammy for Song of the Year.

Topping the charts for six weeks, the US version of *Rubber Soul* opens on a different note than its UK counterpart, starting with the more acoustic, country-styled 'I've Just Seen A Face' (a leftover from the British edition of the *Help!* album). The UK version of the album begins with the Anglo-soul strut 'Drive My Car'.

Number One singles: None

Grammy awards: Song of the year – Michelle

Label: US: Capitol; UK: Parlophone

Recorded in: London, UK

Personnel:
John Lennon (d. 1980)
Paul McCartney
George Harrison (d. 2001)
Ringo Starr
George Martin
Mal Evans (d. 1976)

Producer:
George Martin

THE MAJOR RECORD LABELS

The power of the big record labels during the 1960s is hard to overstate. The top 20 albums of the 1960s sold 127 million units in total, but 98 million of those sales were concentrated in the hands of only six labels – Columbia, Parlophone (of which Apple was a division), Capitol, Atlantic, RCA Victor and CBS. The explosive rise of record sales during the 1960s, which in the US alone went from $600 million in 1960 to US$1.2 billion in 1970 – made the major labels cultural powerhouses. Because a good label was a pre-requisite for success in the 1960s, artists were desperate to sign up, many of them falling foul to harsh contractual terms which saw them give away the rights to their music.

▲ **BACK COVER**

US:

1 **I've Just Seen A Face (2:04)**
2 **Norwegian Wood (This Bird Has Flown) (2:00)**
3 **You Won't See Me (3:19)**
4 **Think For Yourself (2:16)**
5 **The Word (2:43)**
6 **Michelle (2:42)**
7 **It's Only Love (1:53)**
8 **Girl (2:26)**
9 **I'm Looking Through You (2:27)**
10 **In My Life (2:27)**
11 **Wait (2:16)**
12 **Run For Your Life (2:18)**

Total album length: 29 minutes

UK:

1 **Drive My Car (2:30)**
2 **Norwegian Wood (This Bird Has Flown) (2:00)**
3 **You Won't See Me (3:19)**
4 **Nowhere Man (2:44)**
5 **Think For Yourself (2:16)**
6 **The Word (2:42)**
7 **Michelle (2:42)**
8 **What Goes On? (2:50)**
9 **Girl (2:33)**
10 **I'm Looking Through You (2:27)**
11 **In My Life (2:27)**
12 **Wait (2:16)**
13 **If I Need Someone (2:23)**
14 **Run For Your Life (2:18)**

Total album length: 35 minutes

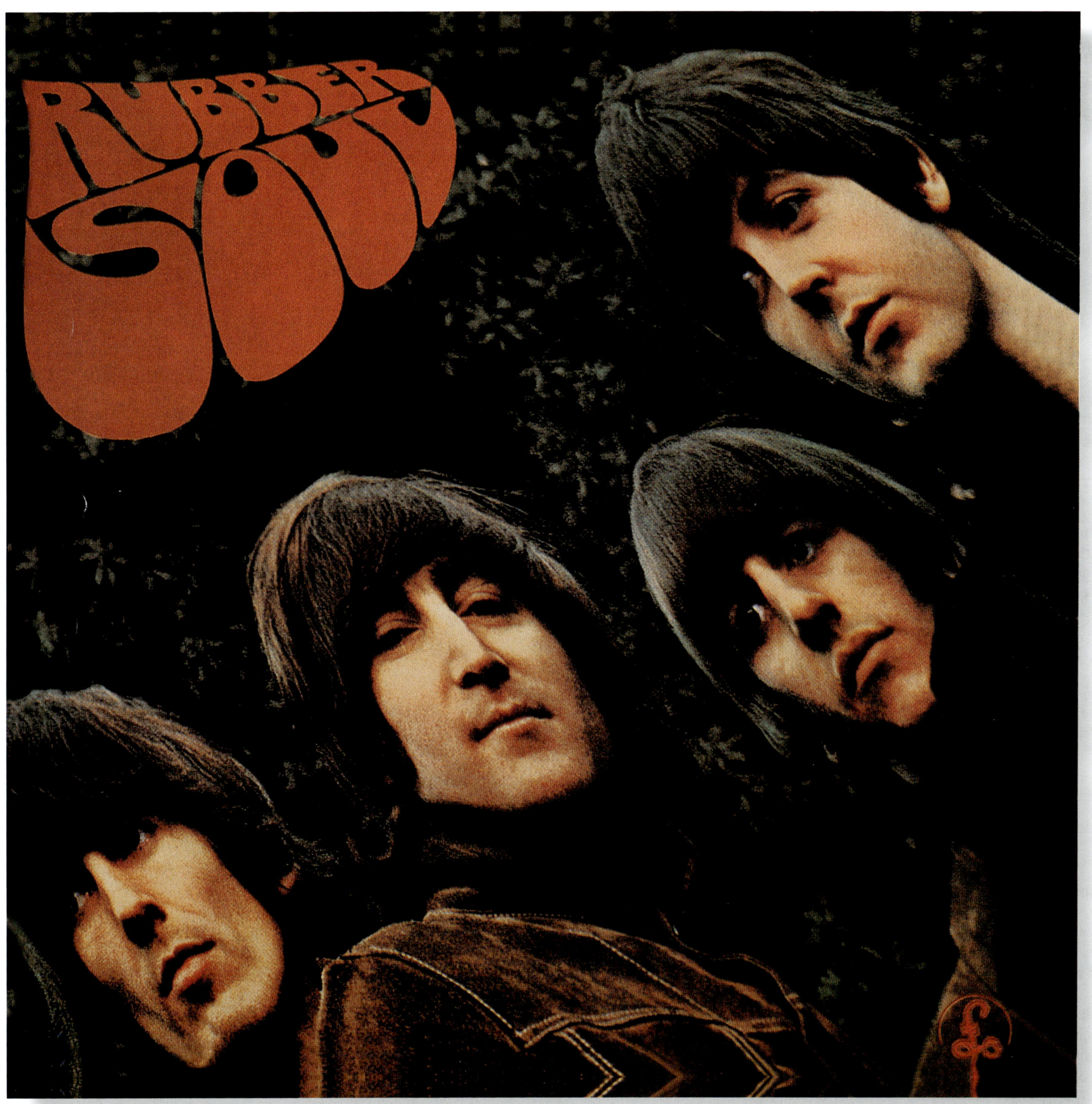
RUBBER SOUL

1960s
5

Led Zeppelin

| • **Album sales:** 10,500,000 | • **Release date:** January 1969 |

Led Zeppelin remains one of the most auspicious and influential debuts in pop. Countless late-1960s' rock bands had toiled in the blues field, particularly as psychedelic rock mutated into 'heavy rock', but none with so original and outsized a take on the venerable genre as Led Zeppelin. The album was recorded in 30 hours, it cost a mere £1,782 ($3,198) and by 1975 would gross £3,500,000 ($6,300,000).

Structurally, all the music on *Led Zeppelin* is blues, but the band's treatment of the form is expansive. Tempos are slowed to allow the riffs to gather force and explode with gales of guitar and shrieking vocals, as on the classics 'You Shook Me' and 'Dazed And Confused'.

Acoustic elements are allowed into the traditional folk song 'Babe I'm Gonna Leave You', and 'Black Mountain Side' is a quiet, all-instrumental interlude, but the album is mostly thunderous and unrelenting in its energy and attack. As such the album – and its sequel, *Led Zeppelin II* – has been a source of inspiration to generations of young musicians eager to express such power before audiences.

Led Zeppelin reached Number Six in the album charts in the UK and spent 79 weeks on chart. It reached Number 10 in the US, spending 50 weeks on chart.

Number One singles: None

Grammy awards: None

Label: US & UK: Atlantic

Recorded in: London, UK

Personnel:
Jimmy Page
Robert Plant
John Paul Jones
Jon Bonham (d. 1980)
Sandy Denny (d. 1978)
Viram Jasani

Producers:
Jimmy Page
Peter Grant (d. 1995)

THE COUNTER-CULTURE MOVEMENT

The 1960s counter-culture was essentially a youth backlash, a mass movement critique of the values, norms and ideas of parents and governments. Throughout Europe and the States, a new generation adopted lifestyles consciously chosen for their antithesis to white, middle-class living. Sexual liberation – aided by the advent of the birth control pill in 1962 – was declared, and radical music embraced. Drug experimentation (particularly with psychotropic substances such as LSD) was enshrined by the scientist/philosopher Timothy Leary, whose saying 'tune in, turn on, and drop out' became a mantra for the hippie generation. Hinduism and Buddhism were embraced by many as alternatives to authoritarian Judaeo-Christian systems. The counter-culture movement was also political, with numerous experiments in communitarian living, a violent opposition to the Vietnam War, and a resurgent socialism.

▲ **BACK COVER**

1. **Good Times Bad Times (2:43)**
2. **Babe I'm Gonna Leave You (6:40)**
3. **You Shook Me (6:30)**
4. **Dazed And Confused (6:27)**
5. **Your Time Is Gonna Come (4:41)**
6. **Black Mountain Side (2:06)**
7. **Communication Breakdown (2:26)**
8. **I Can't Quit You Baby (4:42)**
9. **How Many More Times (3:30)**

Total album length: 40 minutes

Sleeve artwork by George Hardie

1960s
4

Sgt. Pepper's Lonely Hearts Club Band

| • **Album sales:** 12,700,000 | • **Release date:** June 1967 |

When The Beatles first arrived in America in February 1964, the magazine *Newsweek* labelled their lyrics 'a catastrophe' and their music 'a near disaster'. Three years later, the same publication was comparing them to T.S. Eliot, Wordsworth and Tennyson. *Sgt. Pepper* was the occasion for the change of heart.

Both *Rubber Soul* (1965) and *Revolver* (1966) had revealed a steep increase in the sophistication of The Beatles' songwriting and recording skills, but neither was as ambitious – or successful at realizing its ambitions – as *Sgt. Pepper*. The album, which was recorded at London's Abbey Road studios using a pioneering eight-track recording process, made Number One in both the UK and US album charts. Embracing styles as far apart as music-hall ('With A Little Help From My Friends'), psychedelia ('A Day In The Life', 'Lucy In The Sky With Diamonds'), Indian ('Within You, Without You'), and classical, with the use of orchestral pieces, *Sgt. Pepper* held the top position for 15 weeks and remained in the charts for nearly three-and-a-half years.

The album sleeve, which was the first to feature cardboard cut-outs, is also notable for Peter Blake's distinctive artwork, featuring models of The Beatles from London's Madame Tussauds.

Number One singles:
None

Grammy awards:
Album of the year; Best contemporary album

Label: US: Capitol;
UK: Parlophone

Recorded in: London, UK

Personnel:
John Lennon (d. 1980)
Paul McCartney
George Harrison (d. 2001)
Ringo Starr
George Martin
Sheila Bromberg
Robert Burns
Mal Evans (d. 1976)
Various other personnel

Producer:
George Martin

THE BEATLES PHENOMENON

In 1961, Brian Epstein, a record store manager in Liverpool, became manager of a local four-piece group called The Beatles. Under Epstein's promotion, and through sheer musical excellence, The Beatles became the biggest pop group in the world, arguably in all history. 'Beatlemania' – a term that defined the hysteria the group attracted – radiated beyond popular music, and also crossed the Atlantic after television appearances in the United States in 1964. Their explosive appearance onto the US pop scene prompted the critics to proclaim 'the British invasion'. Anything to do with Liverpool became a sensation in the United States – the late DJ John Peel recounted being mobbed in the States purely on account of his similar regional accent.

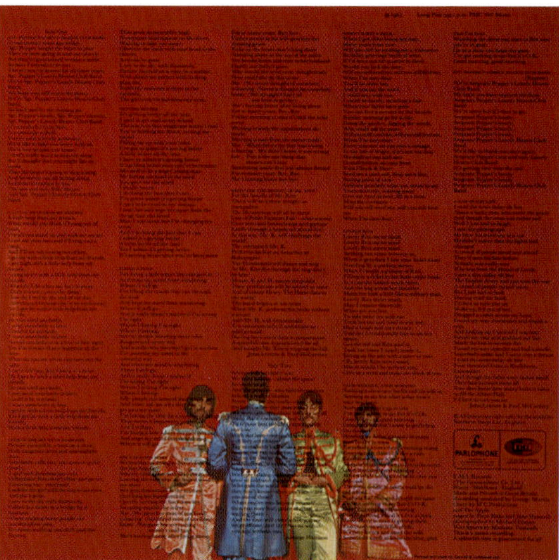

▲ BACK COVER

1 Sgt. Pepper's Lonely Hearts Club Band (2:02)
2 With A Little Help From My Friends (2:44)
3 Lucy In The Sky With Diamonds (3:29)
4 Getting Better (2:48)
5 Fixing A Hole (2:36)
6 She's Leaving Home (3:35)
7 Being For The Benefit Of Mr. Kite (2:37)
8 Within You, Without You (5:06)
9 When I'm Sixty-Four (2:37)
10 Lovely Rita (2:42)
11 Good Morning, Good Morning (2:42)
12 Sgt. Pepper's Lonely Heart's Club Band (Reprise) (1:19)
13 A Day In The Life (5:33)

Total album length: 40 minutes

Sgt PEPPERS
LONELY HEARTS
CLUB BAND
BEATLES

1960s
3

Led Zeppelin II

| • **Album sales:** 13,200,000 | • **Release date:** October 1969 |

In January 1969 Led Zeppelin got the ball rolling with the release of their debut album. Only nine months later they released their second album, *Led Zeppelin II*. It proved even more popular than the first, eventually selling more than 12,000,000 copies in the US alone and hitting Number One spot in both the US and UK, where it enjoyed chart runs of 98 and 138 weeks respectively.

Led Zeppelin II was recorded during the band's US tour and probably owes much of its success to their popularity as a live act. A hit single was also a factor. Though *Led Zeppelin* and *Led Zeppelin II* both received widespread airplay on album-oriented FM stations, the release of 'Whole Lotta Love' as a single took the band's powerful sound to the larger Top 40 AM-radio audience as well. 'Whole Lotta Love' reached Number Four in the US.

The album does not deviate greatly from the approach introduced on the band's debut set. 'Ramble On' is largely acoustic and bare-boned in its arrangement, but the bulk of the programme relies on muscle and electricity. *Rolling Stone* magazine voted the album Number 75 in the 500 greatest albums of all time.

Number One singles: None

Grammy awards: None

Label: US & UK: Atlantic

Recorded in: Various locations, USA

Personnel:
Jimmy Page
John Bonham (d. 1980)
John Paul Jones
Robert Plant
Andy Johns
Chris Huston
Eddie Kramer
George Chkiantz
George Marino

Producer:
Peter Grant (d. 1995)

BBC RADIO

In September 1967, the BBC launched its popular music radio channel, Radio 1, which was to be the powerhouse of popular music broadcasting in the UK for the next 30 years, and which brought Led Zeppelin's 'Whole Lotta Love' to a wide audience.

The radio station was actually created as part of harsh government action against the unregulated 'pirate' radio stations such as Radio London, Radio Caroline and Swinging Radio England. The pirate stations had sizeable audiences, but paid no broadcast fees to artists, so in 1966 they were banned from broadcasting and the BBC announced that it would replace them with a new music station. The first show was hosted by DJ Tony Blackburn. A notable deficiency was that the station broadcast on an AM frequency, and did not have FM stereo as standard for another 21 years.

LED ZEPPELIN II
1 - WHOLE LOTTA LOVE 5:34
2 - WHAT IS AND WHAT SHOULD NEVER BE 4:44
3 - THE LEMON SONG 6:19
4 - THANK YOU 4:47
5 - HEARTBREAKER 4:14
6 - LIVING LOVING MAID (SHE'S JUST A WOMAN) 2:39
7 - RAMBLE ON 4:23
8 - MOBY DICK 4:21
9 - BRING IT ON HOME 4:20
PRODUCED BY JIMMY PAGE
Artwork: David Juniper
Digitally remastered from the original master tapes by Jimmy Page and George Marino at Sterling Sound.
0 7567-82633-2 3
7567-82633-2

▲ **BACK COVER**

1. **Whole Lotta Love (5:34)**
2. **What Is And What Should Never Be (4:44)**
3. **Lemon Song (6:19)**
4. **Thank You (4:47)**
5. **Heartbreaker (4:14)**
6. **Living Loving Maid (She's Just a Woman) (2:39)**
7. **Ramble On (4:23)**
8. **Moby Dick (4:21)**
9. **Bring It On Home (4:20)**

Total album length: 41 minutes

Sleeve artwork by David Juniper

1960s
2

Abbey Road

| • **Album sales:** 13,700,000 | • **Release date:** October 1969 |

Though *Let It Be* was The Beatles' last official album release, *Abbey Road* was their real swan song, a fitting cap to their career and the decade they had dominated. Lennon announced to the other Beatles that he was leaving the band soon after *Let It Be,* but was persuaded to remain quiet in public. Shaking off the creative malaise that had stalled them, the group temporarily shelved that project and reconvened at Abbey Road studios with renewed musical vigour.

Abbey Road is divided into two distinct halves, with the first side comprising stand-alone tracks (opening with Lennon's 'Come Together') and the second featuring an adventurous song suite that justifies its musical pretensions. George Harrison also steps out of Lennon and McCartney's shadow on this LP, penning the album's two best songs, the ebullient 'Here Comes The Sun' and the ballad 'Something'.

A Grammy winner – for Best Engineered Recording – this 1969 release logged 11 straight weeks at Number One. However, the single 'Something' failed to top the charts, reaching Number Three in the US and Number Four in the UK.

Number One singles:
None

Grammy awards:
Best engineered (non-classical) recording

Label: US & UK: Apple

Recorded in: London, UK

Personnel:
John Lennon (d. 1980)
Paul McCartney
George Harrison (d. 2001)
Ringo Starr
George Martin
Billy Preston
Various other personnel

Producers:
George Martin
Geoffrey Emerick (engineer)

LONDON IN THE 1960s

For a few years in the late 1960s, London virtually became the cultural capital of the world and the pace-setter in fashion, music and ideas. In 1966, *Time* magazine proclaimed that London 'swings, it is the scene', and coined the phrase 'swinging London'. This declaration referred to the city's hip youth culture centred on the cult-status music of The Beatles and The Rolling Stones, the mini-skirt fashions of designers such as Mary Quant, the strutting arrogance of the Mods, the ultra trendy shops and cafés of Carnaby Street and the King's Road, the iconic photography of David Bailey, and the general sense of self-importance that imbued the city's intellectuals and fashionistas during this time.

▲ **BACK COVER**

1. **Come Together (4:20)**
2. **Maxwell's Silver Hammer (3:27)**
3. **Something (3:03)**
4. **Oh! Darling (3:26)**
5. **Octopus's Garden (2:51)**
6. **I Want You (She's So Heavy) (7:47)**
7. **Here Comes The Sun (3:05)**
8. **Because (2:45)**
9. **You Never Give Me Your Money (4:02)**
10. **Sun King (2:26)**
11. **Mean Mr Mustard (1:06)**
12. **Polythene Pam (1:12)**
13. **She Came In Through The Bathroom Window (1:57)**
14. **Golden Slumbers (1:31)**
15. **Carry That Weight (1:36)**
16. **The End (2:19)**
17. **Her Majesty (0:23)**

Total album length: 47 minutes

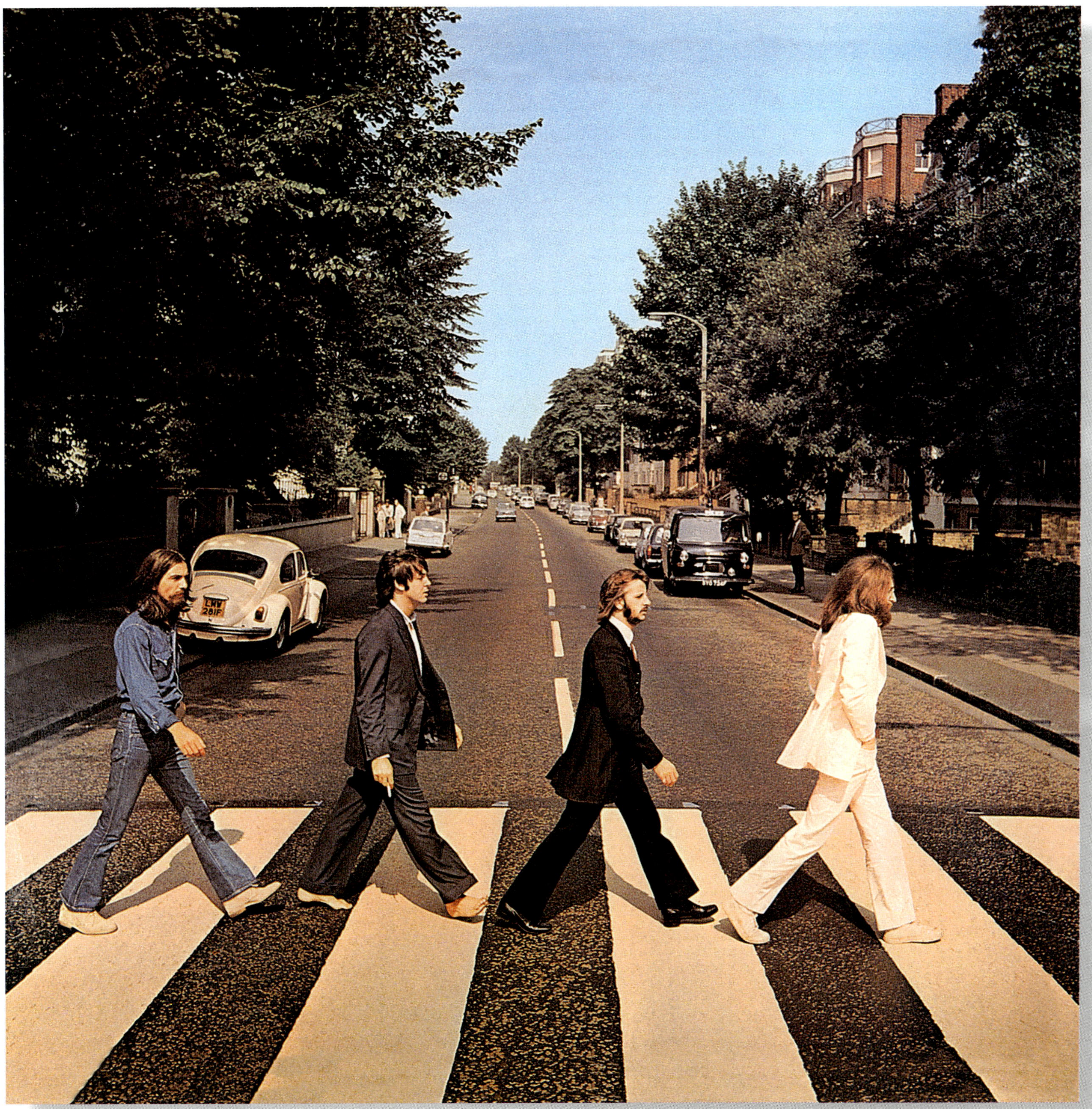
LMW 281F

1960s
1

The Beatles (The White Album)

| • **Album sales:** 20,200,000 | • **Release date:** November 1968 |

In May of 1968, The Beatles gathered at George Harrison's house to record demos and take stock of the wealth of material they had amassed from their recent stay in India. Most of the songs from this time would end up on the mammoth double-album *The Beatles*, commonly known as 'The White Album', released that November.

The album's stark monochromatic cover (with the blind-embossed title intentionally set at an angle), designed by pop artist Richard Hamilton, is visually arresting, but it also provides some indication of the disharmony within the foursome who could not agree on a visual image. Something of this tension can be heard on the album, which is noticeably less cohesive than earlier efforts; producer George Martin has said it would've made a better single disc. By this time, the songwriters were beginning to head in their own directions: John Lennon with the soulful 'Julia'; Paul McCartney with 'Back in the USSR'; and George Harrison with the beautiful 'While My Guitar Gently Weeps', featuring Eric Clapton.

The album reached Number One on both sides of the Atlantic.

Number One singles:
None

Grammy awards:
None

Label: US & UK: Apple

Recorded in: London, UK

Personnel:
John Lennon (d. 1980)
Paul McCartney
George Harrison (d. 2001)
Ringo Starr
Yoko Ono
George Martin
Eric Clapton
Jack Fallon (d. 2006)
The Mike Sammes Singers
Chris Thomas
Various other personnel

Producer:
George Martin

INDIA AND 1960s WESTERN CULTURE

In the counter-culture youth society of the late 1960s, India suddenly became enormously fashionable, a projected antithesis to everything perceived wrong in Western materialist society. Indian spirituality – particularly meditative branches of Hinduism – and Indian fashions, iconography and foods were increasingly imported into Europe and the United States by the end of the decade. The Beatles were at the centre of this movement. George Harrison's interest in eastern mysticism led to The Beatles visiting the Maharishi Mahesh Yogi, a practitioner of transcendental meditation, at Rishikesh in 1968, an experience that was especially formative for Harrison. The sitar, tabla and other Indian instrumentation made frequent appearances in Beatles' records, and in the tracks of many other groups, throughout the 1960s and early to mid-1970s.

▲ **BACK COVER**

1. **Back In The USSR (2:43)**
2. **Dear Prudence (3:57)**
3. **Glass Onion (2:17)**
4. **Ob-la-di-ob-la-da (3:09)**
5. **Wild Honey Pie (1:02)**
6. **The Continuing Story Of Bungalo Bill (3:05)**
7. **While My Guitar Gently Weeps (4:45)**
8. **Happiness Is A Warm Gun (2:44)**
9. **Martha My Dear (2:29)**
10. **I'm So Tired (2:03)**
11. **Blackbird (2:18)**
12. **Piggies (2:05)**
13. **Rocky Racoon (3:41)**
14. **Don't Pass Me By (3:42)**
15. **Why Don't We Do It In The Road? (1:41)**
16. **I Will (1:47)**
17. **Julia (2:54)**
18. **Birthday (2:43)**
19. **Yer Blues (4:01)**
20. **Mother Nature's Son (2:48)**
21. **Everybody's Got Something To Hide Except Me And My Monkey (2:25)**
22. **Sexy Sadie (3:15)**
23. **Helter Skelter (4:30)**
24. **Long Long Long (3:04)**
25. **Revolution 1 (4:16)**
26. **Honey Pie (2:41)**
27. **Savoy Truffle (2:55)**
28. **Cry Baby Cry (3:11)**
29. **Revolution 9 (8:13)**
30. **Good Night (3:12)**

Total album length: 94 minutes

The BEATLES

MICHAEL JACKSON
OFF THE WALL

JOHN TRAVOLTA OLIVIA NEWTON-JOHN
THE ORIGINAL SOUNDTRACK FROM THE MOTION PICTURE
GREASE

The Best-Selling Albums of the 1970s

Describing the 1970s to journalists in early 1980 as "a drag", ex-Beatle John Lennon was noting that the world had become a more dangerous place, with news of war and unrest hitting the headlines on a regular basis. In popular culture, too, the hippy ideals of the 1960s had been swept away by punk and new wave, bringing forth an edgier, more selfish outlook.

In terms of the range and variety of music, however, the decade to which Lennon referred was anything but a drag. The 1970s were a boom period on both sides of the Atlantic, both for the creative output of artists and musicians and for the fortunes of the music industry itself. Record sales, both albums and singles, were growing beyond executives' wildest forecasts. More music was being made available than ever before; newer styles and fresher, more innovative sounds were coming to the fore. Punk, new wave, progressive rock, soul, reggae, dance, disco. They all either burst onto the scene for the first time in the 1970s or, if already established, were developed, enhanced and improved.

Having seen the ideals of the 'peace and love' era amount to little, people approached the 1970s hoping for positive developments. Many looked to the music to provide the answers – or at least a distraction from the real world. People wanted music to reflect the times in which they lived, but they also wanted to use it as a soundtrack to having a good time.

In the 1970s, heavy rock came into its own, thanks largely to British bands such as Led Zeppelin, Deep Purple and the Ozzy Osborne-fronted Black Sabbath. Led Zeppelin accounted for 64 million album sales in the 1970s – with each of the seven albums the band released in the period topping the charts in the UK and getting a Top Two placing in the US. But there was more to UK's rock invasion of the US than a bunch of galvanizing riffs and heavy bass lines. Pink Floyd captured fans everywhere with their deeply constructed compositions, heaping electronic sounds onto guitars and keyboards.

Other bands whose high production values were matched by their ability to turn out albums full of searingly good songs included the Anglo-American Fleetwood Mac. Their album *Rumours* became a Number One album in the US and the UK, and went on to become the second biggest-selling long-player of the decade. Smooth rock was also a forte of the Eagles. At the outset, the band had a distinctly country vibe, but as the albums came and went they developed a sharper sound, nowhere more evident than on their career highlight, *Hotel California*.

It can be argued that the 1970s witnessed a greater breadth and variety of music than any period before or since. Certainly the evolution of music during this time – the speed with which it changed throughout those ten years – resulted in a great swathe of different sounds. There was a readiness on the part of the average music fan to listen to different styles. This was, after all, a time before radio formatting took hold of the airwaves and established creative ghettos. It was a time when an album could work its way up the charts and build upon a groundswell of support. In all, the 1970s were, indeed, a golden age for popular music in all its many forms.

1970s
20

The Long Run

| • **Album sales:** 7,100,000 | • **Release date:** September 1979 |

Follow-up to the hugely successful *Hotel California, The Long Run* took a reported three years to complete, but despite the amount of time expended on putting it together it was never in with a chance of matching its illustrious and mega-selling predecessor. Although the album sold millions and spawned hit singles in 'Heartache Tonight', the title track and the soft rock ballad 'I Can't Tell You Why', it had considerably less of the creative spark of *Hotel California*, and for those prepared to look for them the signs were starting to appear that all was not heading in the right direction for the Eagles. Don Henley's artistic stamp was not much in evidence, unlike on *Hotel California*, with the exception of the title track and the album's closer, 'The Sad Café'. Long-time bassist Randy Meisner had left to pursue a solo career and was replaced by ex-Poco Tim Schmit. Joe Walsh's 'In The City' might not even have been a song destined for an Eagles record, having appeared on the soundtrack to *The Warriors* as a solo song.

Still, all of this didn't prevent the album from topping the US charts, spending 57 weeks in the charts and reaching Number Four in the UK. *The Long Run* was certified platinum in January 1980, less than four months after its release.

Number One singles:
US: Heartache Tonight

Grammy awards:
Best rock vocal performance by a duo or group

Label: US & UK: Asylum

Recorded in: Florida, USA

Personnel:
Don Henley
Glenn Frey
Joe Walsh
Timothy Schmit
Don Felder

Producer:
Bill Szymczyk

SEVENTIES' CONSUMERISM

The 1970s sits in competition with the 1980s as the 'me decade', but has a good claim to the title. While the Eagles sang songs of poetic reflection, much of the rest of adult society was devoted to consumerism. Advances made in computer chip technology (Intel introduced the microprocessor onto the market in 1971) and advances in home entertainment produced a rash of new luxury technologies, including Atari's Pong – the first home games console – and the VCR. For those with greater spending power, they could invest (from 1977) in an Apple II personal computer, which with a whopping 4k of RAM (later upgraded to 48k) retailed in the States for $1298.

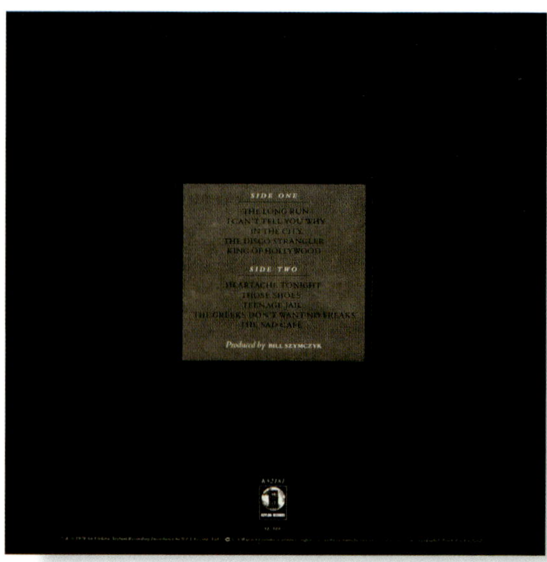

▲ **BACK COVER**

1. **The Long Run (3:43)**
2. **I Can't Tell You Why (4:55)**
3. **In The City (3:45)**
4. **Disco Strangler (2:45)**
5. **King Of Hollywood (6:28)**
6. **Heartache Tonight (4:26)**
7. **Those Shoes (4:54)**
8. **Teenage Jail (3:44)**
9. **The Greeks Don't Want No Freaks (2:20)**
10. **The Sad Café (5:35)**

Total album length: 42 minutes

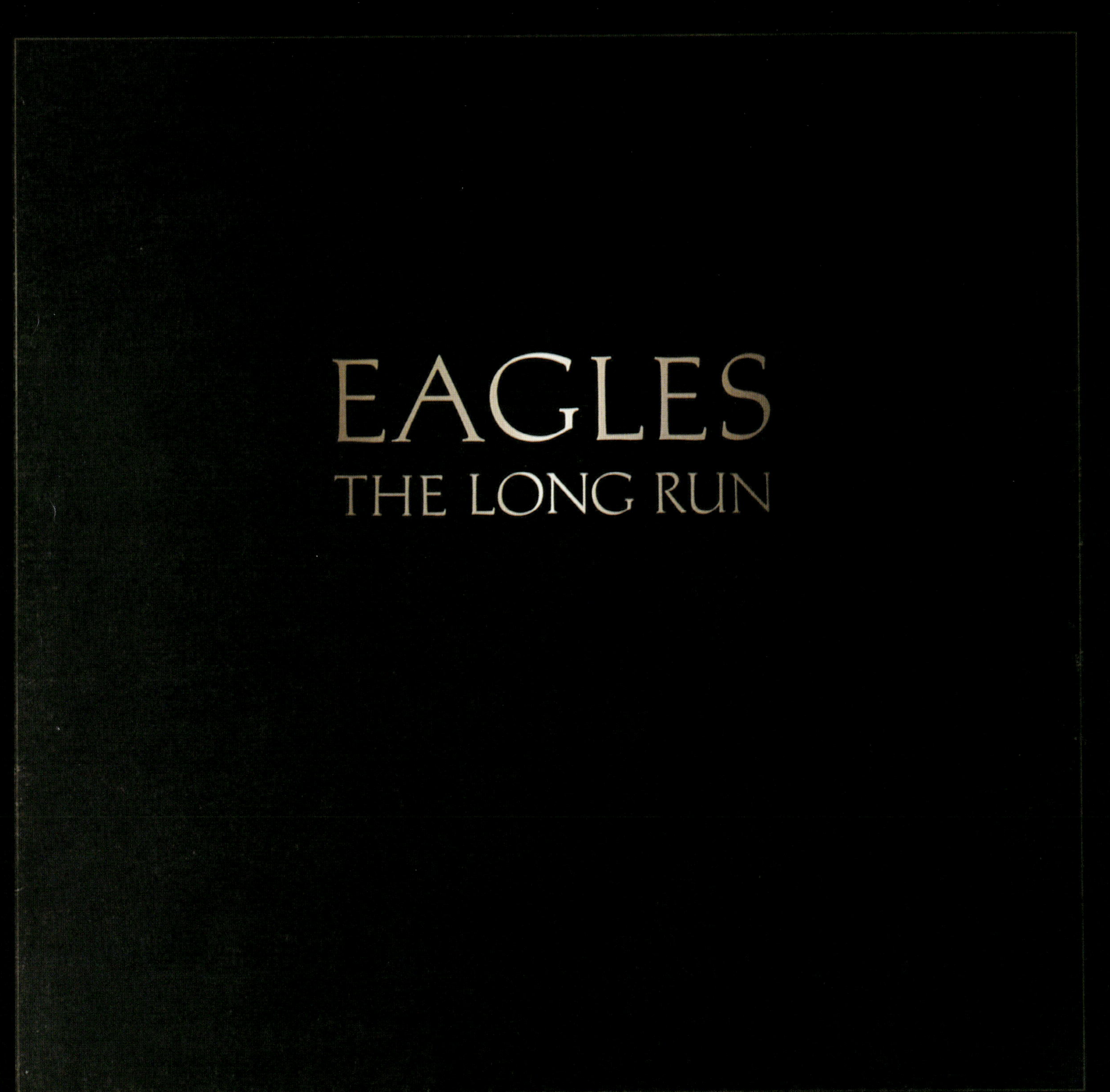

Sleeve artwork by Kosh and Jim Shea

1970s
19

Running On Empty

• Album sales: 7,200,000 | **• Release date:** January 1978

Entering somewhat of a creative lull following some sterling albums – his eponymous debut, *For Everyman, Late For The Sky* and *The Pretender* – *Running On Empty* was regarded by many as lacking ambition, but was nevertheless Browne's most commercially successful of his career to date. It peaked at Number Three in the US and reached Number 28 in the UK.

Browne had exhausted himself emotionally on previous records, laying his soul bare, and the album's title suggests he was indeed close to the edge, or perhaps even the end. Although many of the songs were recorded onstage or in hotel rooms while on the road, it is an album about being on the road, rather than a genuinely 'live' performance album, with songs such as 'The Road', 'Cocaine' and 'The Load Out' – an homage to his road crew – leaving relatively little to the imagination. Still, with two hits in the US in 'The Load Out/Stay' and the title track it served him well. His heartfelt introspection is called upon on 'Love Needs A Heart', an accessible lilting ballad very much in the Browne mould, while one of the album's highlights is the Danny Kortchmar-penned 'Shaky Town'.

Number One singles: None

Grammy awards: None

Label: US & UK: Asylum

Recorded in: Various locations, USA

Personnel:
Jackson Browne
Leland Sklar
Russell Kunkel
David Lindley
Craig Doerge
Danny Kortchmar
Doug Hayward
Rosemary Butler

Producer:
Jackson Browne

THE MUSIC PRESS

While today the music press is of limited impact on the average listener, during the 1970s it could shape the very fashionability of a group or artist. In the US, *Rolling Stone* magazine hit its peak popularity, defining itself as the magazine of the hippie and rock generations. In the UK, *New Musical Express* – a veteran magazine dating back to 1952 – became a critical standard, with defiant, well-crafted, knowing articles that did not shy away from attacking central figures of the music industry. Ironically, after the punk revolution of 1976, *NME* was actually attacked by many as an 'establishment' magazine, but through employing caustic new talent, such as journalists Julie Burchill and Tony Parsons, it retained a committed readership.

▲ **BACK COVER**

1. **Running On Empty (5:27)**
2. **The Road (4:50)**
3. **Rosie (3:41)**
4. **You Love The Thunder (3:56)**
5. **Cocaine (4:54)**
6. **Shaky Town (3:40)**
7. **Love Needs A Heart (3:30)**
8. **Nothing But Time (3:36)**
9. **The Load Out (5:35)**
10. **Stay (3:22)**

Total album length: 42 minutes

JACKSON BROWNE
RUNNING ON EMPTY

1970s
18

Off The Wall

| • **Album sales:** 8,000,000 | • **Release date:** August 1979 |

Despite appearing at the end of the decade, *Off The Wall* is one of the seminal albums of the 1970s. Coming off the back of the disco craze, it is also perhaps one of the slickest pop/dance albums ever recorded, thanks in large part to the efforts of producer Quincy Jones, whose partnership with Jackson helped create the wonderfully full disco/funk sound that pervades much of the record.

And while it may not have spawned as many Number One singles – only 'Don't Stop 'Til You Get Enough' in the US – as his later smash hit album, *Thriller*, it nevertheless marked the point at which Jackson's solo career took an extremely sharp upward curve and the artist became the most recognizable singer on the planet. The album 'only' managed to reach Number Three on the US album charts and Number Five in the UK, but it laid the foundations for the creative purple patch that was to carry Jackson through the 1980s.

With songs written by Jackson, Rod Temperton, David Foster, Carole Bayer Sager and others, *Off The Wall* spawned four Top Ten single hits on both sides of the Atlantic, including the ballad, 'She's Out Of My Life'.

Number One singles: US: Don't Stop 'Til You Get Enough; US: Rock With You

Grammy awards: None

Label: US & UK: Epic

Recorded in: Los Angeles, USA

Personnel:
Michael Jackson (d. 2009)
Louis Johnson
George Duke
John Robinson
Greg Phillinganes
David Williams (d. 2009)
Marlo Henderson
Randy Jackson
Richard Heath
Paulinho da Costa
The Seawind Horns

Producer:
Quincy Jones

MICHAEL AND THE JACKSONS

The Jackson 5 were a family group of five brothers during the early to mid 1970s, yet the talent of young Michael could not be contained within its confines. Signed in 1969 to the Motown label when the eldest, Jackie, was 18 and the youngest, Michael, was 11, The Jackson 5 had four consecutive Number One hits in 1970 alone. Michael stood out as a phenomenally talented dancer and, as he grew older, his talent took the focus from the rest of the group, causing friction. From 1975, the year they moved to Epic Records and renamed themselves The Jacksons, the members started to go their separate ways, particularly Michael. *Off the Wall* (1979) set him aside as a superlative solo act, and he became the world's biggest star during the 1980s.

▲ **BACK COVER**

1. **Don't Stop 'Til You Get Enough (6:05)**
2. **Rock With You (3:40)**
3. **Workin' Day And Night (5:13)**
4. **Get On The Floor (4:39)**
5. **Off The Wall (4:05)**
6. **Girlfriend (3:04)**
7. **She's Out Of My Life (3:38)**
8. **I Can't Help It (4:29)**
9. **It's The Falling In Love (3:48)**
10. **Burn This Disco Out (3:44)**

Total album length: 42 minutes

Sleeve artwork by Mike Salisbury and Steve Harvey

1970s
17

Toys In The Attic

| • **Album sales:** 8,200,000 | • **Release date:** April 1975 |

Seen by many as America's answer to the Rolling Stones, not least due to the camp posturing of singer Steve Tyler and guitarist Joe Perry and the band's obvious enjoyment as they revelled in the fast-lane of rock 'n' roll, Aerosmith's third album confirmed their status as the top live and recorded rock act of the day, at least in their homeland.

Recorded at the Record Plant in New York, and produced by Jack Douglas, *Toys In The Attic* was an immediate success. Tracks such as the epic 'Sweet Emotion', the Zeppelin-esque 'Round And Round', the blues-oriented 'Adam's Apple' and the big-band boogie number, 'Big Ten Inch', combined the band's musical rock 'n' blues influence with an upfront approach to sexual topics. In the US, the single 'Toys In The Attic' stormed the Hot 100, peaking at Number 11, but in the UK, in the grip of the early days of the punk revolution, the record fell on stony ground.

The album is perhaps best known for featuring the first real crossover song in rock in the form of 'Walk This Way', which was remodelled to great effect by rap act Run DMC 11 years later, doing much to rekindle interest in the band. It is one of the few songs in history that has charted in two different decades.

Number One singles: None

Grammy awards: None

Label: US: Columbia; UK: CBS

Recorded in: New York, USA

Personnel:
Steve Tyler
Joe Perry
Tom Hamilton
Brad Whitford
Joey Kramer

Producer:
Jack Douglas

THE ROCK LIFESTYLE

Although there were exceptions, the rock stars of the 1970s generally lived the true 'sex, drugs and rock 'n' roll' lifestyle. Drugs were, ironically, often central to the groups' creativity but usually resulted in group destruction. Luminaries killed by drugs famously include Jimi Hendrix, Janis Joplin and Jim Morrison, but more frequently substance abuse simply rendered people chronically unstable, as in the case of Ozzy Osbourne in Black Sabbath (he was fired and replaced by ex-Rainbow vocalist Ronnie James Dio), or violent, as was horribly demonstrated by Sid Vicious' murder of Nancy Spungen. Sometimes the excesses were (relatively) more benign, such as Led Zeppelin's reputed seafood S&M with groupies, one ex-groupie recounting being beaten with a sea bass.

▲ **BACK COVER**

1. **Toys In The Attic (3:06)**
2. **Uncle Salty (4:10)**
3. **Adam's Apple (4:33)**
4. **Walk This Way (3:41)**
5. **Big Ten Inch Record (2:16)**
6. **Sweet Emotion (4:34)**
7. **No More No More (4:34)**
8. **Round And Round (5:03)**
9. **You See Me Crying (5:12)**

Total album length: 37 minutes

Sleeve artwork by Ingrid Haenke

1970s
16

Bridge Over Troubled Water

| • **Album sales:** 8,300,000 | • **Release date:** February 1970 |

Simon and Garfunkel hit their commercial peak, but also the end of the line with the release of the album *Bridge Over Troubled Water*. The making of what became their final studio album together required 800 studio hours, only emphasizing the diverging paths down which the long-time friends were heading.

While the trademark harmonies were evident on the likes of 'Cecilia' and 'Baby Driver', elsewhere the duo were at loggerheads over song selection. Art Garfunkel rejected Paul Simon's overtly political 'Cuba Si, Nixon No', with Simon turning away his colleague's Bach chorale-like track. Even the gospel-styled title track created tensions. Garfunkel persuaded Simon to pen a third verse to the song, much to the chagrin of its writer, and initially insisted Simon should sing the number himself. Garfunkel's eventual angelic delivery turned it into a landmark recording, though it angered Simon when Garfunkel won all the concert applause for what was his song.

Bridge Over Troubled Water spent 10 weeks as the US Number One, while in the UK its 41-week chart-topping run remains the longest for a pop/rock release. Collectively, as an album and single *Bridge Over Troubled Water* won an unprecedented six Grammy awards. By the end of 1970, Paul Simon had earned over $7 million from the tune.

Number One singles: US & UK: Bridge Over Troubled Water

Grammy awards:
Album of the year; Record of the year; Song of the year; Best contemporary song; Best arrangement accompanying vocalists; Best engineered record

Label: US: CBS; UK: Columbia

Recorded in: New York & Los Angeles, USA

Personnel:
Paul Simon
Art Garfunkel
Hal Blaine
Larry Knechtel (d. 2009)
Fred Carter Jr (d. 2010)
Ernie Freeman Combo
Jimmie Haskell

Producers:
Simon and Garfunkel
Roy Halee

THE NIXON ERA

Simon and Garfunkel's melodies seem to form a soundtrack to a particularly unsettled period in American history. President Richard Nixon entered the White House in 1969, with the Vietnam War still the dominant political issue. Massive war protests were recurrent, and on 4 May 1970 four student protesters were shot dead at Kent State University by National Guardsmen. Nixon withdrew US ground troops from Vietnam by 1973, but there were other problems for the administration. Divorce rates were climbing, and unemployment was high. Abortion was legalized in 1973. Women, ethnic minorities and gays were campaigning for greater status.

The Nixon era came to an end after the Watergate scandal, when in 1974 he resigned to avoid impeachment, being guilty of dirty tricks, including bugging political opponents and cover-ups. Despite bringing US involvement in the Vietnam War to a close, that is what Nixon will be remembered for.

▲ **BACK COVER**

1. **Bridge Over Troubled Water (4:55)**
2. **El Condor Pasa (If I Could) (3:09)**
3. **Cecilia (2:54)**
4. **Keep The Customer Satisfied (2:37)**
5. **So Long, Frank Lloyd Wright (3:45)**
6. **The Boxer (5:12)**
7. **Baby Driver (3:17)**
8. **The Only Living Boy In New York (4:01)**
9. **Why Don't You Write Me (2:46)**
10. **Bye Bye Love (2:52)**
11. **Song For The Asking (1:59)**

Total album length: 36 minutes

Sleeve artwork by Tony Lane

1970s
15

Songs In The Key Of Life

| • **Album sales:** 9,300,000 | • **Release date:** September 1976 |

Stevie Wonder kept bosses at his label Motown waiting for two years for *Songs In The Key Of Life*, but their patience was rewarded by the most ambitious project he had yet conceived.

Having recorded six albums of original material in just over three years, Wonder took his time in crafting this wide-ranging set, spread across two discs and an accompanying four-track EP. At this career point the artist could afford to take his time – six months before the album's release he had signed a seven-year, US$13 million new deal with his record company, at that time the biggest in recording history.

The album became the first by a US artist to debut at Number One on the Hot 100, while delivering chart-topping singles in 'Sir Duke', Wonder's uplifting tribute to Ellington, and the punchy 'I Wish'. With 14 weeks in the top slot, the album also combined the gentleness of 'Love's In Need Of Love Today' with the social awareness of 'Black Man' and 'Village Ghetto Land'. 'Isn't She Lovely', which Wonder refused to edit from its six-and-a-half minutes for single release, honoured the birth of his daughter and even contained her early cries.

Number One singles: US: Sir Duke; I Wish

Grammy awards: Album of the year; Best producer; Best pop vocal (male); Best R&B vocal performance – I Wish

Label: US: Tamla; UK: Tamla Motown

Recorded in: Los Angeles, New York & Sausalito, USA

Personnel:
Stevie Wonder
George Benson
Herbie Hancock
Minnie Riperton (d. 1979)
Various others

Producer:
Stevie Wonder

THE MOTOWN LABEL

By the 1970s, the Motown record label reached the apogee of its success, and had been responsible for bringing some of the greatest African-American artists to the public ear. The company was founded on 14 December 1959 by Berry Gordy, Jr., in Detroit, Michigan. During the 1960s it fostered talent that included The Supremes, Marvin Gaye, Smokey Robinson, Stevie Wonder and The Jackson 5, with the label running 22 hours a day to keep the hits flowing. The late 1970s saw Motown struggle, and fail, to maintain the momentum of the 1960s, although talent such as Lionel Richie and the Commodores ensured that the decade was not free from Number One hits for the label.

▲ BACK COVER

1 **Love's In Need Of Love Today (7:05)**
2 **Have A Talk With God (2:42)**
3 **Village Ghetto Land (3:25)**
4 **Contusion (6:23)**
5 **Sir Duke (3:45)**
6 **I Wish (3:54)**
7 **Knocks Me Off My Feet (4:12)**
8 **Pastime Paradise (3:36)**
9 **Summer Soft (3:27)**
10 **Ordinary Pain (4:14)**
11 **Isn't She Lovely (6:34)**
12 **Joy Inside My Tears (6:29)**
13 **Black Man (8:29)**
14 **Ngiculela-Es Una Historia-I Am Singalong (3:48)**
15 **If It's Magic (3:12)**
16 **As (7:08)**
17 **Another Star (8:28)**
18 **Saturn (4:53)**
19 **Ebony Eyes (4:08)**
20 **All Day Sucker (5:05)**
21 **Easy Goin' Evening (My Mama's Call) (3.56)**

Total album length: 105 minutes

Sleeve artwork by Tony Warren

1970s
14

Grease

| • **Album sales:** 9,400,000 | • **Release date:** May 1978 |

Impresario Robert Stigwood was the man with the Midas touch in 1978. He followed his 1977 disco movie, *Saturday Night Fever,* which made a star of John Travolta, with a film of the stage musical *Grease*. The show had already established itself as a Broadway smash, but its transfer to the big screen, with starring roles for Travolta and Olivia Newton-John, took it to an even higher level of popularity.

The movie, set in a 1950s high school, added four new songs that became the bedrock of its soundtrack. They included the John Farrar-penned 'You're The One That I Want' (the eighth best-selling single of all time with over 1.8 million sales), which, alongside the original score's 'Summer Nights', became worldwide duet smashes for the film's two main stars. The Bee Gees' Barry Gibb wrote the movie's theme song, which sent Frank Valli to Number One in the US for the first time in nearly 16 years. The album was Number One in the US charts for 21 weeks and spent 18 months in the Top 40.

In the UK, sales were almost as impressive. *Grease* spent 12 weeks at Number One and nearly a year in the charts.

Number One singles: Grease; You're The One That I Want

Grammy awards: None

Label: RSO

Recorded in: Los Angeles, USA

Personnel:
Frankie Valli
John Travolta
Olivia Newton-John
Frankie Avalon
Stockard Channing
Cindy Bullens
Sha-Na-Na
Louis St Louis

Producer:
Robert Stigwood

1970s' FILM MUSICALS

***Grease* was by far the biggest musical experience on the cinema screens of the 1970s, grossing US$380 million worldwide upon its release in 1978. It concluded a decade that had already been rich on film musical output. Rock operas such as Andrew Lloyd-Webber's and Tim Rice's *Jesus Christ Superstar* (1973) and The Who's *Tommy* (1975) had no way near the commercial success of *Grease*, but developed popular followings of their own, while *The Rocky Horror Picture Show* (1975) became a cult classic, particularly amongst student audiences. However, there were plenty of embarrassing flops, including Peter Bogdanovich's *At Long Last Love* (1975), which took a critical savaging and only US$1.5 million at the box office, and Martin Scorsese's *New York, New York* (1977).**

▲ **BACK COVER**

1 Grease (2:37)
2 Summer Nights (3:36)
3 Hopelessly Devoted To You (3:00)
4 You're The One That I Want (2:47)
5 Sandy (2:30)
6 Beauty School Dropout (4:02)
7 Look At Me, I'm Sandra Dee (1:38)
8 Greased Lightnin' (3:12)
9 It's Raining On Prom Night (2:57)
10 Alone At A Drive-In Movie (2:22)
11 Blue Moon (2:18)
12 Rock & Roll Is Here To Stay (2:00)
13 Those Magic Changes (2:15)
14 Hound Dog (1:23)
15 Born To Hand Jive (4:39)
16 Tears On My Pillow (2:06)
17 Mooning (2:12)
18 Freddy, My Love (2:40)
19 Rock & Roll Party Queen (2:08)
20 There Are Worse Things I Could Do (2:18)
21 Look At Me, I'm Sandra Dee (1:20)
22 We Go Together (3:14)
23 Love Is A Many Splendored Thing (1:23)
24 Grease (reprise) (2:37)

Total album length: 61 minutes

JOHN TRAVOLTA
OLIVIA NEWTON-JOHN
THE ORIGINAL SOUNDTRACK FROM THE MOTION PICTURE
GREASE
T.M.

1970s
13

The Stranger

| • **Album sales:** 10,300,000 | • **Release date:** September 1977 |

The Stranger delivered on the promise of earlier albums such as *Streetlife Serenade* and *Turnstiles* to become Billy Joel's breakthrough album. Pairing him for the first time with producer Phil Ramone, the nine-track set offered at times a slicker, more commercial version of what had come before.

The album's double Grammy-winning ballad 'Just The Way You Are' gave Billy Joel his first million-selling, Top 10 single, even though he had to be convinced by singers Linda Ronstadt and Phoebe Snow that it was even worthy of inclusion on *The Stranger*. The song has since been covered by more than 200 artists. 'Movin' Out' and 'She's Always A Woman' from the album also became Top 40 hits in their own right, as did 'Only The Good Die Young', despite a ban by Catholic radio stations, which deemed it anti-Catholic. 'Scenes From An Italian Restaurant', a characteristic Joel observation on New York life, was the result of combining three different songs.

Written entirely by its artist, *The Stranger* went on to become Columbia's all-time second biggest seller behind Simon and Garfunkel's *Bridge Over Troubled Water*, although it was kept from ever reaching Number One by the success of the soundtrack to *Saturday Night Fever*.

Number One singles: None

Grammy awards: Record of the year; Song of the year – Just The Way You Are

Label: US: Columbia; UK: CBS

Recorded in: New York, USA

Personnel:
Billy Joel
Liberty DeVitto
Ralph McDonald
Richie Cannata
Steve Khan
Dom Cortese
Steve Burgh (d. 2005)
Hugh MacDonald
Hugh McCracken
Phil Wood
Doug Stegmeyer (d. 1995)
Hiram Bullock (d. 2008)
Dave Brown
Richard Tee (d. 1993)

Producer:
Phil Ramone (d. 2013)

BILLY JOEL'S TROUBLED ROAD

Musical success didn't come easily to Billy Joel. After dropping out of high school in 1964, he tried to make it big with several different bands. All collapsed miserably, the last – the organ and drums duo Attila – breaking up in 1970. Depressed and dispirited by these failures and working as a music critic and jingle writer, Joel made a failed suicide attempt (he drank a bottle of furniture polish), after which he was treated for depression at the Meadowbrook Hospital. In 1971, Joel joined the label Family Productions, a division of Ripp, but a hidden clause meant Joel had actually signed with them for life. Even though he managed to sign to Columbia in 1973, Ripp would take royalties from Joel's record sales until the late 1980s. The Columbia signing was the turning point, but it had taken 10 years of struggle for Joel's childhood dream to finally come alive.

▲ **BACK COVER**

1. **Movin' Out (Anthony's Song) (3:30)**
2. **The Stranger (5:10)**
3. **Just The Way You Are (4:50)**
4. **Scenes From An Italian Restaurant (7:37)**
5. **Vienna (3:34)**
6. **Only The Good Die Young (3:55)**
7. **She's Always A Woman (3:21)**
8. **Get It Right The First Time (3:57)**
9. **Everybody Has A Dream (9:08)**

Total album length: 40 minutes

Sleeve artwork by Jim Houghton

1970s
12

Van Halen

| • **Album sales:** 10,500,000 | • **Release date:** February 1978 |

Founded by guitarist Eddie van Halen and his drum-playing brother Alex, Van Halen's music is arena in scope, but club in attitude. The sound of their debut album was a key element of the band's success; it is upfront and vibrant, and was a big success in the US, certainly for a first record, reaching Number 19 in February 1978, while it managed Number 34 in the UK, no less respectable for a newcomer act.

Intriguingly, the whole thing sounds like it has been recorded live; there is sufficient echo and effects added in the masterful production by Ted Templeman for it to sound that convincing. The album featured a new soloing technique called 'tapping', which utilized both left and right hands on the guitar neck. During the lead-up to the release of the album, Eddie van Halen would play his solos with his back to the audience to hide the technique.

But the production is little without the songs, and tracks such as 'Runnin' With The Devil', the guitar frenzy that is 'Eruption', and the cover of The Kinks' 'You Really Got Me' all illustrate both the dexterity of Eddie's virtuoso guitar playing and singer David Lee Roth's vocal range. And while it was pure good time rock 'n' roll/metal, the band was not averse to mixing things up a bit, as on the eclectic 'Ain't Talkin' 'Bout Love'.

Number One singles: None

Grammy awards: None

Label: US & UK: Warner

Recorded in: Los Angeles, USA

Personnel:
David Lee Roth
Eddie van Halen
Alex van Halen
David Anthony

Producer:
Ted Templeman

THE PULL OF HEADLINE ACTS

The 1970s were a decade in which rock bands such as Van Halen could rise to positions of unprecedented wealth and cultural power. Names such as 10cc, Foreigner, AC/DC, Led Zeppelin and Fleetwood Mac also had prodigious pulling power when they headlined festivals. A two-day 1979 festival at Knebworth, UK, for example, featured Led Zeppelin and Fairport Convention and drew in crowds of 200,000 people on both days. However, even that event had been dwarfed by the Summer Jam rock festival held at the Watkins Glen race track in July 1973. With The Grateful Dead, The Allman Brothers and The Band being the main attractions, 600,000 people attended the one-day event, with an estimated one in three of all Americans between Boston and New York attending the festival.

▲ **BACK COVER**

1. **Runnin' With The Devil (3:32)**
2. **Atomic Punk (3:30)**
3. **Eruption (1:42)**
4. **Feel Your Love Tonight (3:40)**
5. **You Really Got Me (2:37)**
6. **Ain't Talkin' 'Bout Love (3:22)**
7. **Little Dreamer (3:37)**
8. **Ice Cream Man (3:18)**
9. **Jamie's Cryin' (3:30)**
10. **On Fire (3:01)**
11. **I'm The One (3:44)**

Total album length: 35 minutes

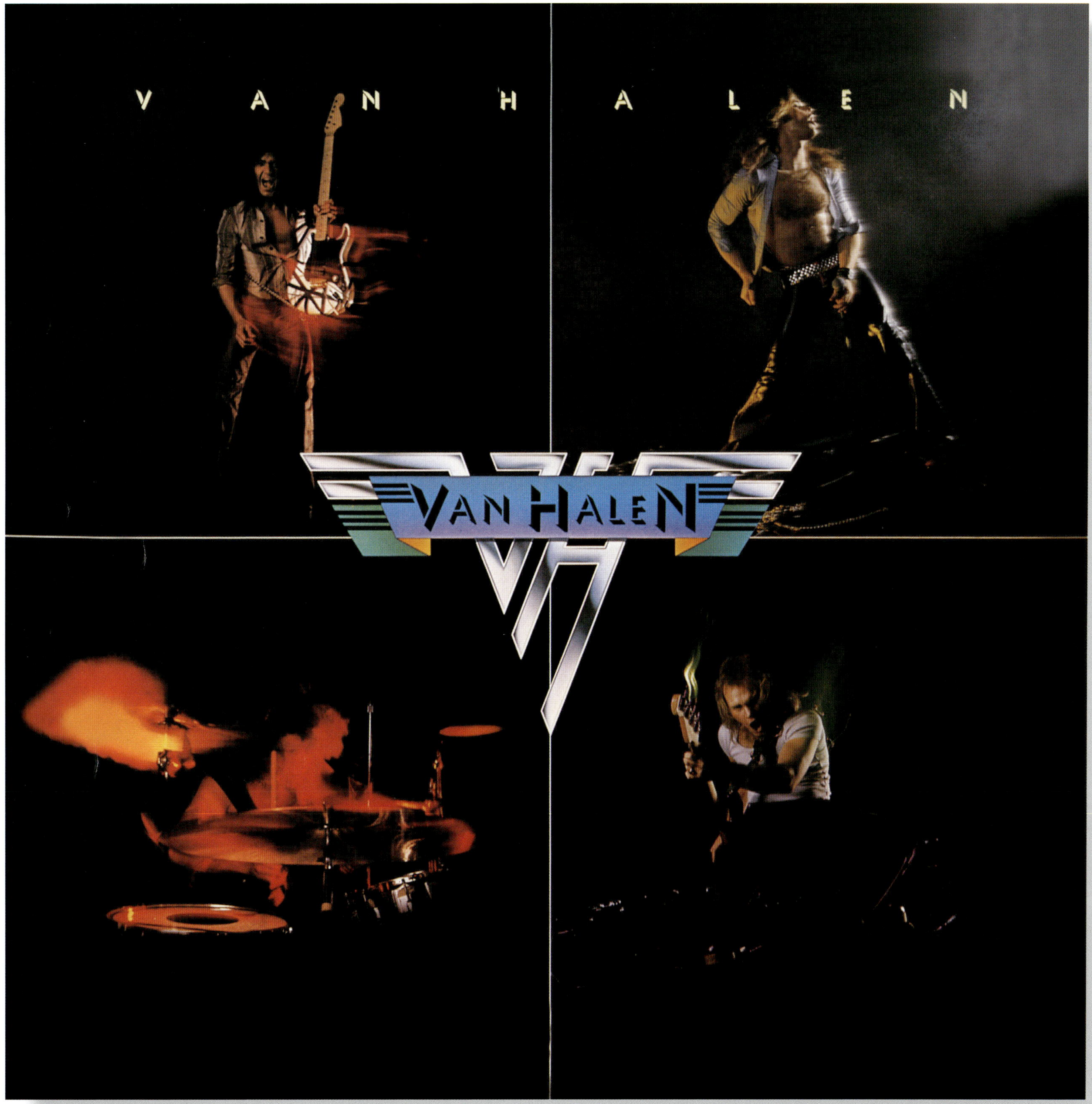

Sleeve artwork by Dave Bhang and Elliot Gilbert

Tapestry

I • **Album sales:** 11,000,000 I • **Release date:** March 1971 I

Carole King tapped into the singer-songwriter movement then taking shape to create an album that set a new watermark for female artists. Unassuming, yet beautifully crafted, this 1971 release paved the way forward for female singer-songwriters, both in terms of the quality of its songs and the honest, highly personal style in which she delivers them.

Together with her husband Gerry Goffin, King had penned a string of hits for others in the previous decade, among them 'Up On the Roof' and 'The Locomotion', but as an artist in her own right *Tapestry* stands as her glorious moment. Two of the album's songs, 'Will You Love Me Tomorrow?' and '(You Make Me Feel Like) A Natural Woman', are reinterpretations from that period with Goffin, but it is the newer songs that notably shine. In 'It's Too Late', knowingly charting the breakdown of a relationship – she had split with Goffin three years earlier – she created a US chart-topping single for herself (it reached Number Six in the UK), while in 'You've Got A Friend' she wrote a US Number One for James Taylor. In turn, Taylor adds backing vocals and guitar to the song's original version.

Tapestry clocked up more than 300 weeks on the US chart, 15 of them at Number One, while it was named Album of the Year at the 1971 Grammys.

Number One singles: US: It's Too Late; You've Got A Friend

Grammy awards: Record of the year; Album of the year; Best pop vocal performance (female); Song of the year – You've Got A Friend

Label: US: Ode; UK: A&M

Recorded in: New York, USA

Personnel:
Carole King
Joni Mitchell
Joel O'Brien
Charles Larkey
Danny Kortchmar
James Taylor
Russ Kunkel
Ralph Schuckett

Producer:
Lou Adler

FEMINISM

Feminism was at its most powerful in the 1970s. The decade produced what has often been described as 'second-wave feminism', setting the period (which began in the mid-1960s) in contradistinction to the women's movements of the 1800s. While some feminists continued to emphasise the equality of men and women, many others in the second wave pointed to the essential differences between men and women, such as in the capacity of motherhood. They also drew on Marxist, linguistic and psychoanalytical models to portray gender as a cultural construct, rather than a biological given. The key voices of second-wave feminism included Germaine Greer and Gloria Steinem.

▲ **BACK COVER**

1. **I Feel The Earth Move (2:57)**
2. **So Far Away (3:56)**
3. **It's Too Late (3:53)**
4. **Home Again (2:30)**
5. **Beautiful (3:06)**
6. **Way Over Yonder (4:46)**
7. **You've Got A Friend (5:07)**
8. **Where You Lead (3:18)**
9. **Will You Love Me Tomorrow? (4:11)**
10. **Smackwater Jack (3:43)**
11. **Tapestry (3:12)**
12. **(You Make Me Feel Like) A Natural Woman (3:39)**

Total album length: 45 minutes

Sleeve artwork by Chuck Beeson, Roland Young and Jim McCrary

1970s
10

Houses Of The Holy

| • **Album sales:** 11,500,000 | • **Release date:** March 1973 |

Ever the ones to surprise fans and critics alike, Zeppelin revealed a new side to their musical creativity with *Houses Of The Holy*. Not only does the album show the band's sense of humour, with off-beat tracks such as the James Brown tribute 'The Crunge', it also mixes up the styles along the way. There is 'cod' reggae with 'D'Yer Mak'er', the ballad-like subtlety of 'The Rain Song', alongside a hard 'n' fast rocking track such as 'The Ocean'. Only on songs such as 'Over The Hills And Far Away' and 'Dancing Days' does the band sound anything like the Zeppelin people had come to know.

Attempts to straddle influences, past and present, did not prevent the album's commercial success. The record found favour, as usual, in the US, where it reached the top of the Hot 100, while it also went to Number One in the UK. 'Over The Hills And Far Away' and 'D'Yer Mak'er' both made the Top 20, and Led Zeppelin's US tour in the summer of 1973 broke the box office records set by The Beatles. On the first two days of the tour alone, over 100,000 fans saw the band in concert.

The title *Houses Of The Holy* is a dedication by the band to their fans who appeared at their venues dubbed 'houses of the holy'; the track 'The Ocean' is also dedicated to the 'sea' of fans that attended Led Zeppelin concerts.

Number One singles:
None

Grammy awards: None

Label: US & UK: Atlantic

Recorded in: London, UK

Personnel:
Robert Plant
Jimmy Page
John Bonham (d. 1980)
John Paul Jones

Producers:
Jimmy Page
Peter Grant (d.1995)

LEGENDARY GUITARISTS

The rock music of the 1970s pushed the guitarist to the forefront in his own right, and many of these musicians became as respected as the frontmen of the groups. Sometimes both guitarist and frontman were one, as in the case of Jimi Hendrix and Eric Clapton. Hendrix excelled in raucous, dirty melodies heavy on the distortion pedal, while Clapton played around with more melodious, song-like blues riffs. Also grinding the 'axe' was, from 1973, Angus Young of AC/DC. Whereas many rock guitarists selected ostentatious instruments, heavily patterned and sometimes double necked, Young handled a simple Gibson SG, but was able to make it come alive through nimble blues riffs and fast power chords. The crowd at AC/DC gigs was commonly heard to chant 'Angus, Angus...', rather than call for the singer.

▲ **BACK COVER**

1. **The Song Remains The Same (5:30)**
2. **The Rain Song (7:38)**
3. **Over The Hills And Far Away (4:50)**
4. **The Crunge (3:17)**
5. **Dancing Days (3:43)**
6. **D'Yer Mak'er (4:22)**
7. **No Quarter (7:00)**
8. **The Ocean (4:31)**

Total album length: 41 minutes

Sleeve artwork by Hipgnosis

1970s
9

Bat Out Of Hell

| • **Album sales:** 15,000,000 | • **Release date:** October 1977 |

Meat Loaf's powerful, uncompromising voice and Jim Steinman's Wagnerian rock epics created the perfect storm to turn *Bat Out Of Hell* into one of the biggest-selling debut albums of all time. Emerging from a Steinman musical set in the future around the story of Peter Pan, the album is practically in a category all by itself, scaling almost operatic heights on the likes of the near 10-minute title track and 'Paradise By The Dashboard Light'.

Such was the ambition of the project that it took four years from its inception to finally earn a release, having been rejected along the way by several record executives before winning finance from a label owned by musician Todd Rundgren, who ended up producing the album. Rundgren, who plays guitar on the record, is the vital third ingredient in a production providing the ideal setting for Steinman's overblown ideas and Meat Loaf's dramatic delivery.

Even after finally winning a release on 21 October 1977, *Bat Out Of Hell* took another six months to crack the US Top 40, peaking at 14 in an 82-week chart run as the extracted 'Two Out Of Three Ain't Bad' became a million seller in its own right. The album's UK chart performance was even more remarkable, setting an all-time run of 471 weeks.

Number One singles: None

Grammy awards: None

Label: US & UK: Epic/ Cleveland International

Recorded in: New York, USA

Personnel:
Meat Loaf
Todd Rundgren
Kasim Sulton
Max Weinberg
John Wilcox
Jim Steinman
Roy Bittan
Cheryl Hardwick
Steven Margoshes
Roger Powell
Jimmy Iovine
John Jansen
Ed Sprague
Mark Thomas
Edgar Winter

Producer:
Todd Rundgren

SEVENTIES' BIKERS

Heavy rock music fell in love with the motorbike from the genre's inception, the bike seeming to represent the personal freedom and hardened character not representative in car culture. The 1970s were a time of biker gangs, the two most famous being the Hell's Angels and the Mongols. The Hell's Angels were actually formed in 1948, but rose to public notice in the 1960s and 1970s, particularly after some of its members beat a man to death at The Rolling Stones' Altamont gig in 1969. Like the Angels, the Mongols hailed from California, and began riding around 1970. Both groups grabbed the attention of the law enforcement agencies, and gained reputations for violence, racism and sexism. However, the Angels and Mongols were only two of 900 outlaw biker gangs recognized in the United States in the 1970s, and they were ranked alongside the Mafia in terms of crime threat.

▲ **BACK COVER**

1. **Bat Out Of Hell (9:51)**
2. **You Took The Words Right Out Of My Mouth (Hot Summer Night) (5:04)**
3. **Heaven Can Wait (4:41)**
4. **All Revved Up With No Place To Go (4:20)**
5. **Two Out Of Three Ain't Bad (5:25)**
6. **Paradise By The Dashboard Light (8:28)**
7. **For Crying Out Loud (8:44)**

Total album length: 46 minutes

Sleeve artwork by Ed Lee and Richard Corben

1970s
8

Saturday Night Fever

| • **Album sales:** 15,400,000 | • **Release date:** November 1977 |

Just a few years before *Saturday Night Fever* hit the screens in 1977, the Bee Gees' music had so fallen out of favour that Atlantic, their record company, refused to release one of their albums. Yet the Bee Gees' soundtrack to *Saturday Night Fever* was so commercially successful that, until the release of Michael Jackson's *Thriller* in 1982, no album could match its sales.

The film tells the story of a young New York Italian-American (John Travolta), his family, friends and girlfriends, and his escape from a dead-end job through disco, where he is 'king of the dance floor'. *Saturday Night Fever* dominated the US album chart for the first half of 1978 with 24 weeks at Number One, and also reached Number One in the UK.

The album that still defines the sound of disco spawned one US and UK Number One single for the Bee Gees ('Night Fever'), two new US Number Ones ('How Deep Is Your Love' and 'Stayin' Alive') and a Number One for Yvonne Elliman with the Bee Gees-penned 'If I Can't Have You'. It also included previous Bee Gee chart-toppers 'Jive Talkin'' and 'You Should Be Dancing'.

Number One singles: US: Stayin' Alive; How Deep Is Your Love; If I Can't Have You; A Fifth Of Beethoven; Jive Talkin'; You Should Be Dancing; US & UK: Night Fever

Grammy awards: Album of the year; Best pop vocal performance; Best arrangement for voices – Stayin' Alive; Producer of the year

Label: US: RSO; UK: Polydor

Recorded in: Paris, France

Personnel:
Robin Gibb (d. 2012)
Maurice Gibb (d. 2003)
Barry Gibb
Yvonne Elliman
Walter Murphy
David Shire
Ralph MacDonald
Kool & The Gang
KC & The Sunshine Band
MFSB
Tavares
The Trammps

Producers:
The Bee Gees
Karl Richardson
Albhy Galuten
Various

THE DISCO PHENOMENON

Disco was initially a club experience rather than a recording and radio event. It was originally a form of beat/dance music popular in the gay, black and Latin American communities, but by the early 1970s was spilling out across the wider club scene. With DJs driving the genre, the music was created specifically for the club turntable, and led to the production of 12in extended play singles by Tom Moulton. Gloria Gaynor's 'Never can Say Goodbye' was the first pure disco hit, but soon the Bee Gees, Donna Summer and many others were pushing the disco beats into public popularity. With the success of both the *Saturday Night Fever* film and album, disco became the most exciting musical genre of the mid to late 1970s.

▲ **BACK COVER**

1. **Stayin' Alive (Bee Gees) (4:45)**
2. **How Deep Is Your Love (Bee Gees) (4:05)**
3. **Night Fever (Bee Gees) (3:33)**
4. **More Than A Woman (Bee Gees) (3:17)**
5. **If I Can't Have You (Yvonne Elliman) (3:00)**
6. **A Fifth Of Beethoven (Walter Murphy) (3:03)**
7. **More Than A Woman (Tavares) (3:17)**
8. **Manhattan Skyline (David Shire) (4:44)**
9. **Calypso Breakdown (Ralph MacDonald) (7:50)**
10. **Night On Disco Mountain (David Shire) (5:12)**
11. **Open Sesame (Kool & The Gang) (4:01)**
12. **Jive Talkin' (Bee Gees) (3:43)**
13. **You Should Be Dancing (Bee Gees) (4:14)**
14. **Boogie Shoes (KC & The Sunshine Band) (2:17)**
15. **Salsation (David Shire) (3:50)**
16. **K-Jee (MFSB) (4:13)**
17. **Disco Inferno (The Trammps) (10:51)**

Total album length: 76 minutes

THE ORIGINAL MOVIE SOUND TRACK
SATURDAY NIGHT
FEVER

1970s
7

Physical Graffiti

| • **Album sales:** 15,600,000 | • **Release date:** February 1975 |

Arriving nearly two years after its predecessor, *Physical Graffiti* was the final confirmation – if confirmation was needed – that Led Zeppelin were more than just any old group. The album topped the US and UK album charts, and shortly after its release the entire Led Zeppelin catalogue of six albums was simultaneously on the Top 200 album chart – a feat never before accomplished.

Physical Graffiti was Zeppelin's first double album and their first release on Swan Song, the record label established by the band in 1974. A number of tracks, notably 'Kashmir' and 'In My Time Of Dying' – redolent of the lengthy blues songs they had recorded in their early career – became live favourites, and featured heavily in a series of dates at London's 21,000 capacity Earl's Court arena, the biggest gigs the band had played in the UK up to that date.

Elsewhere on the album they even managed to pump some funky vibes into the rock composition 'Trampled Under Foot'. There was still room for a lighter touch, and the second record features some classic if unlikely Zeppelin songs, including the bar-room boogie 'Boogie With Stu', the acoustic instrumental 'Bron-Y-Aur', and the hauntingly melodic 'Ten Years Gone'.

Number One singles: None

Grammy awards: None

Label: US & UK: Swan Song

Recorded in: Various locations, UK

Personnel:
Robert Plant
Jimmy Page
John Bonham (d. 1980)
John Paul Jones

Producers:
Jimmy Page
Peter Grant (d.1995)

ROBERT PLANT

Robert Plant remains an archetype of the heavy-rock lead vocalist. He was born in 1948, and during his formative years in England began a deep love for rock 'n' roll and the blues. As a young adult, Plant was talent-spotted by guitarist Jimmy Page and bassist John Paul Jones in 1968, and together with drummer John Bonham they formed Led Zeppelin. Plant became the face of the band, noted for his electrifying stage performances and powerful vocal style. After Bonham's death from alcohol poisoning in 1980, Led Zeppelin disbanded, but Plant has maintained his rock career, with frequent tours, as well as broadening into America with bluegrass-country singer Alison Krauss.

▲ **BACK COVER**

1. **Custard Pie (4:13)**
2. **The Rover (5:37)**
3. **In My Time Of Dying (11:06)**
4. **Houses Of The Holy (4:02)**
5. **Trampled Under Foot (5:36)**
6. **Kashmir (8:28)**
7. **In The Light (8:46)**
8. **Bron-Y-Aur (2:06)**
9. **Down By The Seaside (5:16)**
10. **Ten Years Gone (6:33)**
11. **Night Flight (3:37)**
12. **The Wanton Song (4:09)**
13. **Boogie With Stu (3:53)**
14. **Black Country Woman (4:32)**
15. **Sick Again (4:43)**

Total album length: 88 minutes

Sleeve artwork by Peter Corriston and Mike Doud

1970s
6

Boston

| • **Album sales:** 17,600,000 | • **Release date:** June 1977 |

Boston was one of the few 'corporate rock' albums to contain the germ of something more than the usual bland, edgeless music produced by the group's peers at the time.

The brainchild of Tom Scholz, who recorded countless demos in a home-built basement studio, including six of the eight tracks on the album, Boston's eponymous debut captured millions of US and UK radio listeners with a blend of melodic, well-crafted AOR, spine-tingling harmonies and intelligent instrumentation. It soon became the largest selling debut album of all time and the best-selling debut album by a group. The band quickly went from being virtually unknown to playing sold-out arena shows all over the country.

The record's opening track, 'More Than A Feeling', was an immediate success on US radio and the UK, reaching Numbers Five and 22 respectively. There are thoughtful songs in here too, which while not fitting the 'ballad' blueprint, move in that direction. Noteworthy are 'Hitch A Ride' and the album's closer, 'Let Me Take You Home Tonight'.

Brad Delp's incredibly sopranic vocals and Scholz's fantastic guitar work are both Boston trademarks. This album showcases both of those talents admirably.

Creem Magazine voted the album's cover one of the top 10 album covers of the year in 1977.

Number One singles: None

Grammy awards: None

Label: US & UK: Epic

Recorded in: Los Angeles, USA

Personnel:
Tom Scholz
Brad Delp (d. 2007)
Barry Goudreau
Fran Sheehan
Sib Hashian

Producer:
John Boylan
Tom Scholz

TOM SCHOLZ – MUSIC TECHNICIAN

For a rock musician, Tom Scholz has demonstrated an unusually sophisticated grasp of music technology. He graduated from M.I.T. with a bachelor's and master's degree in mechanical engineering, and while working for Polaroid as a senior product designer he built his own multi-track recording machine, enabling him to record the first Boston album in his apartment. In 1980, Scholz created the Scholz Research and Development company, and during the following decade some of his creations became top-selling products, including the PowerSoak (a device for generating heavy guitar distortion) and the Rockman headphone guitar amp. To date, Scholz has inventor's rights on 34 US patents.

▲ **BACK COVER**

1. **More Than A Feeling (4:45)**
2. **Peace Of Mind (5:03)**
3. **Foreplay Long Time (7:51)**
4. **Rock & Roll Band (3:00)**
5. **Smokin (4:21)**
6. **Hitch A Ride (4:11)**
7. **Something About You (3:48)**
8. **Let Me Take You Home Tonight (4:45)**

Total album length: 38 minutes

Sleeve artwork by Roy Huyssen

1970s
5

Hotel California

| • **Album sales:** 17,900,000 | • **Release date:** December 1976 |

The Eagles moved still further from their early country roots and cranked up the guitars to produce their most rock-flavoured material yet on *Hotel California*. With the addition of guitarist Joe Walsh to the line-up as a replacement for the more country-leaning Bernie Leadon, the band turned out a harder-edged sound for what represents the creative and commercial peak of their incredibly successful career.

Standing, too, as a definitive statement on 1970s' American rock, *Hotel California* was the result of six months' work in Miami's Criteria Studios, with expectations only swelled by a gap of almost 18 months since their last studio effort, *One Of These Nights*. However, the stop-gap *Greatest Hits 1971-75* retrospective ensured that their name had remained at the top of the charts.

The new album provided a metaphor for the excesses of certain aspects of American society and, in particular, Californian life, not least on the epic six-and-a-half-minute title track, made all the more distinctive by duo guitar solos from Walsh and Don Felder. The track, one of five numbers here sung by drummer Don Henley, gave the band a fourth Hot 100 Number One just 10 weeks after fellow album cut 'New Kid In Town' had reached the top. Spread across four separate runs, the album accumulated eight weeks at Number One Stateside in early 1977, while it achieved a Number Two spot in the UK.

Number One singles: US: Hotel California; New Kid In Town

Grammy awards: Record of the year; Best arrangement for voices

Label: US & UK: Asylum

Recorded in: Miami, USA

Personnel:
Don Henley
Glenn Frey
Don Felder
Randy Meisner
Joe Walsh

Producer:
Bill Szymczyk

ROLLING STONE MAGAZINE

For the music-savvy public, *Rolling Stone* magazine was one of the arbiters of taste during the 1970s. The magazine was created in 1967 in San Francisco by music aficionados Jann Wenner and Ralph Gleason. It was, at first, particularly aligned with the hippy movement, and had an underground style of production. On an initial budget of US$7,500, the first issue was put together with the aid of volunteers, and of 40,000 copies printed, sold only 5,000. However, by the 1970s the magazine was firmly set at the cutting edge of music criticism, setting new standards in intelligent music journalism as well as in innovative photography of the stars.

▲ **BACK COVER**

1 **Hotel California (6:30)**
2 **New Kid In Town (5:04)**
3 **Life In The Fast Lane (4:46)**
4 **Wasted Time (4:55)**
5 **Wasted Time (reprise) (1:22)**
6 **Victim Of Love (4:11)**
7 **Pretty Maids All In A Row (4:05)**
8 **Try And Love Again (5:10)**
9 **The Last Resort (7:25)**

Total album length: 43 minutes

Sleeve artwork by John Kosh

1970s
4

Dark Side Of The Moon

| • **Album sales:** 18,500,000 | • **Release date:** March 1973 |

Pink Floyd's eighth album, recorded at London's Abbey Road studios, took more than eight months to produce – an extremely long time for its day. The album was launched at a special listening session at London's Planetarium in January 1973. *Dark Side Of The Moon* topped the US album chart, where it stayed for more than 300 weeks. In the UK the album reached Number Two and has continued to sell well ever since.

The album's first single, 'Money' – which includes a rhythmic accompaniment created from the sampled sounds of clinking coins and cash registers – reached Number 13 on the US Hot 100, although it failed to make a great impression on the UK charts. To make the sampled money sounds fit the 7/4 beat, the tape had to be cut up and stuck back together, using a ruler to make sure the beats were accurate. A second single from the album, 'Us And Them', was released in October 1973, but failed to make it into the Top 100 in either the UK or the US.

A number of voices were used on *Dark Side Of The Moon*, including the band's tour manager and roadie. Paul McCartney's voice was recorded but not actually used.

Number One singles: None

Grammy awards: Best engineered album

Label: Harvest

Recorded in: London, UK

Personnel:
Dave Gilmour
Roger Waters
Rick Wright (d. 2008)
Nick Mason
Barry St. John
Dick Parry
Doris Troy (d. 2004)
Claire Torry
Liza Stuke
Lesley Duncan (d. 2010)

Producer:
Pink Floyd

PINK FLOYD LIVE

Pink Floyd delivered some of the most memorable live gigs in rock history, concerts created as much around outlandish special effects and provocative imagery as the group's haunting sound. The band pioneered the use of a dedicated, touring light-show to augment their music, and also employed a circular movie screen (the band called it 'Mr Screen') onto which were projected films, still images and patterns. Lasers and pyrotechnics became powerful additions to the shows, and during *The Wall* tour a huge fake wall separating band from audience was blown apart in a loud explosion. (During the same tour session musicians in rubber masks played the opening song, a wry comment on the band members' relative anonymity.) Other special effects included a giant inflatable pig which was floated above the audience during tracks from the *Animals* album.

▲ **BACK COVER**

1 **Speak To Me (1:08)**
2 **Breathe In The Air (2:48)**
3 **On The Run (3:50)**
4 **Time (6:49)**
5 **The Great Gig In The Sky (4:44)**
6 **Money (6:22)**
7 **Us And Them (7:49)**
8 **Any Colour You Like (3:26)**
9 **Brain Damage (3:46)**
10 **Eclipse (2:11)**

Total album length: 43 minutes

Sleeve artwork designed by Storm Thorgerson, drawn by George Hardie

1970s
3

Rumours

| • **Album sales:** 19,700,000 | • **Release date:** February 1977 |

Rumours is Fleetwood Mac's 11th and best-selling album. A Number One album on both sides of the Atlantic, *Rumours* debuted at Number 10 and went on to spend 31 weeks at Number One in the US and almost a year in the Top Five, the longest stint in the 1970s. The record produced no fewer than four hit singles for the band – 'Go Your Own Way', 'Don't Stop','You Make Loving Fun' and the US Number One single 'Dreams' (which reached Number 24 in the UK). The record spent 450 weeks on the UK listings.

The group's second album with its most famous lineup – Fleetwood, Buckingham and his then-girlfriend, singer Stevie Nicks, and McVie and his ex-wife, singer and keyboardist Christine McVie – *Rumours* tracks the twin couples as they split. The record features Nicks at her huskiest, and contains bittersweet love songs such as 'Go Your Own Way' and 'I Don't Wanna Know'.

The songwriting duties were once more shared amongst the band, with Buckingham and Nicks pitching in on songs such as 'Go Your Own Way' and 'Dreams', and Christine McVie penning the achingly beautiful 'Songbird', among others. *Rumours* was chosen as the 25th greatest album of all time by the editors of *Rolling Stone* magazine in December 2003.

Number One singles: US: Dreams

Grammy awards: Album of the year

Label: US & UK: Warner

Recorded in: Los Angeles, USA

Personnel:
Lindsey Buckingham
Stevie Nicks
John McVie
Christine McVie
Mick Fleetwood

Producers:
Fleetwood Mac
Richard Dashut
Ken Caillat

1970s FASHIONS

The popular image of 1970s' fashions is of the hippy look – bell-bottom jeans, tie-died shirts/blouses, kaftan and platform-soled shoes. Such dress was certainly an important fashion style of the 70s, but the decade also saw wider experimentation. The 1960s still pervaded the 1970s in the mini skirt, although it was framed by the belt-like micro skirt or the greater coverage of the maxi skirt. As heated cars and home central heating became more prevalent, clothes tended to become lighter, with heavy, long coats being replaced by shorter hip-length jackets. Ethnic clothing became increasingly popular from the mid 1970s, although for evening wear glamour was central, women opting for elaborate dresses with ornate sleeves and necklines or, even, full-length catsuits.

▲ **BACK COVER**

1. **Second Hand News (2:46)**
2. **Dreams (4:17)**
3. **Never Going Back Again (2:14)**
4. **Don't Stop (3:12)**
5. **Go Your Own Way (3:39)**
6. **Songbird (3:21)**
7. **The Chain (4:30)**
8. **You Make Loving Fun (3:36)**
9. **I Don't Wanna Know (3:16)**
10. **Oh Daddy (3:53)**
11. **Gold Dust Woman (4:53)**

Total album length: 39 minutes

1970s

Sleeve artwork by Desmond Strobel

1970s
2

The Wall

| • **Album sales:** 24,300,000 | • **Release date:** December 1979 |

The subject matter of Pink Floyd's 11th album may be bleak – the mental decline of a rock star – but a heavier focus on songs rather than experimental soundscaping gave the album increased appeal. It made Number One in the US and Number Three in the UK, and the single 'Another Brick In The Wall' topped the charts in both countries, 15 weeks in the US. *The Wall* has received an incredible 23 platinum awards since its release, making it the top-selling album of the 1970s and the third best-selling album of all time.

The success of *The Wall* was consolidated with a feature film version in 1982, directed by Alan Parker and starring Bob Geldof. A live show, featuring a construction of the wall, proved so elaborate that it was only staged in four cities.

Bass player and main song writer Roger Waters based *The Wall* on his own experiences of fame, and found little room for drummer Nick Mason or keyboard player Rick Wright – whose cocaine addiction led Waters to soon remove him from the band altogether.

Number One singles:
US & UK: Another Brick in the Wall, Part II

Grammy awards: None

Label: US: Tower; UK: Columbia

Recorded in: Miravel, France; Los Angeles, USA; New York, USA

Personnel:
David Gilmour
Richard Wright (d. 2008)
Roger Waters
Nick Mason
Bruce Johnston
Toni Tenille
Joe Chemay
John Joyce
Stan Farber
Jim Haas

Producers:
Bob Ezrin
David Gilmour
Roger Waters

SEVENTIES' ALIENATION

The 1970s was, in many ways, a philosophically and culturally dark decade. Political disillusionment spread through much of the Western world following the defeat of US-backed South Vietnam by the communist North in 1975, an event compounded by the Watergate scandal that had brought President Nixon's resignation from office in 1974. The literature of the decade often wrestled with ideas of spiritual alienation and loss, with writers such as John Updike and Kurt Vonnegut investigating the loneliness of contemporary existence. Punk and heavy metal were the main musical vehicles of youthful despair, while war films such as *The Deer Hunter* and *Apocalypse Now* were stylized allegories of existential social collapse.

▲ BACK COVER

1 In The Flesh (3:19)
2 The Thin Ice (2:29)
3 Another Brick In The Wall, Part 1 (3:09)
4 The Happiest Days Of Our Lives (1:51)
5 Another Brick In The Wall, Part 2 (3:59)
6 Mother (5:36)
7 Goodbye Blue Sky (2:48)
8 Empty Spaces (2:08)
9 Young Lust (3:30)
10 One Of My Turns (3:37)
11 Don't Leave Me Now (4:17)
12 Another Brick In The Wall, Part 3 (1:14)
13 Goodbye Cruel World (1:17)
14 Hey You (4:42)
15 Is There Anybody Out There? (2:40)
16 Nobody Home (3:24)
17 Vera (1:33)
18 Bring The Boys Back Home (1:27)
19 Comfortably Numb (6:24)
20 The Show Must Go On (1:35)
21 In The Flesh (4:17)
22 Run Like Hell (4:24)
23 Waiting For The Worms (3:58)
24 Stop (0:30)
25 The Trial (5:20)
26 Outside The Wall (1:44)

Total album length: 81 minutes 12 seconds

1970s

Sleeve artwork by Gerald Scarfe

1970s
1

Led Zeppelin IV (Four Symbols)

| • **Album sales:** 24,400,000 | • **Release date:** November 1971 |

By the time Led Zeppelin recorded 'IV' the band was well on the way to becoming the biggest rock 'n' roll outfit in the world. The release of the album, also known as 'Four Symbols' or 'Zoso', on account of the mystical 'runes' adopted by each band member, merely served to confirm the title.

From the opening riff that launches into 'Black Dog' and then refuses to let up with the album's second track, 'Rock And Roll', the album is a testament to rock music in the early 1970s. But Zeppelin also paid heed to their folk/blues roots, with the Tolkienesque 'Battle For Evermore', featuring English folk diva and Fairport Convention vocalist Sandy Denny, and 'Going To California'.

The album is perhaps best known for featuring the eight-minute 'Stairway To Heaven', one of the few songs of its type to be able to live up to the label 'epic'; the track is the most requested song in US rock 'n' roll radio history. Many see the album's closing track, 'When The Levee Breaks', as being equally powerful.

'IV' topped the album chart in the UK, but could only manage the Number Two spot in the US, with single 'Black Dog' only reached Number 12 – bizarre, given the album's status as the best-selling album of the decade and one of the best-selling albums of all time.

Number One singles:
None

Grammy awards: None

Label: US & UK: Atlantic

Recorded in: Hampshire & London, UK; Los Angeles, USA

Personnel:
Robert Plant
Jimmy Page
John Bonham (d. 1980)
John Paul Jones
Sandy Denny (d. 1978)

Producer:
Jimmy Page
Peter Grant

THE MOOG SYNTHESIZER

Robert Moog is a legendary figure in the history of electronic instrument development. Although forms of electronic synthesizers had emerged as far back as the 1920s, the instruments were not really practical sound machines until Moog's synthesizers appeared in 1964.

Moog had begun building electronic instruments around 1961. Aided by fellow technicians Herbert A. Deutsch and Walter Carlos, Moog developed a breakthrough in musical circuitry in 1963 and began making synthesizers the following year. The album *Switched on Bach* was recorded entirely with synthesizers, and the instrument caught on with the big names of pop and rock. Moog brought the synthesizer sound into modern music, a sound which was carried forward by companies such as Roland and Arp.

▲ **BACK COVER**

1 **Black Dog (4:54)**
2 **Rock And Roll (3:40)**
3 **The Battle For Evermore (5:51)**
4 **Stairway To Heaven (8:00)**
5 **Misty Mountain Hop (4:38)**
6 **Four Sticks (4:44)**
7 **Going To California (3:31)**
8 **When The Levee Breaks (7:07)**

Total album length: 42 minutes

Sleeve artwork by Graphreaks and Barrington Coleby

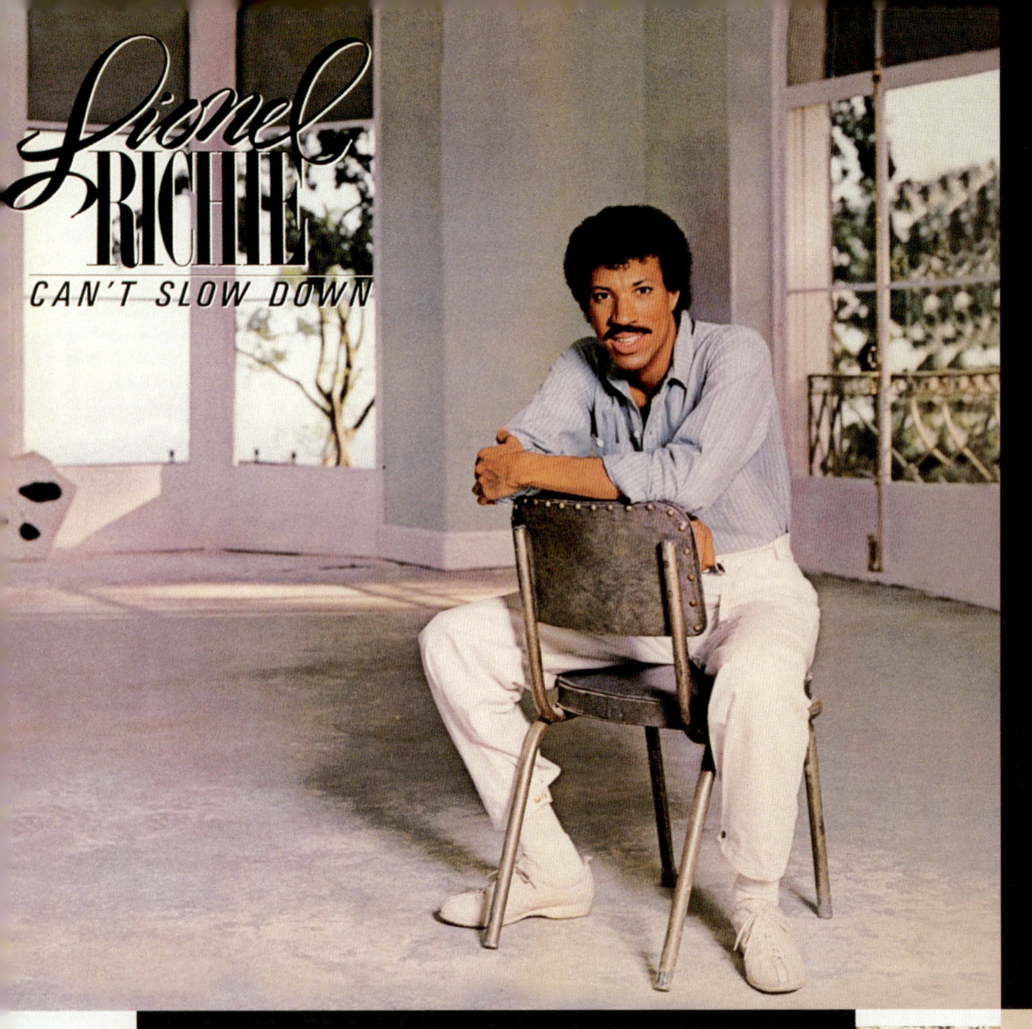
Lionel
RICHIE
CAN'T SLOW DOWN

DEF LEPPARD
Hysteria

Purple Rain
Prince and the Revolution

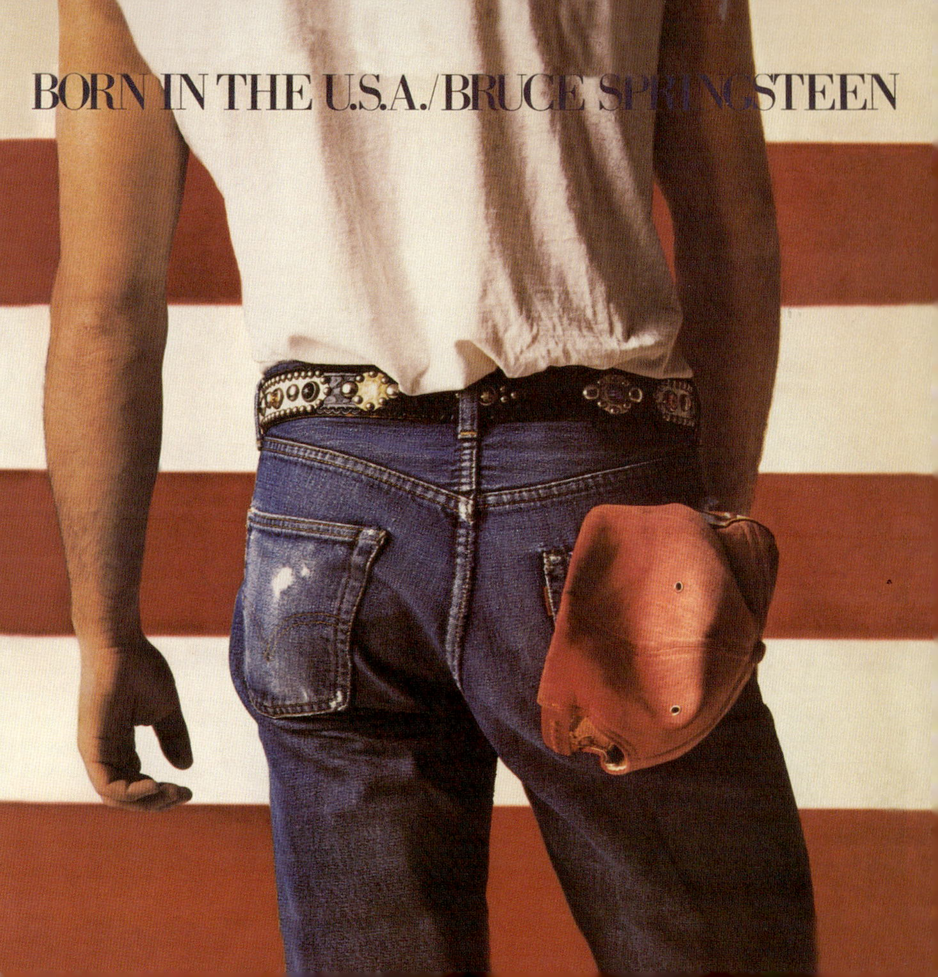
BORN IN THE U.S.A./BRUCE SPRINGSTEEN

The Best-Selling Albums of the 1980s

Because of the huge impact made by British bands such as The Beatles in the 1960s, the US never quite gave up its image of Britain as a magical mystery tour, where London was always swinging. However, album sales in the 1980s showed America's renewed faith in British pop music. Spearheaded by Culture Club, Spandau Ballet and Duran Duran, the Brit-inspired 'New Romantic' movement helped re-establish quality music ideals and provided the perfect accompaniment to new hopeful times.

But album sales during this decade also reflected a taste for more established and mature sounds. In the 1980s, pop music's paranoid obsession with youth greatly disappeared. The generation born in the post-war years demanded music to satisfy and reflect its ever-maturing aspirations, traumas and fears. In 1985, Phil Collins' album *No Jacket Required* tapped into this market.

During the 1980s, albums evolved beyond simple pieces of vinyl sold in a nice cover. Video meant that albums became multi-media packages; images and songs shaped and defined as much by film as they once had been by music alone. Many up-and-coming bands were quick to realize the potential of MTV – exposure on the network could substantially fuel single and album sales. By 1983, no major record label was complete without its own video department. Michael Jackson was one artist who was quick to appreciate the power of video, which became not only an entertainment medium, but a vehicle for social change.

Jackson's *Thriller* was the singer's most successful album of the 80s – almost 30 million copies were sold. Released in December 1982, *Thriller* was Number One in almost every Western country, including the US, where it spent 37 weeks at the top of the album chart. Just as 1980s pop music came to feed off the visual thrills of MTV, many of the top-selling albums of the decade were film soundtracks, such as *Top Gun* and *Dirty Dancing*.

The 1980s may have been an era for revolutionary new media technology, but many albums continued to reflect traditional rock 'n' roll ethics. Of all modern American guitar heroes, none filled the role of working-class-kid-made-good better than Bruce Springsteen. Released in June 1984, *Born in the U.S.A.* was both a celebration and an uncompromising examination of American life. The album spent seven weeks at the top of the US chart.

The 1980s also saw a triumvirate of classic rock albums released by new bands. By 1987, following a series of grinding tours, Def Leppard had become stadium-rock kings. Three years in the making, *Hysteria* hit the US album chart at Number Ten in March 1988. Meanwhile, a former shoe salesman, Jon Bon Jovi, had been moulding his band into stadium headliners. Bon Jovi's album *Slippery When Wet* was released in 1986, by the end of the following year it had sold eight million copies in the US. Guns N' Roses were the real bad boys of rock in the 1980s. Although their career was unruly and controversial, the band produced plenty of magnificent work, including their 1987 release *Appetite For Destruction*.

1980s
20

Top Gun

| • **Album sales:** 10,300,000 | • **Release date:** May 1986 |

One of the best-selling soundtracks of all time, *Top Gun* remains a quintessential collection of 1980s' pop. The film, meanwhile, made a star of the young Tom Cruise, while boosting the careers of Tim Robbins and Meg Ryan.

Two singles dominate the album, Berlin's massive hit, 'Take My Breath Away', which acts as the centrepiece of the film, and Kenny Loggins' 'Danger Zone', both co-written by Italian electronica specialist Giorgio Moroder, who previously scored *Midnight Express*. Canada's Loverboy provided a third single, 'Heaven In Your Eyes', which reached Number 12 on the US chart.

The soundtrack went to Number One in the US, while 'Take My Breath Away' hit Number One in the US and UK, where it stayed for 15 weeks to become the ninth best-selling single in British chart history. The track also won an Oscar for Best Song. Further critical acclaim followed at the Grammys, where Harold Faltermeyer and Steve Stevens won the award for Best Pop Instrumental Performance for 'Top Gun Anthem'.

Number One singles:
US & UK: Take My Breath Away

Grammy awards:
Best pop instrumental performance – Top Gun Anthem

Label: US & UK: Columbia

Recorded in: Various locations

Personnel:
Kenny Loggins
Cheap Trick
Terri Nunn
Ric Olsen
Gloria Estefan
Mike Reno
Matthew Frenette
Scott Smith
Larry Greene
Marietta
Harold Faltermeyer
Steve Stevens
Various other personnel

Producers:
Peter Wolf
Paul Dean
Phil Spector
Giorgio Moroder
Sam Phillips
Various other producers

MACHO METAPHORS

A highly macho film about wannabe fighter pilots, *Top Gun*'s military posturing and gung-ho heroics blazed a trail through cinemas around the world in the mid 1980s, snaring the public's imagination, particularly in America, where the air of invincibility and stunning aerial photography meant the movie pretty much became a two-hour recruiting vehicle for the US Air Force. An early trailer was scored to The Cars' song 'Stranger Eyes', from the album *Heartbeat City*, although the song is not in the movie or on the soundtrack album. Bryan Adams was asked to allow his song 'Only the Strong Survive' on the soundtrack, but he refused permission because he felt that the film glorified war.

▲ **BACK COVER**

1. **Danger Zone (Kenny Loggins) (3:36)**
2. **Mighty Wings (Cheap Trick) (3:51)**
3. **Playing With The Boys (Kenny Loggins) (3:59)**
4. **Lead Me On (Teena Marie) (3:47)**
5. **Take My Breath Away (Love Theme from Top Gun) (Berlin) (4:15)**
6. **Hot Summer Nights (Miami Sound Machine) (3:38)**
7. **Heaven In Your Eyes (Loverboy) (4:04)**
8. **Through Yhe Fire (Larry Greene) (3:45)**
9. **Destination Unknown (Marietta) (3:48)**
10. **Top Gun Anthem (Harold Faltermeyer & Steve Stevens) (4:13)**

Total album length: 37 minutes

ORIGINAL MOTION PICTURE SOUNDTRACK
TOP GUN
KENNY LOGGINS
DANGER ZONE
LOVERBOY
HEAVEN IN YOUR EYES
CHEAP TRICK
MIGHTY WINGS
BERLIN
TAKE MY BREATH AWAY
(LOVE THEME FROM "TOP GUN")
HAROLD FALTERMEYER
& STEVE STEVENS
TOP GUN ANTHEM
MIAMI SOUND
MACHINE
HOT SUMMER NIGHTS
KENNY LOGGINS
PLAYING WITH THE BOYS
TEENA MARIE
LEAD ME ON
MARIETTA
DESTINATION UNKNOWN
LARRY GREENE
THROUGH THE FIRE
Includes the single
DANGER ZONE
by KENNY LOGGINS
plus the U.S. No. 1
TAKE MY BREATH AWAY
by BERLIN
CBS 70296
UP THERE
WITH THE BEST
OF THE BEST.

1980s
19

1984

| • **Album sales:** 10,500,000 | • **Release date:** January 1984 |

Frustrated by his experiences while recording the band's two previous albums, Eddie Van Halen made stringent efforts to exercise greater artistic control with *1984*. A major step included setting up his own studio, where he insisted the album be recorded. He was also successful in persuading his fellow members to allow the use of synthesizers in their music.

Van Halen already had several platinum albums to its name, but Eddie Van Halen was keen to move away from the play-it-safe attitude of the past. Ironically, with *1984* the group would achieve bigger sales than ever before. This was in part due to Eddie Van Halen's performance on Michael Jackson's 'Beat It', which had been a massive hit the previous year. Perhaps learning from Jackson's example, Van Halen also set about filming entertaining videos for the single releases, which helped add a TV-based audience to their fanbase.

Released only nine days into the year for which it was named, the album achieved the Number Two position in the US and Number 15 in the UK.

Number One singles: US: Jump

Grammy awards: None

Label: US & UK: Warner

Recorded in: California, USA

Personnel:
David Lee Roth
Eddie Van Halen
Michael Anthony
Alex Van Halen

Producer:
Ted Templeman

Eddie Van Halen's enthusiasm for synthesizers was vindicated when 'Jump' became a massive hit, reaching Number One in the US and Number Four in the UK. 'Panama' and 'I'll Wait' provided two more US Top 20 hits.

The album reached multi-platinum status well before the end of the year, but the success exacerbated existing tensions within the band, and singer Dave Lee Roth quit the following year.

SPANDEX OVER SUBSTANCE

There is little doubt that rock music in the US had lost its way by the early 1980s. Big-haired, spandex-wearing, rock bands were all the rage, but for the purist, image prevailed over substance. Van Halen were one of the few purveyors of the genre to largely maintain their credibility while still carving out chunks of chart action for themselves with hits such as 'Jump' and 'Panama'.

Frontman David Lee Roth left the group in 1985. Despite having a few solo hits of his own, he never repeated the success of the band and suffered the ignominy of being busted trying to buy drugs in New York's Washington Square in 1996.

▲ **BACK COVER**

1. **1984 (1:07)**
2. **Jump (4:04)**
3. **Panama (3:32)**
4. **Top Jimmy (3:02)**
5. **Drop Dead Legs (4:15)**
6. **Hot For Teacher (4:44)**
7. **I'll Wait (4:45)**
8. **Girl Gone Bad (4:35)**
9. **House Of Pain (3:19)**

Total album length: 33 minutes

MCMLXXXIV
VAN HALEN
MCMLXXXIV

1980s
18

Whitney

| • **Album sales:** 10,800,000 | • **Release date:** May 1987 |

Whitney Houston had enjoyed three consecutive Number One hits with tracks from her debut album. She continued the run with songs from her second album, *Whitney*, which sent her into the record books as the first artist ever to have seven consecutive Number Ones in the US. No stranger to breaking records, Houston had earlier made history when *Whitney* became the first album by a female artist to debut at Number One in the *Billboard* chart.

The core production team from her first album, Narada Michael Walden, Michael Masser and Kashif, all returned, ensuring that Houston's crossover appeal was maintained. Sure enough, the first single, 'I Wanna Dance With Somebody (Who Loves Me)', topped several different *Billboard* charts, including Adult Contemporary, R&B, and the Hot 100 (not to mention the UK singles chart).

By this time, Whitney was confident enough to record her own rendering of the show tune 'I Know Him So Well', duetting with her mother, Cissy Houston. Although *Whitney* contained no less than four US Number One hits, sales fell a few million short of Houston's debut album.

Number One singles: US & UK: I Wanna Dance With Somebody (Who Loves Me); US: Didn't We Almost Have It All; So Emotional; Where Do Broken Hearts Go

Grammy awards: Best female pop vocal performance

Label: US & UK: Arista

Recorded in: N/A

Personnel:
Whitney Houston (d. 2012)
Cissy Houston
Paul Jackson Jr
Kenny G
Kashif
Robbie Buchanan
Randy Jackson
Roy Ayers
Paulinho Da Costa
Various other personnel

Producers:
John 'Jellybean' Benitez
Narada Michael Walden
Michael Masser
Kashif

THE MONEY DECADE

The 1980s, while a period of gross unemployment in many industrial sectors, saw unimaginable inflation of salaries in many professional sectors, particularly those of finance, IT and advertising. For example, in Wall Street in 1981 consultants were paid a total of around $0.4 billion. By 1986, that figure had risen to $2 billion dollars on the back of profits of $5.5 billion. London experienced a similar wealth explosion. The new wealth pushed consumerism to the extreme, with property, cars, luxury holidays and hi-tech electronic equipment being the chief purchases.

▲ **BACK COVER**

1. **I Wanna Dance With Somebody (Who Loves Me) (4:52)**
2. **Just The Lonely Talking Again (5:34)**
3. **Love Will Save The Day (5:25)**
4. **Didn't We Almost Have It All (5:07)**
5. **So Emotional (4:37)**
6. **Where You Are (4:11)**
7. **Love Is A Contact Sport (4:19)**
8. **You're Still My Man (4:18)**
9. **For The Love Of You (5:33)**
10. **Where Do Broken Hearts Go (4:38)**
11. **I Know Him So Well (4:30)**

Total album length: 53 minutes

1980s

Sleeve artwork by Marl Larson and Richard Avedon

1980s
17

Can't Slow Down

| • **Album sales:** 11,000,000 | • **Release date:** October 1983 |

Lionel Richie's rise to solo superstardom parallels with that of his 'We Are The World' co-writer Michael Jackson. Both had become the main attraction in the groups they performed with, and had achieved enviable success with their first solo albums. Richie had already given Motown its biggest single to date ('Endless Love', performed with Diana Ross). However, as with Jackson, these early triumphs were eclipsed by the release of his second solo album, *Can't Slow Down*, in 1983.

During his Commodores career, Richie had gradually steered the band away from rigid soul and funk towards a more commercial pop sound. This shift was fully realised with *Can't Slow Down*, Motown's biggest selling album. It won Richie Grammys for Album of the Year and Producer of the Year, an honour he shared with David Foster and James Anthony Carmichael.

Five of the album's tracks, 'All Night Long', 'Penny Lover', 'Stuck on You', 'Running With The Night' and 'Hello' went on to become hit singles in the US. In 1984, Richie performed 'All Night Long' before a worldwide audience at the closing ceremony of the Los Angeles Olympics.

Number One singles: US & UK: Hello

Grammy awards: Album of the year; Producer of the year (non-classical)

Label: US & UK: Motown

Recorded in: California, USA

Personnel:
Lionel Richie
David Cochrane
Sonny Burke
Darrell Jones
Carlos Rios
Steve Lukather
Louie Shelton
John Hobbs
Reginald 'Sonny' Burke
David Foster
Michael Boddicker
Greg Phillinganes
Abraham Laboriel
Nathan East
Paul Leim
John Robinson
Jeff Porcaro (d. 1992)
Paulinho Da Costa
Richard Marx
Various other personnel

Producers:
Lionel Richie
James Anthony Carmichael
David Foster

AFRICAN-AMERICAN MUSIC IN THE 1980s

During the 1980s the paths of African-American music diverged to form two separate movements, with some limited crossover. On the one side was pop-soul, a broad style that concentrated on ballads or funk style. The classic representatives of pop-soul were artists such as Michael Jackson, Whitney Houston, Lionel Richie and Prince. Conversely, hip-hop took African-American music in an entirely different direction. Hip-hop's thumping drum-and-bass backbeats, often accentuated by rap vocals, were pioneered by artists such as LL Cool J, Afrika Bambaata & The Soulsonic Force and Grandmaster Flash. Hip-hop also entered into controversy, often taking as its subject matter sex, drugs, race and the police.

▲ **BACK COVER**

1. **Can't Slow Down (4:43)**
2. **All Night Long (All Night) (6:25)**
3. **Penny Lover (5:35)**
4. **Stuck On You (3:15)**
5. **Love Will Find A Way (6:16)**
6. **The Only One (4:24)**
7. **Running With The Night (6:02)**
8. **Hello (4:11)**

Total album length: 41 minutes

Lionel
RICHIE
CAN'T SLOW DOWN

1980s
16

Like A Virgin

I • **Album sales:** 11,000,000 I • **Release date:** November 1984 I

Madonna had already reached the Top 10 with singles from her first album. However, it was the release of her second album, *Like A Virgin,* that not only turned her into a superstar, but saw her become one of the lasting cultural icons of the 1980s and 1990s.

Always far more astute than her early image as a singer/dancer might have suggested, Madonna carefully planned her next assault on the world. She brought in former Chic guitarist Nile Rodgers, the producer of David Bowie's hit *Let's Dance*, to work on the album. *Like A Virgin* was completed sometime before the buzz around Madonna's first self-titled album began to die down. In fact, the release of 'Like A Virgin', the first single from the album, had to be delayed while the Top Five single 'Lucky Star', from *Madonna*, gradually climbed down the charts.

Number One singles: US: Like A Virgin

Grammy awards: None

Label: US & UK: Sire

Recorded in: New York, USA

Personnel:
Madonna
Nile Rodgers
Lenny Pickett
Rob Sabino
Bernard Edwards (d. 1996)
Tony Thompson (d. 2003)
Jimmy Bralower
Curtis King
Frank Simms
George Simms
Brenda King

Producer:
Nile Rodgers

When released, 'Like A Virgin' topped the charts in the US and reached Number Three in the UK. At its peak, the single was selling 75,000 copies per day in the US alone. Three other singles followed: 'Material Girl', 'Angel' and 'Dress You Up', all of which became Top Five hits on both sides of the Atlantic.

Like A Virgin was certified platinum the month after release, and was six-times platinum by the end of the following year.

SHOCKING THE PUBLIC

While there was no doubting the quality of Madonna's music, she also built her fame upon the ability to shock, particularly through pushing her heavy sexuality. She began releasing solo records in 1982, with sexually provocative videos and lyrics giving her instant notoriety. In 1985, *Playboy* and *Penthouse* magazine released nude photographs of Madonna dating back to 1977, and in the same year the erotic film *A Certain Sacrifice*, which Madonna had made in 1979, was also released. The sexual content of Madonna's personality was most forcibly expressed in the 1990s with singles such as 'Justify My Love' and 'Erotic', accompanied by explicit videos, and the publication of her book *Sex*, a soft-porn photo book which, despite critical animosity to the publication, helped the *Erotica* album to sell two million copies.

▲ **BACK COVER**

1. **Material Girl (4:01)**
2. **Angel (3:55)**
3. **Like A Virgin (3:39)**
4. **Over And Over (4:12)**
5. **Love Don't Live Here Anymore (4:50)**
6. **Dress You Up (4:01)**
7. **Shoo-Bee-Doo (5:17)**
8. **Pretender (4:30)**
9. **Stay (4:06)**

Total album length: 38 minutes

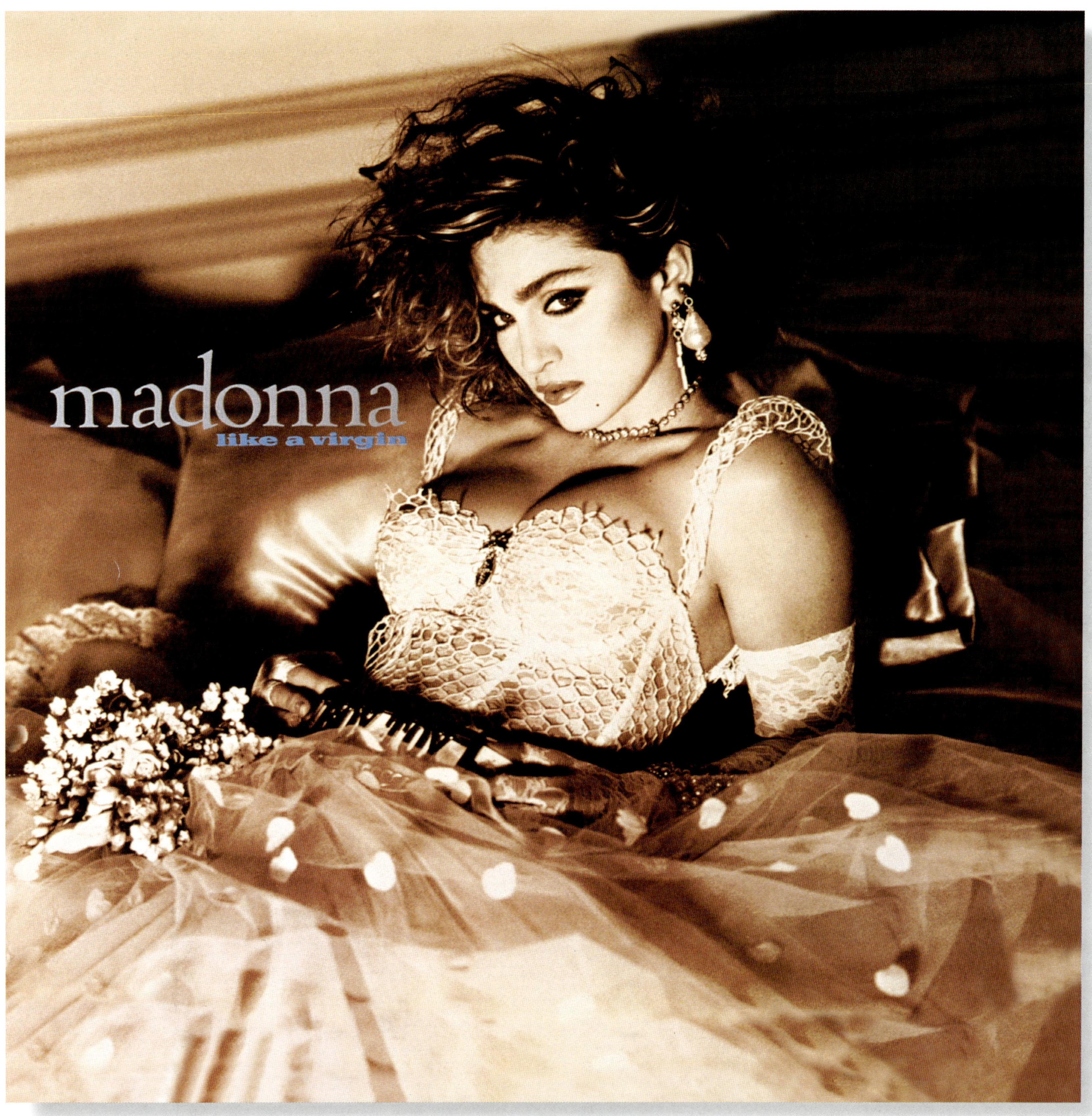

Sleeve artwork by Jeffery Kent Ayeroff and Steven Meisel

1980s
15

Faith

• Album sales: 11,400,000 | **• Release date:** October 1987

Following the break-up of pop duo Wham! in 1986, George Michael commenced his bid for solo stardom the following year with the release of 'I Want Your Sex'. Complete with a controversial video, the single was promptly banned by a number of radio stations and thereby secured Michael the publicity to ensure that his debut solo album, *Faith*, wouldn't go unnoticed.

Clearly conscious of the need to prove himself as a serious musician in both the public and the critical eye, George Michael not only wrote all the songs on *Faith*, but also produced and arranged the album, performed most of the vocal tracks, played many of the instruments, and even had a hand in the sleeve design.

Faith went to Number One in both the UK and the US, with George Michael becoming the first white solo artist to top the *Billboard* R&B album chart. The album was particularly well-received in the US, producing four Number One singles and earning a Grammy Award. Peaking at Number Two, 'Faith' was the most successful of the singles on the UK chart.

Number One singles: US: Faith; Father Figure; Monkey; One More Try

Grammy awards: Album of the year

Label: US: Columbia; UK: Epic

Recorded in: Denmark; and London, UK

Personnel:
George Michael
Hugh Burns
Lord Monty
Lee Fothergill
J.J. Belle
Roddy Matthews
Robert Ahwai
John Altman
Mark Chandler
Steve Waterman
Malcolm Griffiths
Jamie Talbot
Steve Sidwell
Paul Spong
Shirley Lewis
Various other personnel

Producers:
George Michael
David Austin

GAY ARTISTS

George Michael would not openly declare himself gay until 1998, following his arrest for 'lewd conduct' in a Beverley Hills' public toilet. The 1980s, however, saw openly homosexual and transsexual artists become major pop successes. Bands such as Culture Club, Bronski Beat and Dead or Alive were fronted by figures who declared their sexual make-up in dress, lyrics and public statements. Despite some opposition, particularly from the Christian right in the United States, the sexuality of these performers did not detract from chart success. Culture Club, for example, had seven Top 10 hits in the UK and nine in the US during the 1980s, with Boy George's image inspiring millions to emulate his androgynous style.

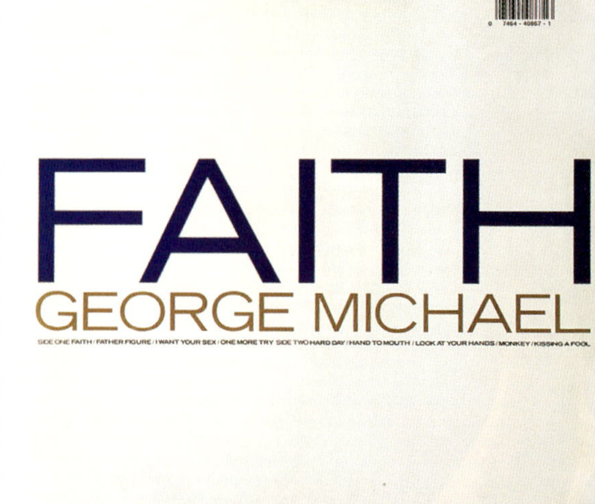

▲ **BACK COVER**

1 **Faith (3:16)**
2 **Father Figure (5:36)**
3 **I Want Your Sex, Pt. 1 & 2 (9:17)**
4 **One More Try (5:50)**
5 **Hard Day (4:48)**
6 **Hand To Mouth (4:36)**
7 **Look At Your Hands (4:37)**
8 **Monkey (5:05)**
9 **Kissing A Fool (4:35)**
10 **Hard Day (Remix) (6:30)**
11 **A Last Request (I Want Your Sex, Pt. 3) (3:48)**

Total album length: 53 minutes

Sleeve artwork by Stylorouge and George Michael

1980s
14

The Joshua Tree

| • **Album sales:** 12,700,000 | • **Release date:** March 1987 |

Even before 1987, U2 were well on their way to becoming one of the world's biggest bands, with a performance on Live Aid in 1985 bringing them worldwide attention. The release of *The Joshua Tree* two years later was eagerly anticipated and the album set a new record by going platinum within 28 hours of release. It went on to top the album charts on both sides of the Atlantic and won a Grammy for Album of the Year. The album's first single, 'With Or Without You', reached Number One on the *Billboard* Hot 100 and Number Four in the UK. The band topped the US charts again with the second single, 'I Still Haven't Found What I'm Looking For', which peaked at Number Six in the UK.

While making the album, U2 continued to work with Brian Eno and Daniel Lanois, and also brought back former collaborator Steve Lillywhite to mix four songs. The opening track, 'Where The Streets Have No Name', was nearly dropped after its complex arrangement caused problems in the studio. It later became a Top 10 single in the UK and reached Number 13 in the US.

Around 20 tracks were recorded for *The Joshua Tree*, prompting thoughts of releasing a double album. A stronger single disc release was ultimately decided upon.

Number One singles: US: I Still Haven't Found What I'm Looking For

Grammy awards: Album of the year; Best rock performance by a duo or group with vocal; Best performance music video

Label: US & UK: Island

Recorded in: Dublin, Ireland

Personnel:
Bono
The Edge
Adam Clayton
Larry Mullen Jr
Daniel Lanois
Brian Eno
Paul Barrett
Steve Lillywhite

Producers:
Daniel Lanois
Brian Eno

THE LIVE AID CONCERT

Live Aid is one of the great cultural landmarks of the 1980s. In November 1984, the single 'Do They Know It's Christmas', written by Bob Geldof and Midge Ure, was recorded by 36 of the UK's top musicians and artists, with all proceeds going towards famine relief in Ethiopia. A total of £8 million was raised and the single became the best-selling record in history at that time. Following up the success, Geldof then organized the world's biggest charity rock concert. Live Aid was performed in the United Kingdom and United States on 13 July 1985. Featuring 60 of the world's greatest groups and artists, the two concerts were watched live by 162,000 people and on television by 1.9 billion worldwide. The day raised $70 million in disaster relief.

▲ **BACK COVER**

1. **Where The Streets Have No Name (5:37)**
2. **I Still Haven't Found What I'm Looking For (4:37)**
3. **With Or Without You (4:56)**
4. **Bullet The Blue Sky (4:32)**
5. **Running To Stand Still (4:18)**
6. **Red Hill Mining Town (4:52)**
7. **In God's Country (2:57)**
8. **Trip Through Your Wires (3:32)**
9. **One Tree Hill (5:23)**
10. **Exit (4:13)**
11. **Mothers Of The Disappeared (5:14)**

Total album length: 50 minutes

Sleeve artwork by Steve Averill and Anton Corbijn

1980s
13

Hysteria

| • **Album sales:** 13,000,000 | • **Release date:** July 1987 |

Def Leppard had experienced their first taste of rock superstardom, albeit largely US-based, with the release of their 1983 album *Pyromania*. However, plans to build on this success proved problematic to say the least.

'Mutt' Lange declined an offer to produce the follow-up album, deciding to take a break after recording The Cars' *Heartbeat City*. Working instead with Meat Loaf songwriter Jim Steinman, Def Leppard began recording tracks in Holland in 1984, before deciding that the producer's style wasn't appropriate for their music. At Lange's suggestion, the band instead turned to Nigel Green, who had been an engineer on their second album, *High 'n' Dry*.

Then, on New Year's Eve 1984, drummer Rick Allen lost his left arm in an automobile accident. He successfully learnt to use a custom-made drum kit, and rejoined Def Leppard in the studio in 1985. Lange came back on board, but was dissatisfied with the existing recordings and the album was started again, virtually from scratch.

Recording continued throughout 1986. *Hysteria* was finally released in 1987, but initial sales were slow and the first single, 'Women', failed to chart. Fortunes changed with the release of 'Animal', the second of the seven singles eventually released from the album.

Number One singles: US: Love Bites

Grammy awards: None

Label: US: Mercury; UK: Vertigo

Recorded in: Hilversum, Netherlands; Dublin, Ireland; Paris, France

Personnel:
Joe Elliott
Steve Clark (d. 1991)
Phil Collen
Rick Savage
Rick Allen

Producer:
Robert John 'Mutt' Lange

RICK ALLEN'S BATTLE

On 31 December 1984, Def Leppard drummer Rick Allen was driving along the A57 near Sheffield in his vintage Corvette Stingray. He lost control, the car overturned and Allen's left arm was torn off at the shoulder. Medical teams were unable to re-attach the arm, so it looked as if Allen's days as a drummer were over, something the rest of the band would not accept. An electronic custom drum kit was built for Allen, replacing left-arm functions with a series of foot pedals. Today, the kit mixes electronic drum pads with acoustic snare, bass and cymbals, although the electronic sounds can be selected from acoustic samples.

▲ **BACK COVER**

1 **Women** (5:41)
2 **Rocket** (6:34)
3 **Animal** (4:02)
4 **Love Bites** (5:46)
5 **Pour Some Sugar On Me** (4:25)
6 **Armageddon It** (5:21)
7 **Gods Of War** (6:32)
8 **Don't Shoot Shotgun** (4:10)
9 **Run Riot** (4:38)
10 **Hysteria** (5:49)
11 **Excitable** (4:19)
12 **Love And Affection** (4:35)

Total album length: 62 minutes

Sleeve artwork by Laurie Lewis and Ross Halfin

1980s
12

Bad

| • **Album sales:** 13,000,000 | • **Release date:** August 1987 |

Following *Thriller*, Michael Jackson was arguably the biggest star in the world. However, the spectre of that album's enormous success made recording a follow-up something of an unenviable task. With Quincy Jones and Jackson again co-producing, *Bad*, the resulting album, was a clear attempt to repeat the *Thriller* formula with a tougher edge. The title track was given a cinematic video, directed by Martin Scorsese, and starring Wesley Snipes alongside a newly leather-clad Jackson.

Once again Jackson managed to set new records when the debut single, 'I Just Can't Stop Loving You', became the first ever to enter the US chart in top position. Four more songs made it to the US Number One spot: 'Bad', 'The Way You Make Me Feel', 'Man In The Mirror' and 'Dirty Diana'. In the UK, only 'I Just Can't Stop Loving You' topped the charts, but another three singles reached the Top Three.

The subsequent worldwide *Bad* tour, which lasted from September 1987 until December 1988, brought in a gross revenue of US$124 million.

Number One singles: US & UK: I Just Can't Stop Loving You; US: Bad; Dirty Diana; The Way You Make Me Feel; Man In The Mirror

Grammy awards: None

Label: US & UK: Epic

Recorded in: California, USA

Personnel:
Michael Jackson (d. 2009)
Stevie Wonder
David Williams
Eric Gale
Steve Stevens
Bill Bottrell
Dann Huff
Michael Landau
Paul Jackson Jr
Larry Williams
Kim Hutchcroft
Gary Grant
Jerry Hey
John Barnes
Kevin Maloney
Jimmy Smith (d. 2005)
Various other personnel

Producers:
Quincy Jones
Michael Jackson (d. 2009)

MTV

The 1980s saw video become a near essential tool of music promotion, and from 1981 music video found a streetwise new channel on which to broadcast – MTV. MTV (standing for 'Music Television') began broadcasting from New York City – and its availability throughout the United States spread alongside the expansion of cable television networks. The show was initially presented in a chart-listing format, and its first video shown was 'Video Killed The Radio Star' by Buggles. Its power grew rapidly, with many big-name artists relying on MTV to promote their music to an eventually global audience. In 1984, MTV's confidence was sufficient to launch the MTV Music Video Awards, which have since become one of the biggest dates in the music industry calendar.

▲ **BACK COVER**

1. **Bad (4:06)**
2. **The Way You Make Me Feel (4:59)**
3. **Speed Demon (4:01)**
4. **Liberian Girl (3:53)**
5. **Just Good Friends (4:05)**
6. **Another Part Of Me (3:53)**
7. **Man In The Mirror (5:18)**
8. **I Just Can't Stop Loving You (4:10)**
9. **Dirty Diana (4:52)**
10. **Smooth Criminal (4:16)**
11. **Leave Me Alone (4:37) (bonus track)**

Total album length: 48 minutes

Sleeve artwork by Nancy Donald and Tony Lane

1980s
11

Live/1975–85

| • **Album sales:** 13,200,000 | • **Release date:** October 1986 |

Much of Bruce Springsteen's reputation, prior to the career turning point that was *Born in the U.S.A.*, had been built on the strength of his live shows, during which he regularly performed for over three hours. It was appropriate, then, that Springsteen would follow up his most successful album with a long-awaited live collection demonstrating the very strengths that had taken him so far.

Presented as a potted history of Springsteen's life and music over the previous decade, *Live/1975–85* starts with songs recorded during 1975's *Born To Run* tour and ends with his worldwide *Born In The U.S.A.* tour.

It includes a live version of the Patti Smith song 'Because the Night' and cover versions of Woody Guthrie's 'This Land Is Your Land' and Tom Waits' 'Jersey Girl'.

Despite its ambitious breadth (no less than five LPs, 40 tracks, a three-and-a-half hour running time), *Live/1975–85* debuted at Number One in the US album charts.

Number One singles: None

Grammy awards: None

Label: US: Columbia; UK: CBS

Recorded in: Various locations

Personnel:
Bruce Springsteen
Nils Lofgren
Clarence Clemons (d. 2011)
Roy Bittan
Danny Federici (d. 2008)
Stan Harrison
Garry Tallent
Steve Van Zandt
Max Weinberg
Various other personnel

Producers:
Jon Landau
Chuck Plotkin

THE COMPACT DISC

In the early 1980s, music became increasingly available in a new format – the compact disc. Digitally recorded tapes had been produced during the 1970s, but the 11.4cm (4.5in) discs read on an optical laser drive revolutionized music recording and had a major effect on composition. Typical length of play on one of the new CDs was around 74 minutes, up to 15 or 20 minutes more music than LPs could contain. Furthermore, it was claimed that CDs were not vulnerable to the scratches and damage of LPs – a claim we now know to be untrue. The clarity of a CD recording, however, was undeniable and the format's star quickly ascended. In the US in 1983, 30,000 CD players and 800,000 CDs were sold. By 1990, 9.2 million players and 288 million CDs were sold each year in the States.

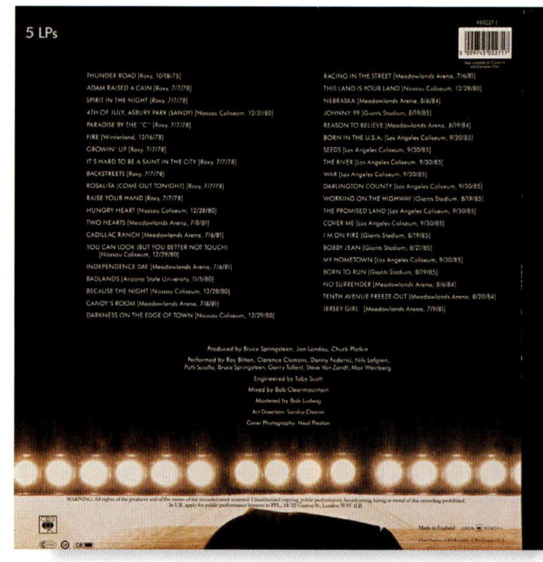

▲ **BACK COVER**

1 **Thunder Road (5:41)**
2 **Adam Raised A Cain (5:25)**
3 **Spirit In The Night (6:22)**
4 **4th Of July, Asbury Park (Sandy) (6:29)**
5 **Paradise By The "C" (3:34)**
6 **Fire (3:12)**
7 **Growin' Up (7:57)**
8 **It's Hard To Be A Saint In The City (4:37**
9 **Backstreets (7:27)**
10 **Rosalita (Come Out Tonight) (9:59)**
11 **Raise Your Hand (5:13)**
12 **Hungry Heart (4:27)**
13 **Two Hearts (3:05)**
14 **Cadillac Ranch (4:50)**
15 **You Can Look (But You Better Not Touch) (3:51)**
16 **Independence Day (5:09)**
17 **Badlands (5:15)**
18 **Because The Night (5:18)**
19 **Candy's Room (3:09)**
20 **Darkness On The Edge Of Town (4:24)**
21 **Racing In The Streets (8:13)**
22 **This Land Is Your Land (4:17)**
23 **Nebraska (4:16)**
24 **Johnny 99 (4:21)**
25 **Reason To Believe (5:19)**
26 **Born In The U.S.A. (6:07)**
27 **Seeds (5:11)**
28 **The River (11:37)**
29 **War (4:51)**
30 **Darlington County (5:12)**
31 **Working On The Highway (3:59)**
32 **The Promised Land (5:32)**
33 **Cover Me (6:58)**
34 **I'm On Fire (4:24)**
35 **Bobby Jean (4:26)**
36 **My Hometown (5:08)**
37 **Born To Run (5:02)**
38 **No Surrender (4:42)**
39 **Tenth Avenue Freeze-Out (4:18)**
40 **Jersey Girl (6:30)**

Total album length: 216 minutes

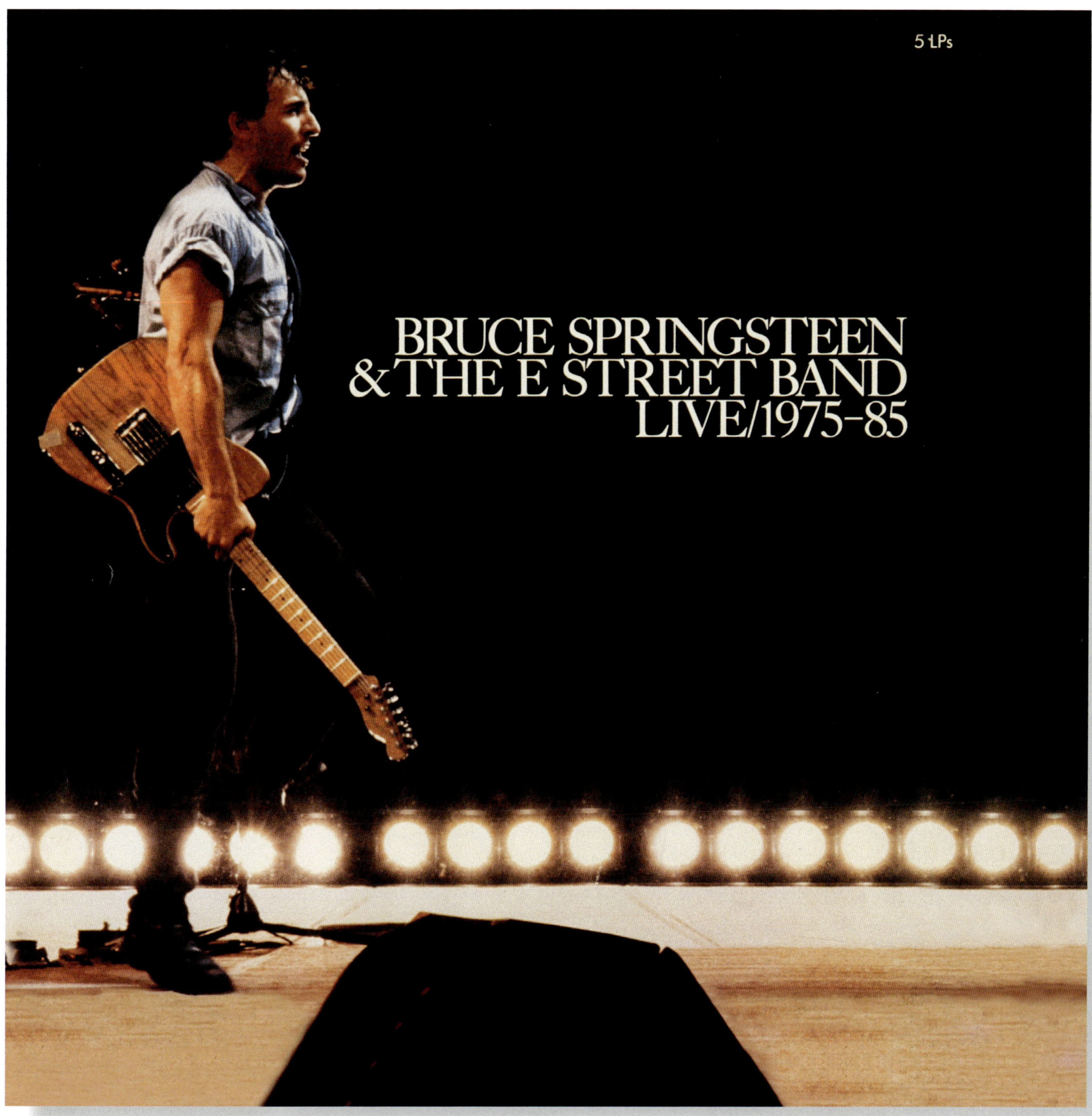

Sleeve artwork by Sandra Choron and Neal Preston

1980s
10

Brothers In Arms

| • **Album sales:** 13,500,000 | • **Release date:** May 1985 |

Dire Straits had spent some years building a reputation for writing solid songs performed by expert musicians who were also superb live performers. All this served as little warning of the impact that *Brothers In Arms* would have, both on the group's career, and on the public's regard for them. Buoyed by the Top 40 success of the first single 'So Far Away', released earlier in the year, the album went platinum in the UK and entered the charts at Number One, a position it held for three weeks.

Much of the album's commercial success can be attributed to 'Money For Nothing', which features Sting singing 'I want my MTV' to the melody of the Police's 'Don't Stand So Close To Me'. Supported by a cutting-edge computer animated video, which guaranteed heavy rotation on the new music channels, the single reached Number One in the US and Number Four in the UK, won a Grammy for Best Music Video, and became the band's only million-selling single.

Other singles followed, including 'Walk of Life', which reached Number Seven in the US and Number Two in the UK. The song 'Brothers in Arms', while less successful on the charts, is remembered as having been the first CD-single to be sold commercially. With a pressing of only 400 copies, it has since become a sought-after collector's item.

Number One singles: US: Money For Nothing

Grammy awards: Best music video, short form; Best rock performance by a duo or group with vocal

Label: US: Warner; UK: Vertigo

Recorded in: Monserrat, West Indies; London, UK; New York, USA

Personnel:
Mark Knopfler
Hal Lindes
Guy Fletcher
Alan Clark
John Illsley
Terry Williams
Sting
Michael Becker (d. 2007)
Randy Becker
Various other personnel

Producers:
Neil Dorfsman
Mark Knopfler

ANIMATED VIDEO

Although the video for 'Money for Nothing' was cutting edge at the time, computer animation (CA) had been in development since the 1950s. However, it was during the early 1970s that the computer-generated images reached refinement, with Cornell University producing architectural walk-throughs on screen, and Pennsylvania University creating rudimentary human-figure animation. The first computer-animated film, *Hunger,* was produced by Canadian Rene Jodoin in 1974, and by the late 1970s fully articulated human forms could be generated on screen. During the 1980s, CA emerged as a viable, then preferable, alternative to stop-motion filming, and landmark movies such as *Tron* (1982) demonstrated that entire worlds could be manifested on screen.

▲ **BACK COVER**

1. **So Far Away (5:12)**
2. **Money For Nothing (8:26)**
3. **Walk Of Life (4:12)**
4. **Your Latest Trick (6:33)**
5. **Why Worry (8:31)**
6. **Ride Across The River (6:57)**
7. **The Man's Too Strong (4:40)**
8. **One World (3:40)**
9. **Brothers In Arms (6:59)**

Total album length: 55 minutes

1980s

Sleeve artwork by Sutton Cooper

1980s
9

Dirty Dancing

| • **Album sales:** 13,500,000 | • **Release date:** September 1987 |

The impressive sales of the *Dirty Dancing* soundtrack were largely the result of the track '(I've Had) The Time Of My Life'. A duet sung by Jennifer Warnes and former Righteous Brother Bill Medley, the ballad reached Number One in the US, won a Grammy, and earned an Academy Award for Best Song. The single sold over 36,000,000 copies.

For such a huge success, the song had fairly inauspicious origins. Songwriter Franke Previte had recently been dropped by MCA when producer Jimmy Lenner invited him to write a song for *Dirty Dancing* (what Previte didn't know was that he was one of over 100 artists who had been extended the invitation). The filmmakers instantly realised that the submitted song was the perfect number for the final scene.

Other singles followed: 'Hungry Eyes' provided Eric Carmen with a Top Ten hit in the US, while even the film's star, Patrick Swayze, hit the charts with 'She's Like The Wind'.

Number One singles: US: (I've Had) The Time Of My Life

Grammy awards: Best pop performance by a duo or group with vocal

Label: US & UK: RCA

Recorded in: Various locations

Personnel:
Jennifer Warnes
Maurice Williams
Tony Kiley
Mick Anker
Neville Henry
Bill Medley
Bruce Channel
Tom Johnston
Ronnie Spector
Estelle Bennet (d. 2009)
Nedra Talley
Merry Clayton
Wendy Fraser
Patrick Swayze (d. 2009)
Alfie Zappacosta
Maurice Williams
Various other personnel

Producers:
Peter Wilson
Michael Lloyd
Phil Spector
Leon Medica
Eric Carmen
Alfie Zappacosta

BLOCKBUSTER MOVIES OF THE 80s

While films such as *Dirty Dancing* and *Footloose* pulled in good money for the studios, they were dwarfed in box office performance by the decade's major genre – the action adventure. The two power names in the industry were George Lucas and Steven Spielberg. Lucas opened the decade with the second of the *Star Wars* trilogy, *The Empire Strikes Back* (1980), following up with *Return of the Jedi* in 1983. With Spielberg, Lucas also launched the Indiana Jones series with 1981's *Raiders of the Lost Ark,* while Spielberg directed *E.T. The Extra Terrestrial* (1982). *Raiders* took US$242 million and won four Oscars and *E.T.* grossed just short of US$400 million.

▲ BACK COVER

1 (I've Had) The Time Of My Life (Jennifer Warnes) (4:47)
2 Be My Baby (The Ronettes) (2:37)
3 She's Like The Wind (Patrick Swayze) (3:51)
4 Hungry Eyes (Eric Carmen) (4:06)
5 Stay (Maurice Williams & the Zodiacs) (1:34)
6 Yes (Merry Clayton) (3:15)
7 You Don't Own Me (The Blow Monkeys) (3:00)
8 Hey! Baby (Bruce Channel) (2:21)
9 Overload (Alfie Zappacosta) (3:39)
10 Love Is Strange (Mickey & Sylvia) (2:52)
11 Where Are You Tonight? (Tom Johnston) (3:59)
12 In The Still Of The Night (The Five Satins) (3:03)

Total album length: 39 minutes

Sleeve artwork by Pam Rodi and Adger Cowans

1980s
8

No Jacket Required

| • **Album sales:** 13,900,000 | • **Release date:** February 1985 |

Phil Collins had gradually established himself as a solo artist of note with two previous albums released outside the Genesis envelope. Although he remained insistent during the 1980s that he wasn't about to leave the group, *No Jacket Required* arrived during a period when Phil Collins was a far bigger name than Genesis. He was even able to recruit former Genesis frontman Peter Gabriel to perform backing vocals for 'Take Me Home', as well as Sting (on 'Long Long Way To Go', a song that Collins would perform to memorable effect at Live Aid).

The title was inspired after Collins was stopped from entering the bar at Chicago's Ambassador Hotel (where he was staying with Robert Plant) because his leather jacket wasn't deemed to be a 'proper' jacket.

Number One singles: US: One More Night; Sussudio

Grammy awards: Album of the year; Best male pop performance; Producer of the year (non-classical)

Label: US: Atlantic; UK: Virgin

Recorded in: London, UK

Personnel:
Phil Collins
Daryl Stuerner
Arif Mardin (d. 2006)
The Phoenix Horns
Don Mynck
Lee Sklar
Helen Terry
Peter Gabriel
Sting
Various other personnel

Producers:
Phil Collins
Hugh Padgham

The album won Collins the 1985 Grammy award for Album of the Year, affirming him as an artist with a fair degree of commercial clout, and consolidating his solo efforts alongside the respect he had already garnered for skills as both a producer and drummer. It reached the Number One spot in charts across the world, and spawned three hit singles: 'Sussudio', 'Take Me Home' and 'One More Night'.

THE GRAMMY AWARDS

The Recording Academy, the organization responsible for the Grammy awards, was formed by a group of music professionals in 1957. Their objective was to recognize and reward the achievements of exceptional artistes and recording professionals through a peer recognition system. It has become one of the largest arts organizations in the United States, and the Grammy awards ceremonies are at the top of the music industry calendar. The awards themselves cover 105 categories, are presented annually, and cover all fields of music making. The Recording Academy also involves itself in legal issues surrounding the music industry, from protecting artists' contractual rights to combating music piracy.

▲ **BACK COVER**

1. **Sussudio (4:23)**
2. **Only You Know And I Know (4:20)**
3. **Long Long Way To Go (4:20)**
4. **I Don't Wanna Know (4:12)**
5. **One More Night (4:47)**
6. **Don't Lose My Number (4:46)**
7. **Who Said I Would (4:01)**
8. **Doesn't Anybody Stay Together Anymore (4:18)**
9. **Inside Out (5:14)**
10. **Take Me Home (5:51)**

Total album length: 50 minutes

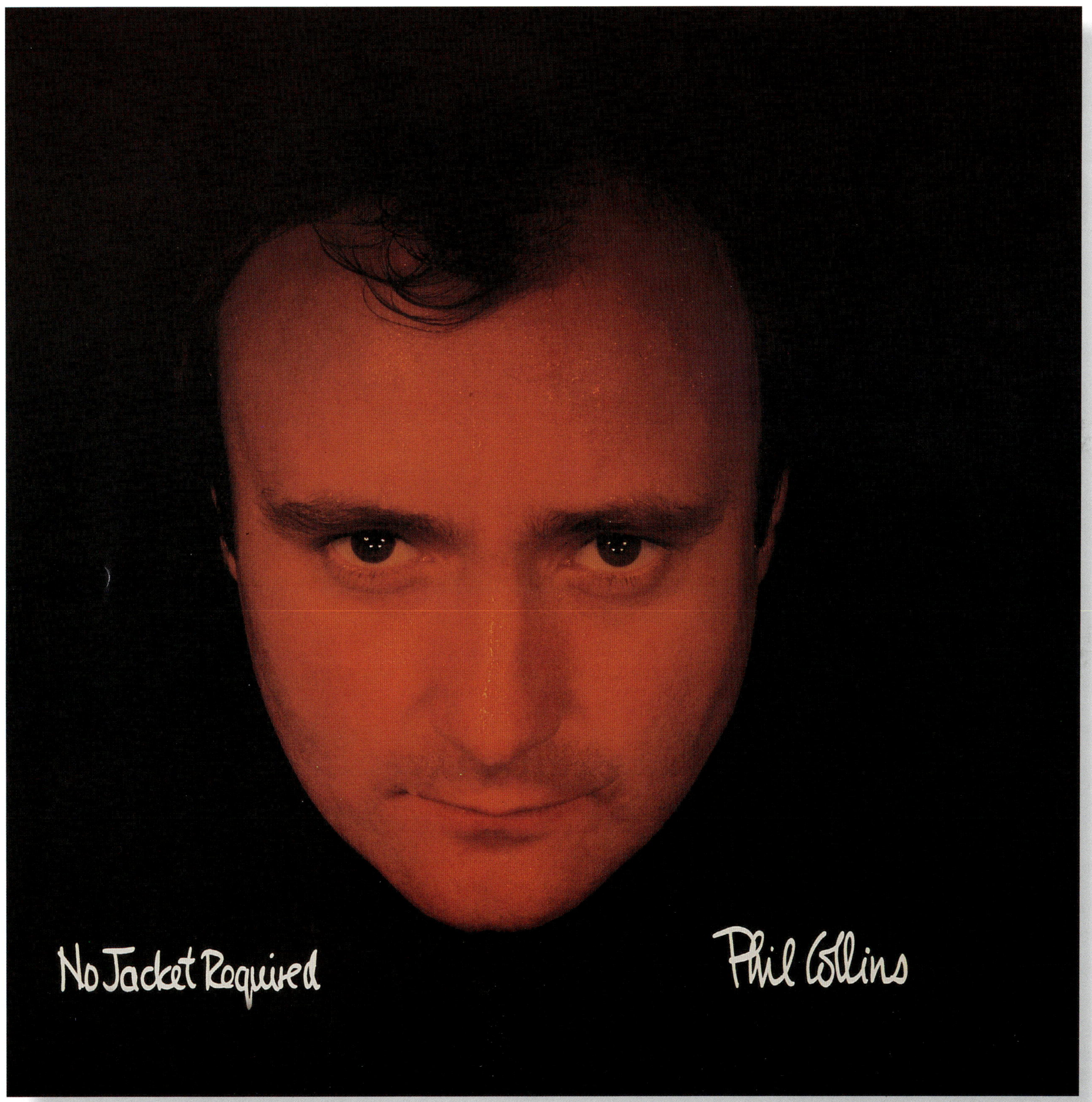
No Jacket Required
Phil Collins

1980s
7

Slippery When Wet

| • **Album sales:** 14,100,000 | • **Release date:** August 1986 |

With only a few minor hits to their name, Bon Jovi had failed to scale the heights of rock stardom with their first two albums. The group therefore decided to tailor their third album into a surefire bestseller.

Bringing songwriter Desmond Child on board as a collaborator, the band put together a total of 30 songs which were then auditioned for focus groups consisting of teenagers from New York and New Jersey. Both the final selection and the running order were determined by the results from these auditions. The first choice of sleeve image (that of a busty woman clad in a wet T-shirt) was also ditched in favour of the inoffensive water-textured sleeve.

A further change in emphasis saw the single releases from the album supported by videos that tended to show off Jon Bon Jovi's pin-up good looks, bolstered by his carefully styled hair.

The resulting album, *Slippery When Wet*, became the biggest selling rock album of 1987 (though metal fans took exception to its pop-oriented content) and went multi-platinum. Two singles, 'You Give Love A Bad Name' and 'Livin' On A Prayer', reached Number One in the US (Number 14 and Number Four, respectively, in the UK) and Bon Jovi became one of the biggest rock acts in the world.

Number One singles: US: You Give Love A Bad Name; Livin' On A Prayer

Grammy awards: None

Label: US: Mercury; UK: Vertigo

Recorded in: Vancouver, Canada

Personnel:
Jon Bon Jovi
Richie Sambora
Dave Bryan
Alec John Such
Hugh McDonald
Tico Torres
Bruce Fairbairn (d. 1999)
Lema Moon
Tom Keenlyside

Producer:
Bruce Fairbairn (d. 1999)

OFFENSIVE LANGUAGE

While Bon Jovi was toning down its cover for *Slippery When Wet*, a dramatic change had occurred in the music industry, this time relating to lyrics. Concomitant with the rise of rap music and some of the extremes of heavy metal, sexist, racist, anti-law and explicit lyrics had become commonplace. Concerns over the lyrics led to the formation of the Parents' Music Resource Center (PMRC) in the United States. Headed by Tipper Gore (the wife of then senator Al Gore) and other powerful women, the PMRC successfully pressurized the Senate and the Recording Industry Association of America (RIAA) into introducing 'voluntary' warnings of explicit content on the covers of all albums from 1985. In 1990 this system was standardized to the now-familiar sticker declaring – 'Parental Advisory: Explicit Lyrics'.

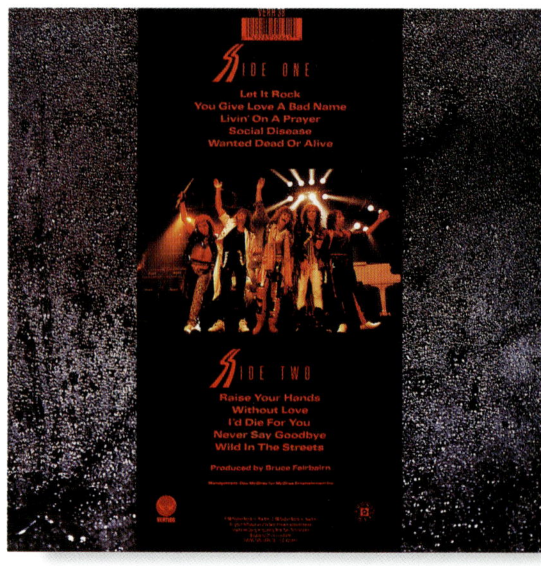

▲ **BACK COVER**

1 **Let It Rock (5:25)**
2 **You Give Love A Bad Name (3:43)**
3 **Livin' On A Prayer (4:09)**
4 **Social Disease (4:18)**
5 **Wanted Dead Or Alive (5:09)**
6 **Raise Your Hands (4:17)**
7 **Without Love (3:31)**
8 **I'd Die For You (4:30)**
9 **Never Say Goodbye (4:49)**
10 **Wild In The Streets (3:56)**

Total album length: 44 minutes

Sleeve artwork by Bill Levy and Mark Weiss

1980s
6

Whitney Houston

I • **Album sales:** 14,300,000 I • **Release date:** February 1985 I

For an album that would hit the record books as the biggest selling debut by a female artist, *Whitney Houston* got off to an inauspicious start. Houston had signed in 1983 to Arista, whose boss, Clive Davis, is commonly credited with discovering her. Davis was determined to make her debut album a success by recruiting only the best songwriters and producers for the task. Despite Davis' enthusiasm, many established producers were unwilling to throw their lot in with an unproven artist, and the album only started to get off the ground after Kashif came forward with a demo for 'You Give Good Love'. In the end, the label spent over $250,000 dollars in recording *Whitney Houston*, an unheard of amount for an artist's first recording.

Released on Valentine's Day, the album built up momentum, reaching Number One spot later in the year, a position it held for 14 weeks. Such was its popularity that *Whitney Houston* was still the bestselling album in 1986, the year after its release.

Number One singles: US & UK: Saving All My Love For You; US: How Will I Know; Greatest Love Of All

Grammy awards: Best Female Pop Vocal Performance – Saving All My Love For You

Label: US & UK: Arista

Recorded in: N/A

Personnel:
Whitney Houston (d. 2012)
Cissy Houston
Neil Vineberg
Paul Pesco
Ira Siegel
Corrado Rustici
Paul Jackson Jr
Kenny G
Vincent Henry
Jerry Hey
Marc Russo
Wayne Wallace
Robbie Buchanan
Preston Glass
Kashif
Teddy Pendergrass (d. 2010)
Tom Scott
Various other personnel

Producers:
Narada Michael Walden
Kashif
Michael MasserJ

NIGHTCLUBS IN THE 1980s

While the 1970s were the era of disco, the 1980s were the era of nightclub. The 1970s saw much of nightclubs' focus being directed towards Friday and Saturday nights, the primary nights on which people went out. However, with the sheer diversity of the 1980s' music scene, nightclubs now found that they could open speciality nights throughout the week to cater for various different interests, such a gothic night, New Romantic night, and hip-hop night. Outside professional clubs, numerous underground clubs also sprang up, particularly with the onset of rave culture in the mid-1980s, which spread out from the UK to the US. Raves – music dance events held in venues ranging from basements to abandoned factories – could attract tens of thousands of people, and were targeted by the police for their ignorance of health and safety legislation, and for prolific drug use (mainly of Ecstasy). Rave events continued into the 1990s, but during that decade they became less underground and more mainstream club events.

▲ **BACK COVER**

1. **You Give Good Love (4:37)**
2. **Thinking About You (5:26)**
3. **Someone For Me (5:01)**
4. **Saving All My Love For You (3:58)**
5. **Nobody Loves Me Like You Do (3:49)**
6. **How Will I Know (4:36)**
7. **All At Once (4:29)**
8. **Take Good Care Of My Heart (4:16)**
9. **Greatest Love Of All (4:51)**
10. **Hold Me (6:00)**

Total album length: 47 minutes

WHITNEY HOUSTON

Sleeve artwork by Dom Davenport

1980s
5

Purple Rain

| • **Album sales:** 14,400,000 | • **Release date:** August 1984 |

Prince's previous album, *1999*, had brought the singer considerable success in the US, but it was his soundtrack to the 1984 film *Purple Rain* that was to turn him and backing band The Revolution into global superstars. The album spent 24 weeks at the top of the US album charts, reached Number Seven in the UK, and gave Prince his first two US Number One singles with 'When Doves Cry' and 'Let's Go Crazy'. The title track reached Number Two in the US, while 'I Would Die 4 U' and 'Take Me With U' charted in the *Billboard* Hot 100.

With a reputation for lyrical lewdness, Prince retained his right to shock with tracks such as 'Darling Nikki', but there was a growing sense of maturity in the starkly arresting 'When Doves Cry'. The album won Prince two Grammy awards and an Academy Award for Best Song Score.

In addition to making the soundtrack, Prince took the starring role in *Purple Rain*, a loosely autobiographical film about a young Minneapolis rock musician struggling to make it big. The movie grossed over $68 million dollars at the US box office and functioned as an extended promotional video for the album. Coupled with the record-breaking success of his 1984–85 *Purple Rain* tour, the hype helped make the album into the biggest hit of Prince's career.

Number One singles: US: When Doves Cry; Let's Go Crazy

Grammy awards: Best album or original score for a motion picture; Best rock performance by a duo or group with vocal

Label: US & UK: Warner

Recorded in: Los Angeles, USA

Personnel:
Prince
Wendy Melvoin
Lisa Coleman
Matt Fink
Brown Mark
Bobby Z
Apollonia
Novi Novog
David Coleman (d. 2004)
Suzie Katayama

Producers:
Prince
The Revolution

ALTERNATIVE 1980s FASHIONS

While the 1980s was the decade of power dressing, with male and female professionals donning wide-shouldered power suits, it was also the decade of extreme fashion experimentation. What you wore depended on the movement to which you belonged. If you were a New Romantic, frills, lace and historical pastiche were the order of the day, creating a dandyish, narcissistic look accented by heavy, bright make-up. The Goths, by contrast, dressed with a Bela Lugosi morbidity, with black the obligatory colour scheme, and styles that included references to fetish wear. Massive crimped-and-back-combed hairstyles usually completed the Gothic look, along with skull motif boot-lace ties and other ghoulish jewellery.

▲ BACK COVER

1 Let's Go Crazy (4:39)
2 Take Me With U (3:54)
3 The Beautiful Ones (5:15)
4 Computer Blue (3:59)
5 Darling Nikki (4:15)
6 When Doves Cry (5:52)
7 I Would Die 4 U (2:51)
8 Baby I'm a Star (4:20)
9 Purple Rain (8:45)

Total album length: 44 minutes

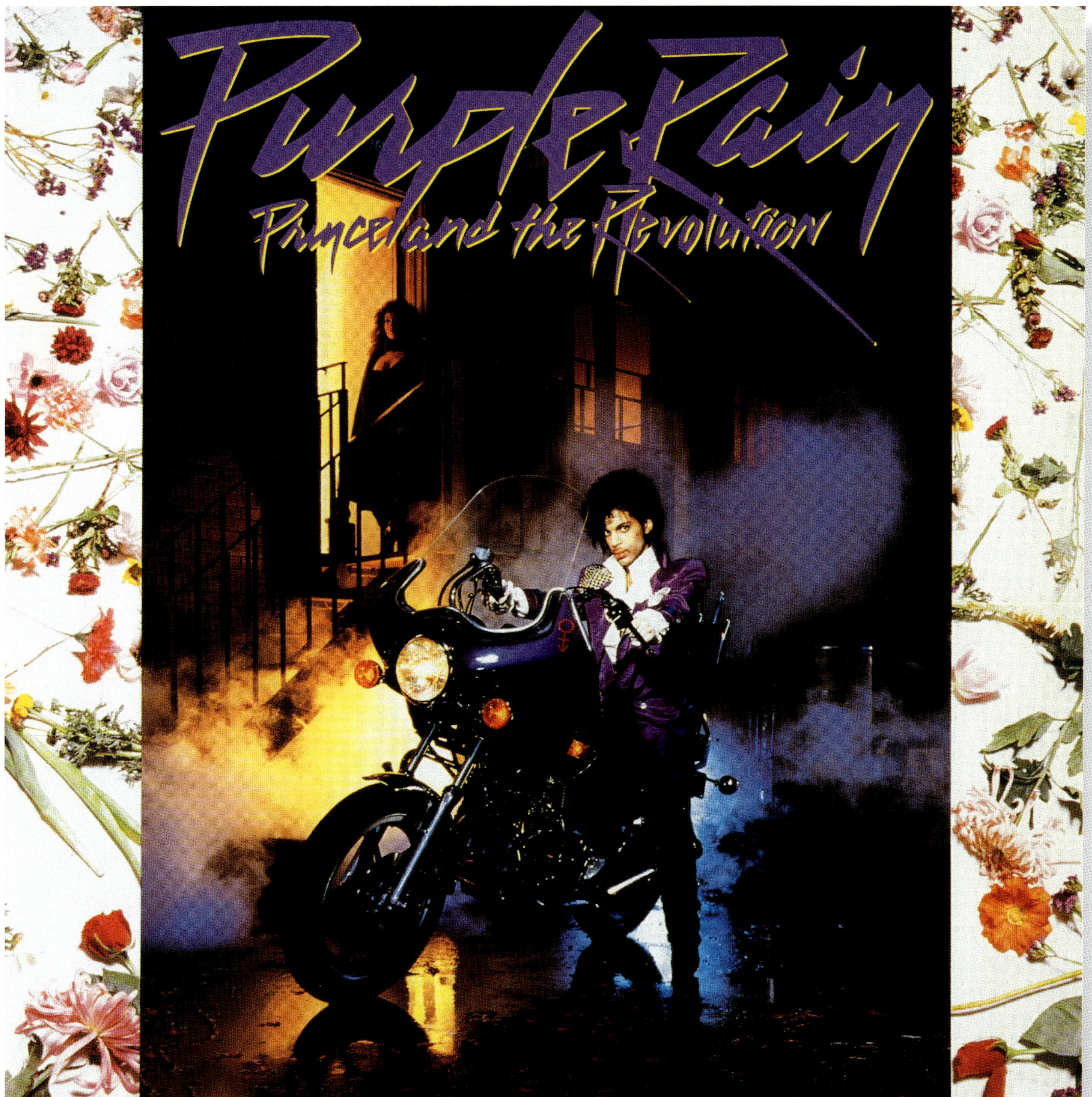
Purple Rain
Prince and the Revolution

1980s
4

Born In The U.S.A.

| • **Album sales:** 16,500,000 | • **Release date:** June 1984 |

Prior to the 1984 release of *Born In The U.S.A.*, Bruce Springsteen's career was qualified largely through strong reviews, healthy sales and a loyal following, but he stopped short of unqualified mainstream stardom. Since the release of *Born To Run* in 1975, his songs had grown increasingly cynical and downbeat. Although *Born In The U.S.A.* continued this trend, its stadium-bound production helped create The Boss's greatest popular success. While commercially-minded ears were drawn by the anthemic sound of singles like the title track, loyal fans were rewarded by songs that continued to focus on the working classes and the disenfranchised.

The first single, 'Dancing In The Dark', illustrated most startlingly how Springsteen was broaching new musical ground with its keyboard hook, while the video is now famous for featuring a teenage Courtney Cox dancing with Springsteen.

Although *Born In The U.S.A.* failed to yield any number one singles, seven of 12 tracks went on to become Top 10 hits in the US, while the album itself stayed in both the US and UK charts for more than two years.

Number One singles:
None

Grammy awards:
Best male rock vocal performance – Dancing In The Dark

Label: US: Columbia; UK: CBS

Recorded in: New York, USA

Personnel:
Bruce Springsteen
Steve Van Zandt
Clarence Clemons (d. 2011)
Danny Federici (d. 2008)
Roy Bittan
Garry Tallent
Max Weinberg
Ruth Jackson
Richie Rosenberg

Producers:
Bruce Springsteen
Jon Landau
Chuck Plotkin
Steve Van Zandt

US SOCIAL PROBLEMS IN THE 1980s

The 1980s were a curious cultural period for the United States. At the same time as affluence spread on a wider scale than ever before, certain social and economic problems intensified. Gang violence created virtual war zones of inner-city areas, bolstered by the easy proliferation of automatic firearms and high unemployment amongst African-Americans and Hispanics. Thus, in the mid 1980s, New York alone was seeing around 2,200 murders a year, compared to only 600 a year during the 1960s. Such violence in turn led the Reagan administration to declare a 'war on drugs', spurred by rising crack cocaine usage, and the penalties for drug possession became ferociously harsh. Also making its presence felt in the 1980s was the spread of HIV/AIDS, which tore through the gay community, African-Americans and worked its way out into all sectors of US society.

▲ **BACK COVER**

1. **Born In The U.S.A. (4:39)**
2. **Cover Me (3:26)**
3. **Darlington County (4:48)**
4. **Working On The Highway (3:11)**
5. **Downbound Train (3:35)**
6. **I'm On Fire (2:36)**
7. **No Surrender (4:00)**
8. **Bobby Jean (3:46)**
9. **I'm Goin' Down (3:29)**
10. **Glory Days (4:15)**
11. **Dancing In The Dark (4:01)**
12. **My Hometown (4:33)**

Total album length: 46 minutes

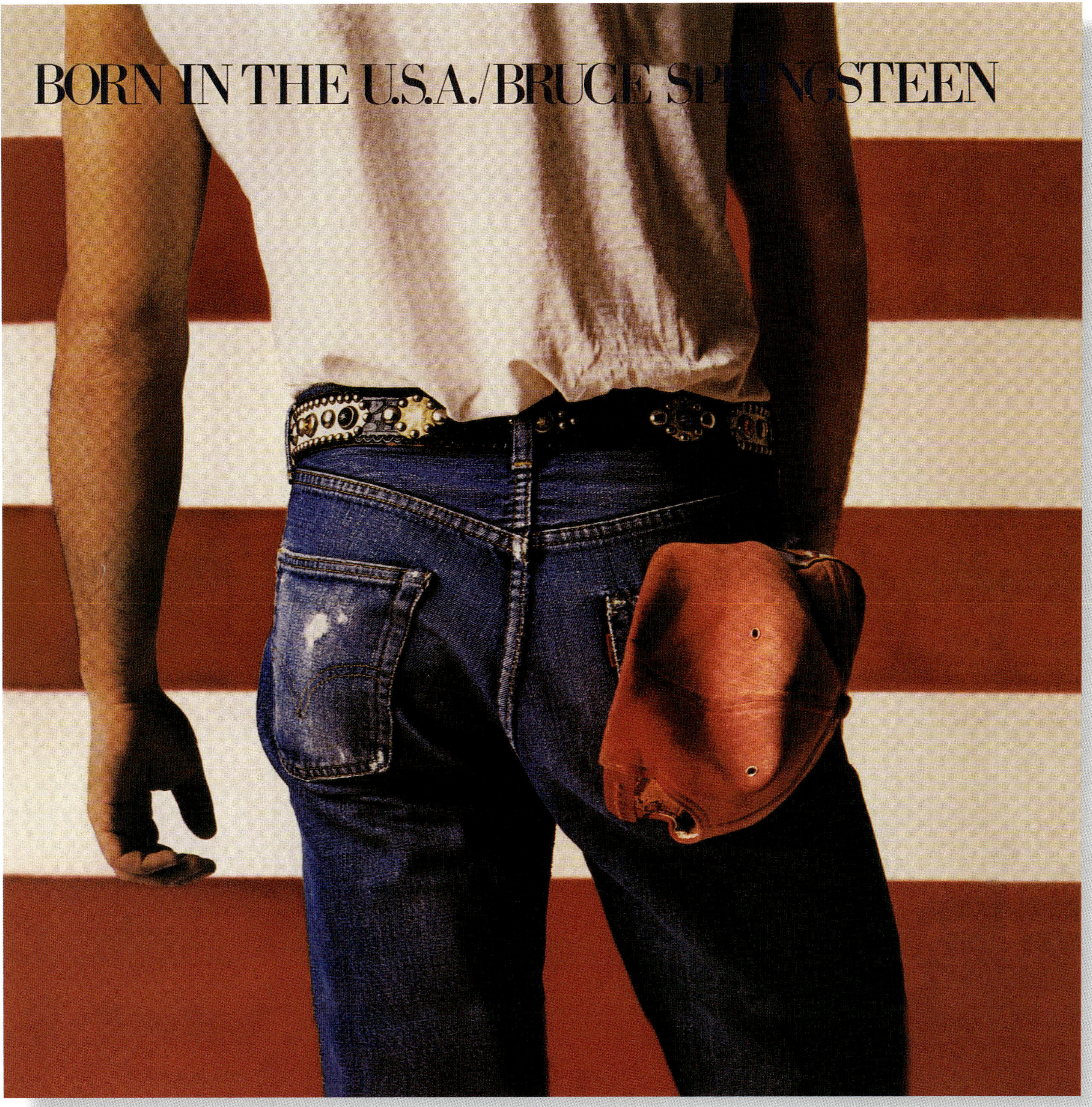

Sleeve artwork by Andrea Klein and Annie Leibovitz

1980s
3

Appetite For Destruction

| • **Album sales:** 17,100,000 | • **Release date:** July 1987 |

Just as heavy metal seemed to be getting too long in the tooth to remain credible, Guns N' Roses arrived. The group successfully re-energised the genre with shameless gusto, and made the basic tenets of hard rock, as well as the accompanying attitude, fashionable once again.

Following an independent live EP release, Guns N' Roses were signed by Geffen in 1986, who launched their debut album, *Appetite For Destruction*, the following year.

Appetite For Destruction took its time to get noticed. Its potential for success was marred initially by the original sleeve, depicting a violent rape, which saw it banned by several major retailers. The cover was subsequently redesigned, and the album reissued.

'Welcome To The Jungle' started to get airplay on radio and TV music channels early in 1988 (and was also featured on the soundtrack of the movie *The Dead Pool*, starring Clint Eastwood). However, it was 'Sweet Child O' Mine' that finally proved the album's selling point. The song was picked up by MTV and quickly made it to Number One in the US pop charts (although only 24 in the UK), helping the album to reach Number One in July 1988, a year after its release. 'Welcome To The Jungle' was subsequently re-released. A further single, 'Paradise City', made it into the Top 10 in the US and UK in 1989.

Number One singles: US: Sweet Child O' Mine

Grammy awards: None

Label: US & UK: Geffen

Recorded in: California, USA

Personnel:
Axl Rose
Slash
Izzy Stradlin
Duff McKagan
Steven Adler

Producer:
Mike Clink

AXL ROSE

Axl Rose was a true wild-child of the 1980s, living the dream of sex, drugs and rock 'n' roll. Born in Lafayette, Indiana, on 6 February 1962, and named William Bruce Bailey, he had a difficult, abusive upbringing in the hands of his father and then stepfather, the latter a religious zealot who tried to force William into a repressive religious mould. Axl Rose – William changed his name at the age of 17 – rebelled, fell into trouble with the law, joined rock bands, and ended up being a founding member of Guns N' Roses in 1985. Rose was noted for his shrieking vocals and his excessive lifestyle of rock, alcohol, drugs, parties and women. He also had a volatile temper, attacking a fan at a gig in St Louis, Missouri, and walking out on the band during a live gig in Montreal in 1991 (both incidents sparked riots). Throughout the 1990s, Rose held a dictatorial grip over a continually disintegrating/reforming band.

▲ **BACK COVER**

1. **Welcome To The Jungle (4:32)**
2. **It's So Easy (3:21)**
3. **Nightrain (4:26)**
4. **Out Ta Get Me (4:20)**
5. **Mr. Brownstone (3:46)**
6. **Paradise City (6:45)**
7. **My Michelle (3:38)**
8. **Think About You (3:49)**
9. **Sweet Child O' Mine (5:54)**
10. **You're Crazy (3:16)**
11. **Anything Goes (3:25)**
12. **Rocket Queen (6:14)**

Total album length: 53 minutes

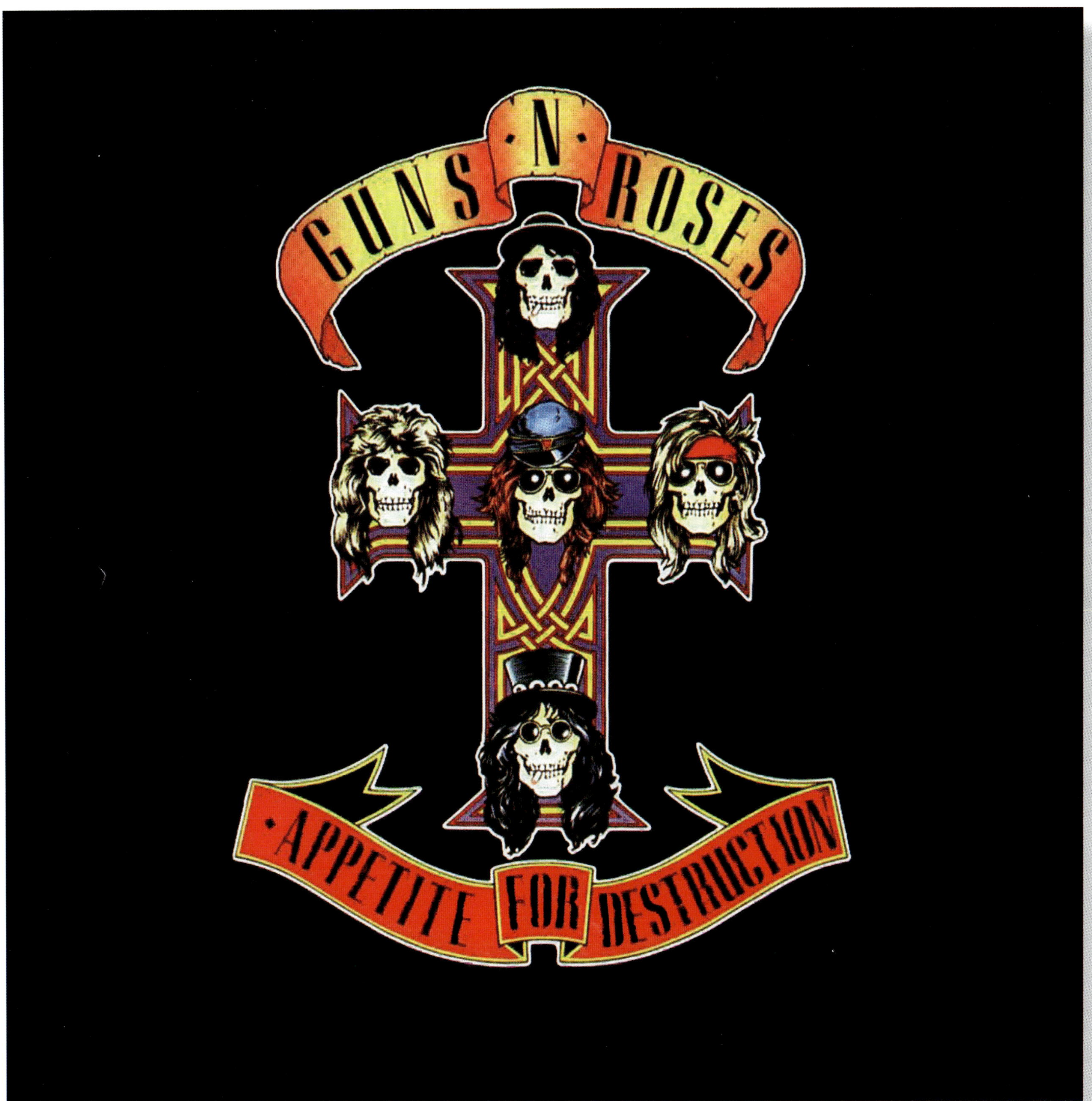

Sleeve artwork by Michael Hodgson and Robert Williams

1980s
2

Back In Black

| • **Album sales:** 22,100,000 | • **Release date:** July 1980 |

The February 1980 death of AC/DC's lead singer, Bon Scott, came close to curtailing the rock band's recent rise to international status. Nevertheless, with a new singer, Brian Johnson, and the recently recruited Robert John 'Mutt' Lange continuing on production, AC/DC managed a return to the record stores just five months later with their biggest album. *Back In Black* was certified platinum within two months of release and transformed AC/DC into one of the biggest rock groups in the world.

Lange, brought on board for the previous album, *Highway To Hell*, had managed to fine tune the band's raucous hard rock sound into something altogether more viable commercially and approaching the anthemic at times. Meanwhile, Brian Johnson proved not only a capable match for Bon Scott on vocals, but in many ways surpassed the late singer.

Number One singles: None

Grammy awards: None

Label: US & UK: Atlantic

Recorded in: Nassau, Bahamas

Personnel:
Brian Johnson
Angus Young
Malcolm Young
Cliff Williams
Phil Rudd

Producer:
Robert John 'Mutt' Lange

A number of the album's strongest tracks, 'Rock & Roll Ain't Noise Pollution' and 'You Shook Me All Night Long', enjoyed success in the singles charts, while 'Hells Bells' became something of a signature track.

The massive sales of *Back In Black* also prompted the American release of the band's 1976 album *Dirty Deeds Done Dirt Cheap*, which had been previously available only in Europe and, in a different form, Australia.

BON SCOTT

Bon Scott was to be AC/DC's frontman for six years, during which time he took the group to superstardom. He was born Ronald Belford Scott in Kirriemuir, Scotland, on 9 July 1946, and dropped out of school at 15 to play with a rock group. By the late 1960s, he was already a recording artist, his fame concentrated in Australia, where his family had moved when he was young. Following stints with the Fraternity and the Valentines, in 1973 Scott had a serious motorbike accident, and was in a coma for several months. A year after his recovery he joined AC/DC, and between 1974 and the end of the decade, the group climbed higher up the charts with their albums. In true rock 'n' roll style, however, Scott developed problems with alcohol, and on 19 February 1980 he died after a heavy drinking bout.

▲ **BACK COVER**

1 **Hells Bells (5:09)**
2 **Shoot To Thrill (5:14)**
3 **What Do You Do For Money Honey (3:33)**
4 **Given The Dog A Bone (3:30)**
5 **Let Me Put My Love Into You (4:12)**
6 **Back In Black (4:13)**
7 **You Shook Me All Night Long (3:28)**
8 **Have A Drink On Me (3:57)**
9 **Shake a Leg (4:03)**
10 **Rock & Roll Ain't Noise Pollution (4:12)**

Total album length: 42 minutes

AC/DC

1980s
1

Thriller

| • **Album sales:** 31,100,000 | • **Release date:** December 1982 |

Michael Jackson had already released one career-defining solo album with the Quincy Jones production *Off The Wall*. This, nevertheless, did little to prepare the world for the behemoth that was 1982's *Thriller*. The album had it all: rock, soul, pop, Jackson's distinctive vocals, and a celebrated selection of collaborators.

The first single, 'The Girl Is Mine', reached the Top 10 on both sides of the Atlantic, but it was the ambitious videos for 'Billie Jean' and 'Beat It' that would provide the foundation for the album's success. Thanks in part to Eddie Van Halen's powerhouse guitar solo, 'Beat It' was readily embraced by MTV, making Jackson the first black artist to find success on the network. Equally, Jackson's star power helped gain an extensive audience for the new channel.

An unprecedented seven of the album's nine tracks became Top 10 hits in the US. The success of *Thriller*, and the impact of the videos, redefined expectations within the music industry for ever.

Number One singles: US & UK: Billie Jean; US: Beat It

Grammy awards: Album of the year; Record of the year – Beat It; Best male pop vocal performance – Thriller; Best male rock vocal performance – Beat It; Producer of the year; Best male R&B vocal performance – Billie Jean; Best R&B song – Billie Jean; Best video album

Label: US & UK: Epic

Recorded in: California, USA

Personnel:
Michael Jackson (d. 2009)
Paul McCartney
Vincent Price (d. 1993)
Eddie Van Halen
Janet Jackson
LaToya Jackson
James Ingram
Dean Parks
David Foster
Larry Williams
Jerry Hey
David Paich
Various other personnel

Producers:
Michael Jackson (d. 2009)
Quincy Jones

THE POWER OF VIDEO

The 'Thriller' single video demonstrated that while good music would always sell, its marketability would be dramatically improved with striking video visuals. Made in 1983, the video was unusual through its length – at 17 minutes it stood more as a mini film than a pop track – and featured plot and dialogue as well as stunning dance and song scenes. The film featured Jackson transforming into a werewolf and also a zombie, and was directed by John Landis, who had directed the film *An American Werewolf In London.* The film's graphic horror attracted accusations of occultism, which Jackson rejected. It is open to speculation whether the *Thriller* album would have become the best-selling album of all time were it not for the controversy and influence of the video.

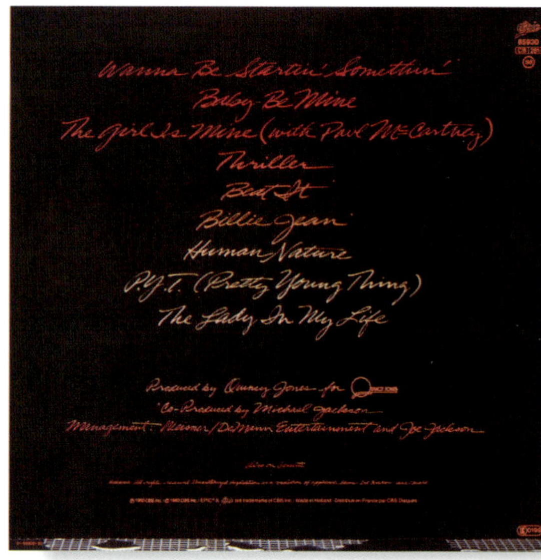

▲ **BACK COVER**

1. **Wanna Be Startin' Somethin' (6:02)**
2. **Baby Be Mine (4:20)**
3. **The Girl Is Mine (3:42)**
4. **Thriller (5:57)**
5. **Beat It (4:17)**
6. **Billie Jean (4:57)**
7. **Human Nature (4:05)**
8. **P.Y.T. (Pretty Young Thing) (3:58)**
9. **The Lady In My Life (4:57)**

Total album length: 42 minutes

Sleeve artwork by Dick Zimmerman

PEARL JAM

Dixie Chicks

SUPERNATURAL
HE WORLDWIDE PHENOMENON
Over 13 million copies sold
9 GRAMMY AWARDS
including
ALBUM OF THE YEAR
Includes the singles
"SMOOTH"
(Song of the Year &
Record of the Year)
plus "Maria Maria".
Santana
180g
audiofile vinyl
special limited
edition

Alanis
Morissette
jagged little pill

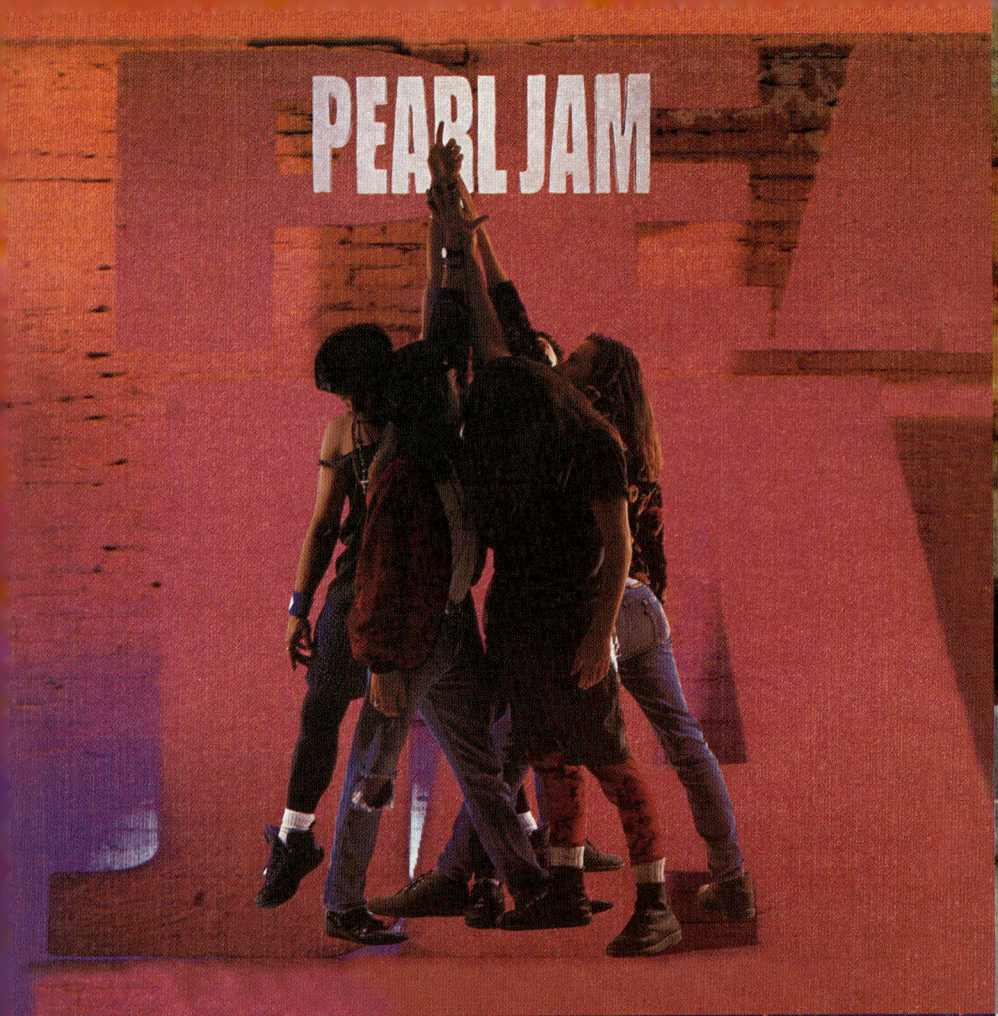

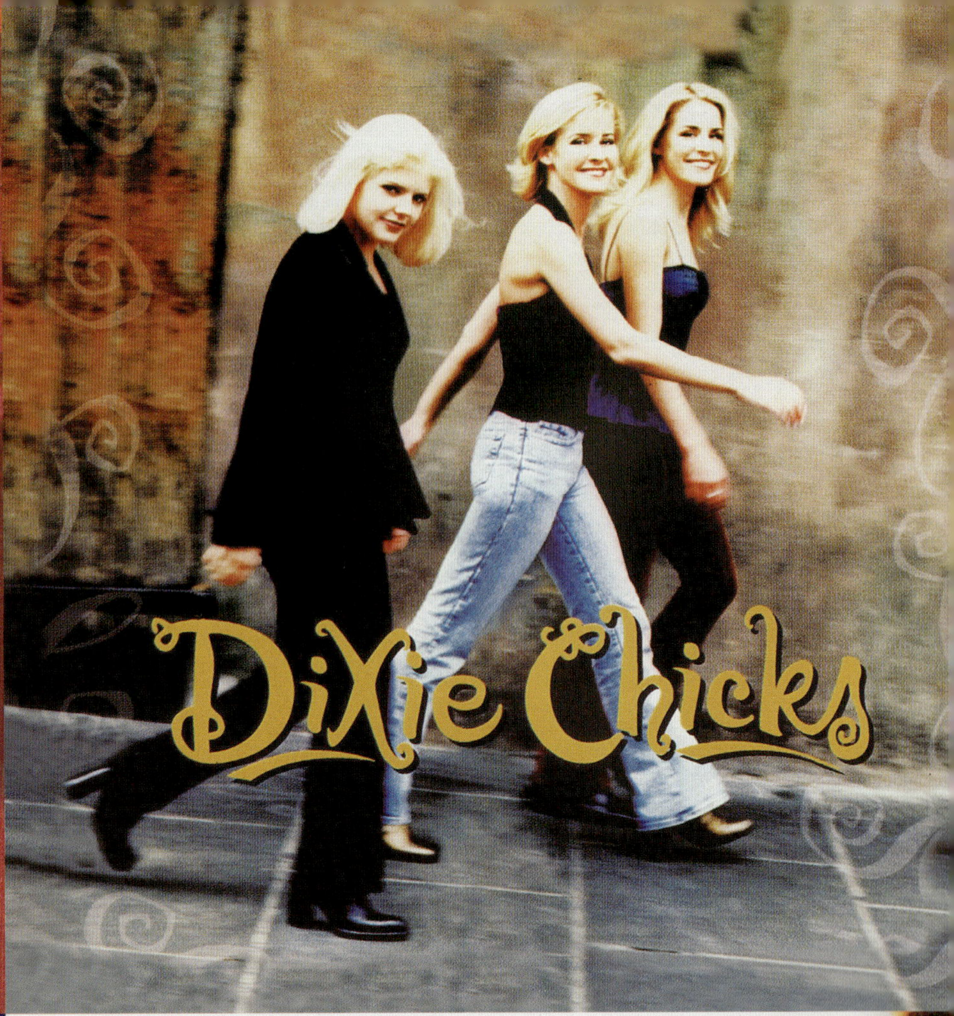

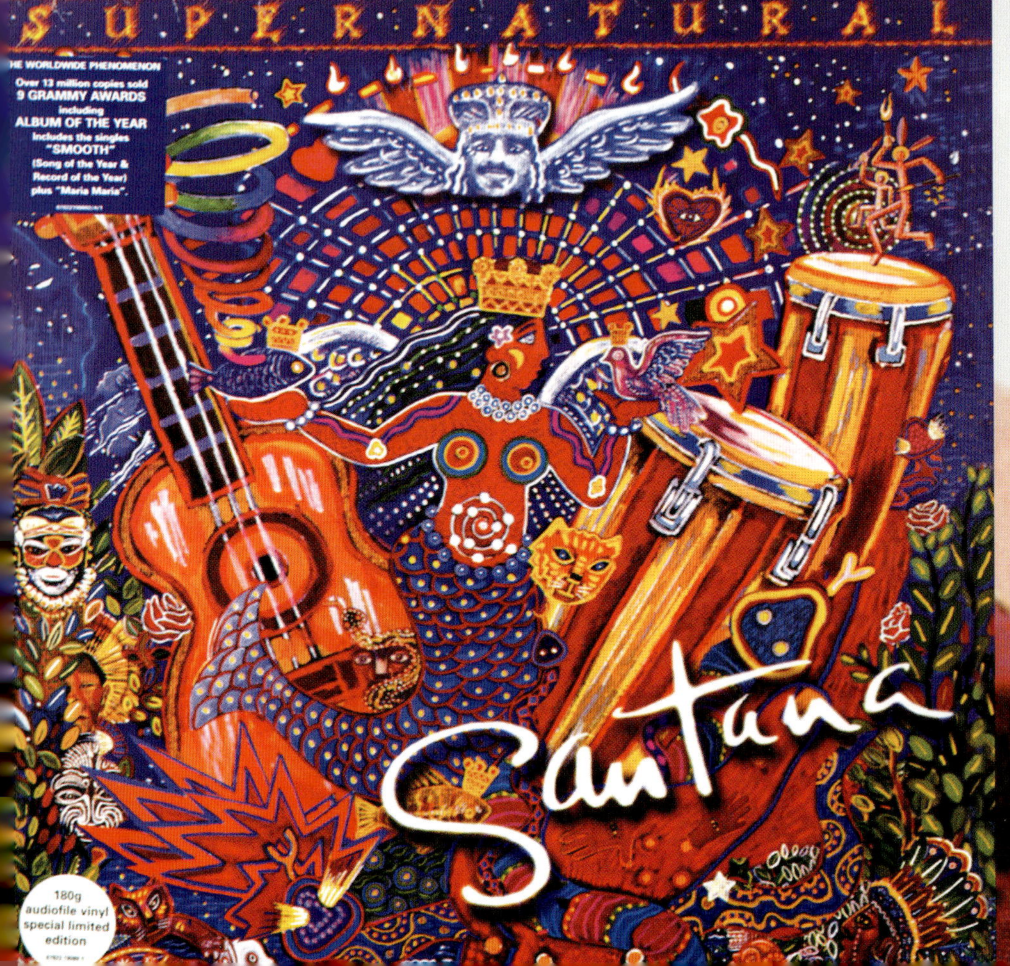

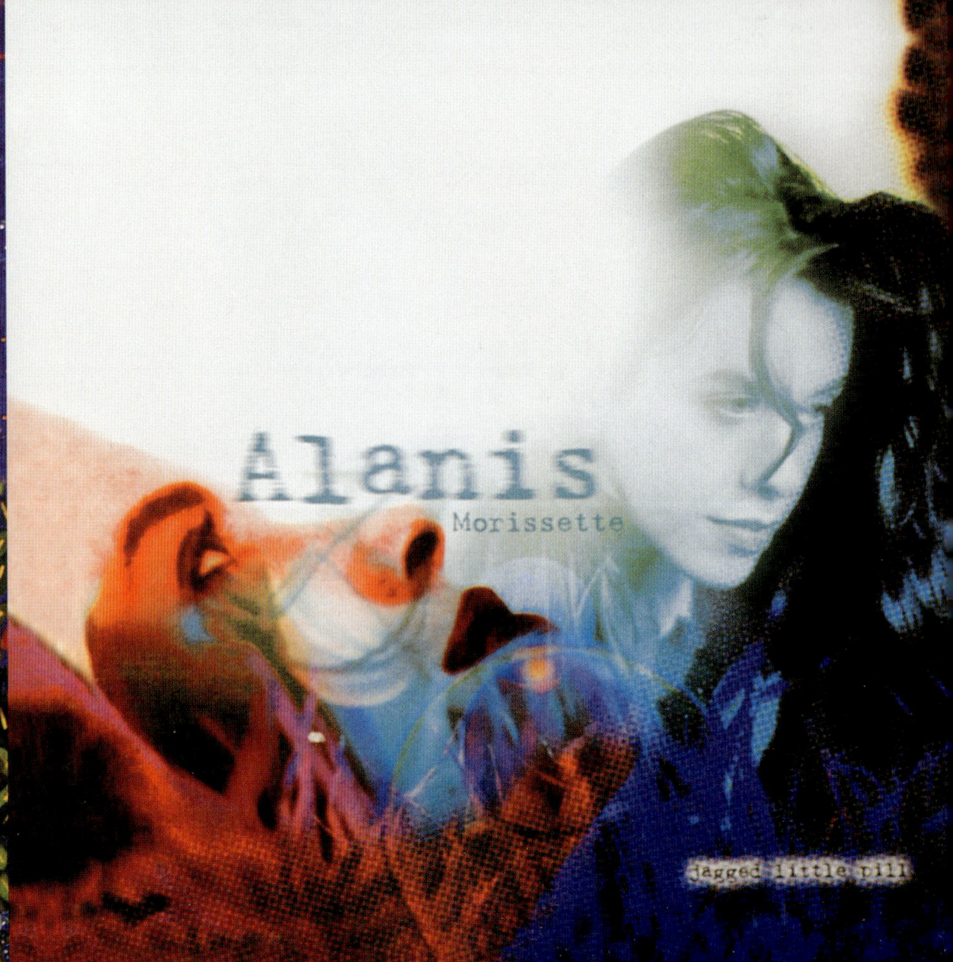

The Best-Selling Albums of the 1990s

In the 1990s, the album charts opened up to encompass a greater variety of sounds and styles than ever before. Grunge bands like Pearl Jam and Nirvana brought guitar rock and a punk aesthetic back into the mainstream. Hip-hop finally began to reap the commercial rewards it had promised for so long, silencing those who had dismissed it as a passing fad, and other urban sounds, from R&B to dance, filled the charts. There was room, too, for strong, commercial pop. But it was country music that really dominated the decade in the US, with artists such as Garth Brooks and Shania Twain helping reinvigorate the genre. Hot on Shania Twain's trail came Dixie Chicks, three cowgirl divas who crossed barriers with their dramatic album *Wide Open Spaces* to become the bestselling country act of 1998. Another successful female artist of the 90s was Celine Dion. Her *Titanic* love theme 'My Heart Will Go On' was a classic pop epic, melting the iciest heart. The song helped make the *Titanic* soundtrack and Dion's own album *Let's Talk About Love*, into multi-platinum best-sellers.

The 1990s also had its fair share of boy bands. The decade's pre-eminent example, Backstreet Boys, were named after Backstreet Market, a shopping area in Orlando, Florida. Legend has it that Backstreet Boys landed a major recording deal after their co-manager, Donna Wright, phoned a Jive Records' executive on her mobile phone from one of their early concerts. The executive heard the screaming crowd and the band was signed up the next day. The 1990s saw a plethora of former television child stars grow up and turn into hot chart material. Two members of *NSYNC, the decade's other chart-topping boy band, had cut their teeth working on the Disney Channel's Mickey Mouse Club, as had Britney Spears. She and *NSYNC's Justin Timberlake later dated, and the antics of the two young pop icons were destined to fuel the gossip columns for years.

Meanwhile, 1980s' stadium-rock bands such as Bon Jovi and Def Leppard were increasingly sidelined by the new heavy metal movement represented by bands like Metallica. In 1999, the RIAA gave them a diamond award for selling more than 10 million copies of their album, *Metallica*. The 1990s also saw fresh developments in rap music, hip-hop and R&B that would feed the record industry for many years to come. Mariah Carey, with her impish looks and a seven octave voice, became the best-selling R&B diva of the 1990s. It was during the 90s that the R&B boy band Boyz II Men became extremely popular – their tight harmony style quickly gained them plenty of attention.

The 1990s began with some commentators wondering whether the growing popularity of computer games would stop kids from spending money on music; the decade ended with many in the industry expressing concerns about the affects of illegal downloading on record sales. But 1990s' music was anything but in a crisis – the album charts show an industry in fine health, in terms of both profits and the diversity of music available. The great virtue of 1990s' music was that it never settled into a niche or grew complacent, but continued to innovate.

1990s
20

II

| • **Album sales:** 12,000,000 | • **Release date:** August 1994 |

When the first single from an album shoots to the top of the charts in the US, only to be replaced two months later by the follow-up, the album has definitely hit the big time. This was what happened with Boyz II Men's second album, simply titled *II*, and the tracks 'I'll Make Love To You' and 'On Bended Knee'.

If ever a second album consolidated a band's reputation, this was it. Shawn Stockman, Michael McCary and Nathan and Wanya Morris infuse their album with R&B and soul flavours. Working with some of the hottest talent around, including Babyface, Jimmy Jam and Terry Lewis, the band turned out an album that both played to the dance floor and showed off the Philadelphia quartet's stunning vocal interplay.

Generally, the slower numbers showed best the band's penchant for technically impressive vocal gymnastics, of which they had become pre-eminent exponents. Their vocal prowess is displayed to most stunning effect on the closing track – an audacious 'a capella' rendition of Paul McCartney's 'Yesterday'.

Number One singles: US: I'll Make Love To You; On Bended Knee

Grammy awards: Best R&B album; Best R&B performance by a duo or group with vocals

Label: US: Motown UK: Dts

Recorded in: Various locations

Personnel:
Shawn Stockman
Michael S McCary
Nathan Morris
Wanya Morris

Producers:
Dallas Austin
Jimmy Jam
Babyface
Terry Lewis
L A Reid
Tony Rich

1990s' FASHIONS

Boy bands such as Boyz II Men became global fashion role models in a decade that shifted away from the fashion experimentation of the 1980s. Generally speaking, the 1990s were about dressing down, rejecting the consumerist fashion displays of the previous decade. Jeans, T-shirts and trainers returned as standards, although the brand of these items was important, and for women clothing shapes became more figure-hugging while rejecting the shoulder-pads and glitzy jewellery accentuations of the 1980s. Also for women was a revived emphasis on cleavage, aided by the return of the Wonderbra as a fashion essential, cleverly marketed in a campaign using supermodel Eva Herzigova.

▲ **BACK COVER**

1. **Thank You (4:34)**
2. **All Around The World (4:56)**
3. **U Know (4:46)**
4. **Vibin' (4:27)**
5. **I Sit Away (4:34)**
6. **Jezebel (6:06)**
7. **Khalil (Interlude) (1:41)**
8. **Trying Times (5:23)**
9. **I'll Make Love To You (4:07)**
10. **On Bended Knee (5:29)**
11. **50 Candles (5:06)**
12. **Water Runs Dry (3:21)**
13. **Yesterday (3:07)**

Total album length: 58 minutes

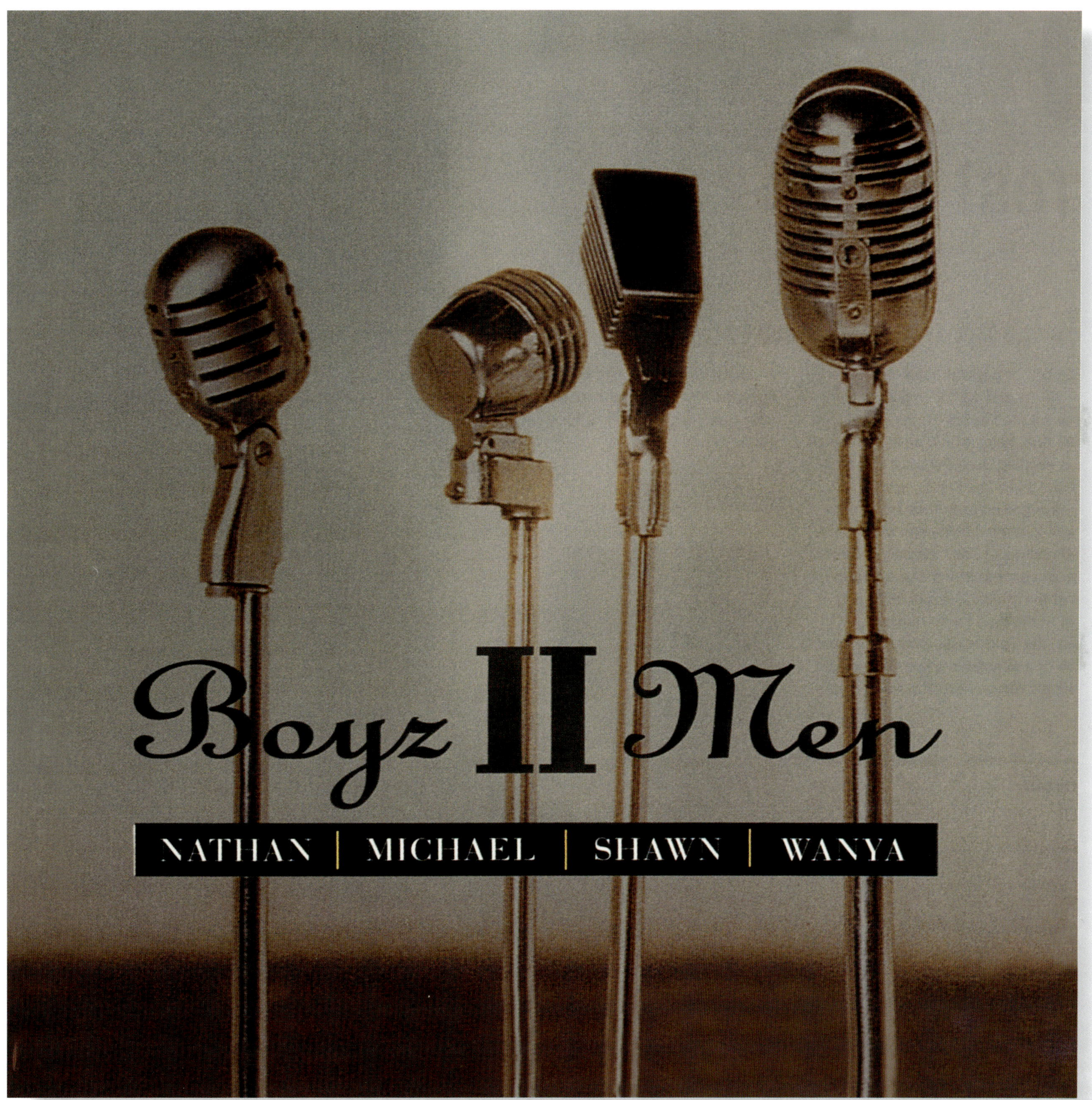
Boyz II Men
NATHAN | MICHAEL | SHAWN | WANYA

1990s
19

Forrest Gump

| • **Album sales:** 12,200,000 | • **Release date:** August 1994 |

This selection of popular music from the 1950s, 1960s and 1970s – collected together for the *Forrest Gump* soundtrack – was a powerful one. Many of the most significant artists of the preceding decades were included, from Aretha Franklin to The Doors, usually performing a strong song from their repertoire.

While any well-compiled collection of classics stands a good chance of chart success, this had the advantage of accompanying one of the most popular films of the 1990s. Despite attracting some criticism at the time for its reactionary political stance, the Tom-Hanks-starring *Forrest Gump*, the tale of a simpleton's journey through some of America's recent historical milestones (Vietnam War, civil rights movement, Watergate scandal, AIDS), proved a massive box-office smash and won the Oscar for Best Picture in 1995.

Number One singles: None

Grammy awards: None

Label: US & UK: Epic

Recorded in: Various locations

Personnel: Various artists

Producers: Various producers

EPIC MOVIES

Although most movie genres (apart from musicals) enjoyed successes during the 1990s, it was the historical epic which dominated the box office. Blockbusters included *Dances with Wolves* (1991), *Unforgiven* (1992), *Schindler's List* (1993), *Forrest Gump* (1994), *Braveheart* (1995), *The English Patient* (1996) and *Titanic* (1997). The average budget for a Hollywood production reached $58 million by 1998. Such films, plus a worldwide economic improvement and an increase in the numbers of multiplexes in Europe and the United States, corrected the general downturn in audience figures of the early 1990s. This upturn continued despite the spread of DVD viewing from around 1997.

▲ **BACK COVER**

1 Hound Dog (Elvis Presley) (2:16)
2 Rebel Rouser (Duane Eddy) (2:22)
3 But I Do (Henry, Clarence 'Frogman') (2:18)
4 Walk Right In (The Rooftop Singers) (2:33)
5 Land Of 1000 Dances (Wilson Pickett) (2:25)
6 Blowin' In The Wind (Joan Baez) (2:36)
7 Fortunate Son (Creedence Clearwater Revival) (2:18)
8 I Can't Help Myself (The Four Tops) (2:43)
9 Respect (Aretha Franklin) (2:27)
10 Rainy Day Women #12 & 35 (Bob Dylan) (4:35)
11 Sloop John B (The Beach Boys) (2:56)
12 California Dreamin' (The Mamas & the Papas) (2:39)
13 For What It's Worth (Buffalo Springfield) (2:38)
14 What The World Needs Now Is Love (Jackie DeShannon) (3:13)
15 Break On Through (The Doors) (2:27)
16 Mrs Robinson (Simon & Garfunkel) (3:51)
17 Volunteers (Jefferson Airplane) (2:04)
18 Let's Get Together (The Youngbloods) 4:36
19 San Francisco (Scott McKenzie) (2:58)
20 Turn! Turn! Turn! (The Byrds) (3:54)
21 Aquarius/Let The Sunshine In (The Fifth Dimension) (4:48)
22 Everybody's Talkin' (Harry Nilsson) (2:44)
23 Joy To The World (Three Dog Night) (3:16)
24 Stoned Love (The Supremes) (2:59)
25 Raindrops Keep Falling On My Head (BJ Thomas) (3:00)
26 Mr. President (Randy Newman) (2:46)
27 Sweet Home Alabama (Lynyrd Skynyrd) (4:43)
28 Running On Empty (Jackson Browne) (4:56)
29 It Keeps You Runnin' (The Doobie Brothers) (4:13)
30 I've Got To Use My Imagination (Gladys Knight & the Pips) (3:30)
31 Go Your Own Way (Fleetwood Mac) (3:39)
32 On The Road Again (Willie Nelson) (2:29)
33 Against The Wind (Bob Seger) (5:33)
34 Forrest Gump Suite (Alan Silvestri) (8:49)

Total album length: 114 minutes

34 American Classics on 2 CDs
Forrest Gump
The Soundtrack
Special Collectors' Edition

1990s
18

Breathless

| • **Album sales:** 12,200,000 | • **Release date:** October 1992 |

Kenny G's light and breezy style has won him the considerable accolade of the best-selling saxophonist of all time and *Breathless* is one of his best-selling albums.

Having risen to prominence in the 1980s, by the 1990s Kenny G was a global artist much favoured by middle-of-the-road and easy-listening radio stations. Although derided by jazz purists, his fluid phrasing and mellow style earned him an army of fans. Criticism from the jazz *cognoscenti* was of no matter to Kenny G, who, by his own admission, was simply a pop instrumentalist, and a very popular one at that.

The former horn man for Barry White's Love Unlimited Orchestra certainly delivers some great, feelgood pop cuts on *Breathless*, ranging from 'The Joy Of Life' to 'End Of The Night' and 'Forever In Love'. Legendary rhythm and blues singer Aaron Neville adds to the celebration with a welcome vocal on 'Even If My Heart Would Break'. Peabo Bryson adds vocal colour on the soulful 'By The Time This Night Is Over'.

Number One singles: None

Grammy awards: Best instrumental composition

Label: US & UK: Arista

Recorded in: Seattle, Sausalito, & Los Angeles, USA

Personnel:
Kenny G
Peabo Bryson
Aaron Neville
Dean Parks
Michael Thompson
Walter Afanasieff
Dan Shea
Vail Johnson
John Robinson
Paulinho Da Costa

Producers:
Kenny G
Walter Afanasieff
David Foster
Dan Shea

JAZZ AROUND THE NEW MILLENNIUM

Kenny G's easy-listening style of jazz was part of something of a renaissance for jazz in the 1990s and 2000s. Back in the 1960s and 1970s, much of the jazz world had turned to experimental sounds that appealed to very selective audiences, with a consequential freefall in album purchases. However, during the 1980s certain 'smooth jazz' or 'soul jazz' practitioners such as Sade, Curiosity Killed the Cat and Simply Red revived the jazz sound for a mainstream audience. Such 'popular' jazz was maintained and advanced in the 2000s by the likes of Michael Bublé, Norah Jones and Jamie Cullum.

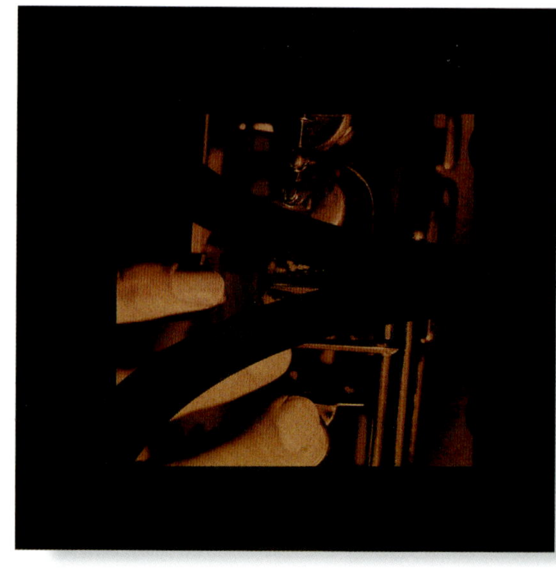

▲ **BACK COVER**

1 **The Joy Of Life (4:19)**
2 **Forever In Love (4:58)**
3 **In The Rain (4:59)**
4 **Sentimental (6:34)**
5 **By The Time This Night Is Over (4:45)**
6 **End Of The Night (5:21)**
7 **Alone (5:24)**
8 **Morning (5:13)**
9 **Even If My Heart Would Break (4:58))**
10 **G Bop (4:05)**
11 **Sister Rose (6:13)**
12 **A Year Ago (5:15)**
13 **Homeland (4:32)**
14 **The Wedding Song (3:21)**

Total album length: 70 minutes

KENNY G
BREATHLESS

1990s
17

The Woman In Me

| • **Album sales:** 12,300,000 | • **Release date:** July 1995 |

Shania Twain's newfound romantic and professional partnership with studio-ace 'Mutt' Lange propelled the songstress from country darling to global megastar. Lange's production skills had thus far seen him polishing up metal acts such as Def Leppard and AC/DC, making them shine for a mainstream audience. His partnership with Twain found him attempting to take country to a pop audience.

What the writing team of Twain and Lange produces is a sassy combination of witty, well-crafted lyrics, strong melodies and hooks, all shown off to best effect by deft arrangements.

Twain's solid yet agile voice is just as at home with the traditional country of 'Who's Bed Have Your Boots Been Under?' as it is with the rockier 'You Win My Love' or the balladry of 'Home Ain't Where His Heart Is (Anymore)'.

Many pop acts have been fashioned by studio svengalis, but Twain – with a little help from Lange – is one act who invented herself. *The Woman In Me* is where the big story started.

Number One singles: None

Grammy awards: Best country album

Label: US & UK: Mercury

Recorded in: St Anne des Lacs, Canada; Nashville, USA

Personnel:
Shania Twain
Larry Byrom
Dann Huff
Brent Rowan
Brent Mason
Billy Crain
John Hughey (d. 2007)
Paul Franklin
Sam Bush
Ron Hajacos
Joe Spivey
Glen Duncan
Hargus 'Pig' Robbins
David Hungate
Various other personnel

Producer:
Robert John 'Mutt' Lange

'MUTT' LANGE

Shania Twain's husband/producer Robert John 'Mutt' Lange is a seminal force behind Shania's music, with an impressive track record in the rock industry. Born on 16 November 1948, Lange became heavily involved with rock music during his teen years, and began working as a record producer in 1976. From 1979 to 1980, Lange achieved high standing by producing AC/DC's *Highway To Hell* and *Back in Black* albums, and in 1981 he received a Grammy nomination for Producer of the Year for work on Foreigner's *4*. He subsequently became one of the most sought after producers in music, and over the next two decades worked with the likes of the Cars, Def Leppard, Billy Ocean and Bryan Adams. Lange and Twain married in 1993 and they had a son in 2001. They divorced in 2010, after Lange's affair with Twain's friend Marie-Anne Thiebaud. In 2011, Twain married Thiebaud's ex-husband, Frederic Thiebaud.

▲ **BACK COVER**

1. **Home Ain't Where His Heart Is (Anymore) (4:12)**
2. **Any Man Of Mine (4:07)**
3. **Whose Bed Have Your Boots Been Under? (4:25)**
4. **(If You're Not In It For Love) I'm Outta... (4:30)**
5. **The Woman In Me (Needs The Man In You) (4:50)**
6. **Is There Life After Love? (4:39)**
7. **If It Don't Take Two (3:40)**
8. **You Win My Love (4:26)**
9. **Raining on Our Love (4:38)**
10. **Leaving Is The Only Way Out (4:07)**
11. **No One Needs To Know (3:04)**
12. **God Bless The Child (1:30)**

Total album length: 48 minutes

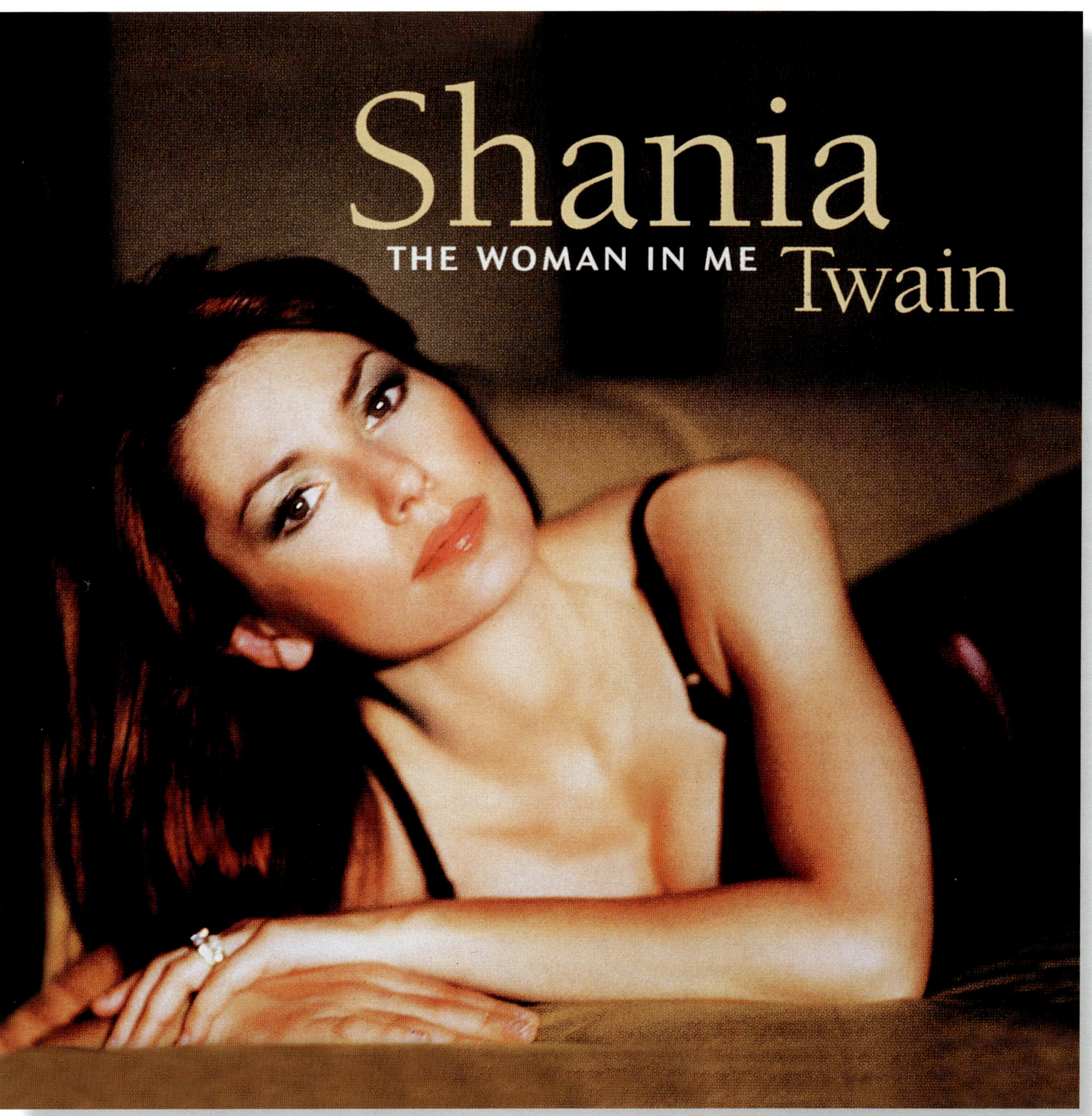

1990s

1990s
16

Yourself Or Someone Like You

| • **Album sales:** 12,400,000 | • **Release date:** October 1996 |

Influences as wide as Pearl Jam, REM, Tom Petty, early Van Morrison – even a hint of The Velvet Underground – are among the sources that inform this impressive alternative rock debut. In the wake of the Seattle grunge outbreak, Matchbox 20's writer and singer Rob Thomas continued to fly the flag, while sticking within the parameters of mainstream album rock.

Favouring the solid workmanlike approach, Thomas delivers a clutch of confident, well-crafted frill-free songs all benefiting from his sturdy delivery. *Yourself Or Someone Like You* falls into the category of an all-time classic US rock album, standing proud in its own terms, but harking back to halcyon moments in modern American music's rich heritage.

Content-wise, the Georgia group tackle a trawl through contemporary Americana taking in troubled love, unrealized dreams and urban confusion. Monosyllabic titles, like 'Push', 'Damn' and 'Argue', emphasise the no-mess approach.

Initially dismissed by some as a flash in the pan, Matchbox 20 proved their critics wrong and stayed the distance. *Yourself Or Someone Like You* may have never topped the charts, but it sold and sold. Within two years it was five times platinum and by 2000 it had doubled that.

Number One singles: None

Grammy awards: None

Label: US & UK: Lava – Atlantic

Recorded in: Atlanta, USA

Personnel:
Rob Thomas
Kyle Cook
Adam Gaynor
Brian Yale
Paul Doucette

Producer:
Matt Serletic

A WORLD ONLINE

Sales of albums such as *Yourself Or Someone Like You* have been aided, and at the same time hampered, by the expanding access of global markets to online stores. In 1994 about three million people in the United States had Internet access, but by 1998 that figure had rocketed to 100 million people, and over 200 million by the early 2000s. Globally, in 2014, three billion people had internet access, almost 40 per cent of the world's population. By 2014, global recorded music sales topped US$15 billion in revenue.

▲ **BACK COVER**

1 **Real World (3:50)**
2 **Long Day (3:45)**
3 **3 A.M. (3:46)**
4 **Push (3:59)**
5 **Girl Like That (3:45)**
6 **Back 2 Good (5:40)**
7 **Damn (3:20)**
8 **Argue (2:58)**
9 **Kody (4:03)**
10 **Busted (4:15)**
11 **Shame (3:35)**

Total album length: 46 minutes

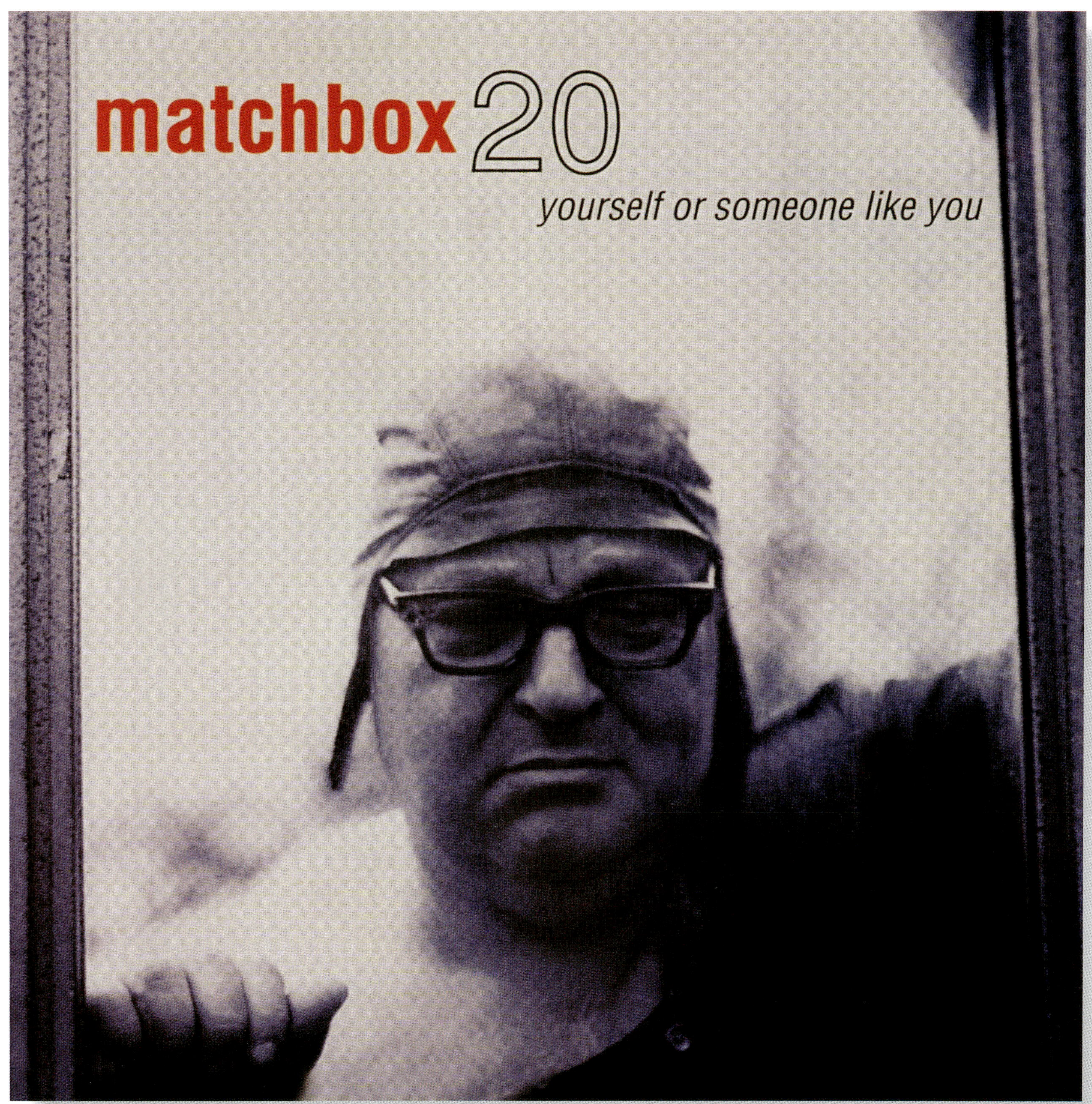

Sleeve artwork by Valerie Wagner, Katrin Thomas and Chris Cuffaro

1990s
15

Wide Open Spaces

| • **Album sales:** 12,700,000 | • **Release date:** January 1998 |

Sweet harmonies, exemplary acoustic country playing and deft, understated arrangements have always distinguished albums from the Dixie Chicks. By the time *Wide Open Spaces* came along, the founding sisters, Martie Seidel and Emily Erwin, had been performing together for almost a decade. They were joined and somewhat rejuvenated by the arrival of Natalie Maines on lead vocal duties. The support of a major label, Monument, may have helped draw in a larger audience, but the scintillating three-way vocal interplay, sensitively backed by guitar, fiddle and banjo was enough to command a healthy following in its own right.

The powerful performances are supported by a beguiling blend of defiant mid-tempo rockers and sad, wistful ballads. The album closes with contributions from female writers: Maria McKee's 'Am I The Only One (Who's Ever Felt This Way)' and 'Give It Up Or Let Me Go' by Bonnie Raitt.

Number One singles: None

Grammy awards: Best country album; Best country performance by a duo or group with vocals

Label: US: Monument; UK: Epic

Recorded in: Nashville, USA

Personnel:
Natalie Maines
Emily Burns Erwin
Martie Seidel
Mark Casstevens
Matt Rollings
Lloyd Maines
Tony Paoletta
Billy Crain
Billy Joe Walker Jr
Paul Worley
Bobby Charles Jr
Joe Chemay
Michael Rhodes
Tom Roady
Greg Morrows
George Marinelli
Tommy Nash

Producers:
Jim Burnett
Tony Castle
Blake Chancey
Erik Hellerman
Clarke Schleicher
Ed Simonton
Paul Worley

NASHVILLE

The city of Nashville, Tennessee, is unofficially the global capital of country music. Its rise to this position began in 1925 with a Saturday night radio show nicknamed 'The Grand Ole Opry', which played live country music and eventually became a US-wide hit. Country music record labels also concentrated in the city (there were few labels outside of Nashville interested in the genre) and soon thousands of country performers were heading there to secure radio air time and, if possible, recording contracts. Nashville has retained its hold over the country music industry to this day, although performers such as Shania Twain have begun to challenge the necessity of a Nashville break to become a success in country music.

▲ BACK COVER

1 I Can Love You Better (3:53)
2 Wide Open Spaces (3:44)
3 Loving Arms (3:37)
4 There's Your Trouble (3:10)
5 You Were Mine (3:37)
6 Never Say Die (3:56)
7 Tonight The Heartache's On Me (3:25)
8 Let 'Er Rip (2:49)
9 Once You've Loved Somebody (3:28)
10 I'll Take Care Of You (3:40)
11 Am I The Only One (Who's Ever Felt This Way) (3:25)
12 Give It Up Or Let Me Go (4:55)

Total album length: 44 minutes

Dixie Chicks

1990s
14

Falling Into You

| • **Album sales:** 13,100,000 | • **Release date:** March 1996 |

French-Canadian chanteuse Celine Dion already had legions of fans from the faithful AOR market when this polished collection of songs burst on to the scene, guaranteeing her a surefire winner. For many, the strength of Dion's voice alone is enough, and here it's shown off to dazzling effect across a variety of styles.

Jim Steinman provides Dion with an arresting opener with 'It's All Coming Back To Me Now'. Elsewhere, she effortlessly tackles powerful ballads like Diane Warren's 'Because You Love Me', the theme song from the movie *Up Close And Personal*. The song won the 1997 Grammy for Best Song Written Specifically for a Motion Picture or Television. The album was also nominated for Record Of The Year, Song Of The Year and Best Female Pop Vocal Performance.

Ike and Tina Turner's 'River Deep – Mountain High' also gets the lavish Dion treatment, as does Eric Carmen's haunting 'All By Myself'.

Number One singles: US: Because You Loved Me

Grammy awards: Best pop album; Album of the year

Label: US: 550 Music; UK: Epic

Recorded in: Various locations

Personnel:
Celine Dion
Gary 'Headman' Hasse
Paul Buckmaster
Aldo Nova
Jeff Smallwood
Ottmar Liebert
Steve Farris
Tim Pierce
Eddie Martinez
Michael Thompson
Andre Coutu
Chris Taylor
Basile Leroux
David Foster
Roy Bittan
Various other personnel

Producers:
Jim Steinman
David Foster
Rick Nowels
Billy Steinberg
Ric Wake

DIANE WARREN

Born in 1956, Diane Warren went on to become a songwriter of legendary status, the musical mind behind some of the greatest tracks of the 1980s and 1990s. Her songs have included 'I Don't Want to Miss a Thing' (performed by Aerosmith), 'How Do I Live' (Leanne Rimes), 'Un-Break My Heart' (Toni Braxton) and 'If I Could Turn Back Time' (Cher), and the list of artists who have had success with her tracks includes Celine Dion, Gloria Estefan, Barbra Streisand, Faith Hill, Tim McGraw and Ricky Martin. The consistent quality of Warren's tracks has won her three Grammys, five ASCAP Songwriter of the Year awards, and, twice, BMI Songwriter of the Year. Her songs – which now number over 800 – have also appeared in over 50 movies, and her company, Realsongs, is one of the biggest music factories in the United States.

▲ **BACK COVER**

1 It's All Coming Back To Me Now (7:37)
2 Because You Loved Me (Theme from *Up Close And Personal*) (4:33)
3 Falling Into You (4:18)
4 Make You Happy (4:31)
5 Seduces Me (3:46)
6 All By Myself (5:12)
7 Declaration Of Love (4:20)
8 Dreaming Of You (5:07)
9 I Love You (5:30)
10 If That's What It Takes (4:12)
11 I Don't Know (4:38)
12 River Deep – Mountain High (4:10)
13 Call The Man (6:08)
14 Fly (2:58)

Total album length: 68 minutes

FALLING INTO YOU
Céline
DION

1990s
13

Ten

| • **Album sales:** 13,200,000 | • **Release date:** August 1991 |

Pearl Jam's debut album, *Ten*, was released just one month before Nirvana's *Nevermind.* Although the Pearl Jam album didn't catch as big a wave initially, it stayed around longer and eventually outsold Nirvana in the US. Guitarist Stone Gossard and bassist Jeff Ament who, together with singer Eddie Vedder, wrote most of the album, had paid their dues in metal rock bands, and the influence shows. Of all the groups that forged the Seattle grunge sound, it was Pearl Jam that made it most accessible, purveying a radio friendliness that didn't alienate fans of more traditional rock forms.

It was vocalist Vedder, with his gravelly baritone and tortured, passionate delivery, who was pivotal in identifying Pearl Jam with the Seattle sound.

Ament and Gossard had been in an earlier band, Mother Love Bone, but in 1990 its singer, Andrew Wood, died from a heroin overdose. When they teamed up with Vedder their first choice for a band name was Mookie Blaylock, after the NBA basketball star. The group changed the name to Pearl Jam before their debut effort was released. The album title, *Ten*, is taken from the number on Mookie Blaylock's vest.

Number One singles: None

Grammy awards: None

Label: US & UK: Epic

Recorded in: Seattle, USA

Personnel:
Eddie Vedder
Mike McCreedy
Stone Gossard
Jeff Ament
Dave Krusen
Walter Gray
Rick Parasher
Tim Palmer

Producers:
Rick Parasher
Pearl Jam

GRUNGE

Grunge's originality is arguable, as its distorted guitar sound and thumping percussion was characteristic of numerous other forms of rock and metal. However, grunge was clearly reacting against the macho posturing of stadium rock, and eschewed self-promoting guitar solos and male-power lyrics. The genre began mainly with Seattle-based bands such as Nirvana, Pearl Jam and Soundgarden in 1991, and Nirvana's Number One album *Nevermind* became the maternal soundtrack of the genre. Grunge was popular with disaffected youth, and had a laid-back dress code that was easily mastered. Grunge's decline began with the suicide of Nirvana frontman Kurt Cobain in 1994 and ended with the break-up of Soundgarden in 1997. Grunge musicians had often defied mainstream commercialism, so there was little industry support to carry it through the bad times.

▲ **BACK COVER**

1 Once (3:51)
2 Even Flow (4:53)
3 Alive (5:40)
4 Why Go (3:19)
5 Black (5:48)
6 Jeremy (5:18)
7 Oceans (2:41)
8 Porch (3:30)
9 Garden (4:58)
10 Deep (4:18)
11 Release (6:30)

Total album length: 51 minutes

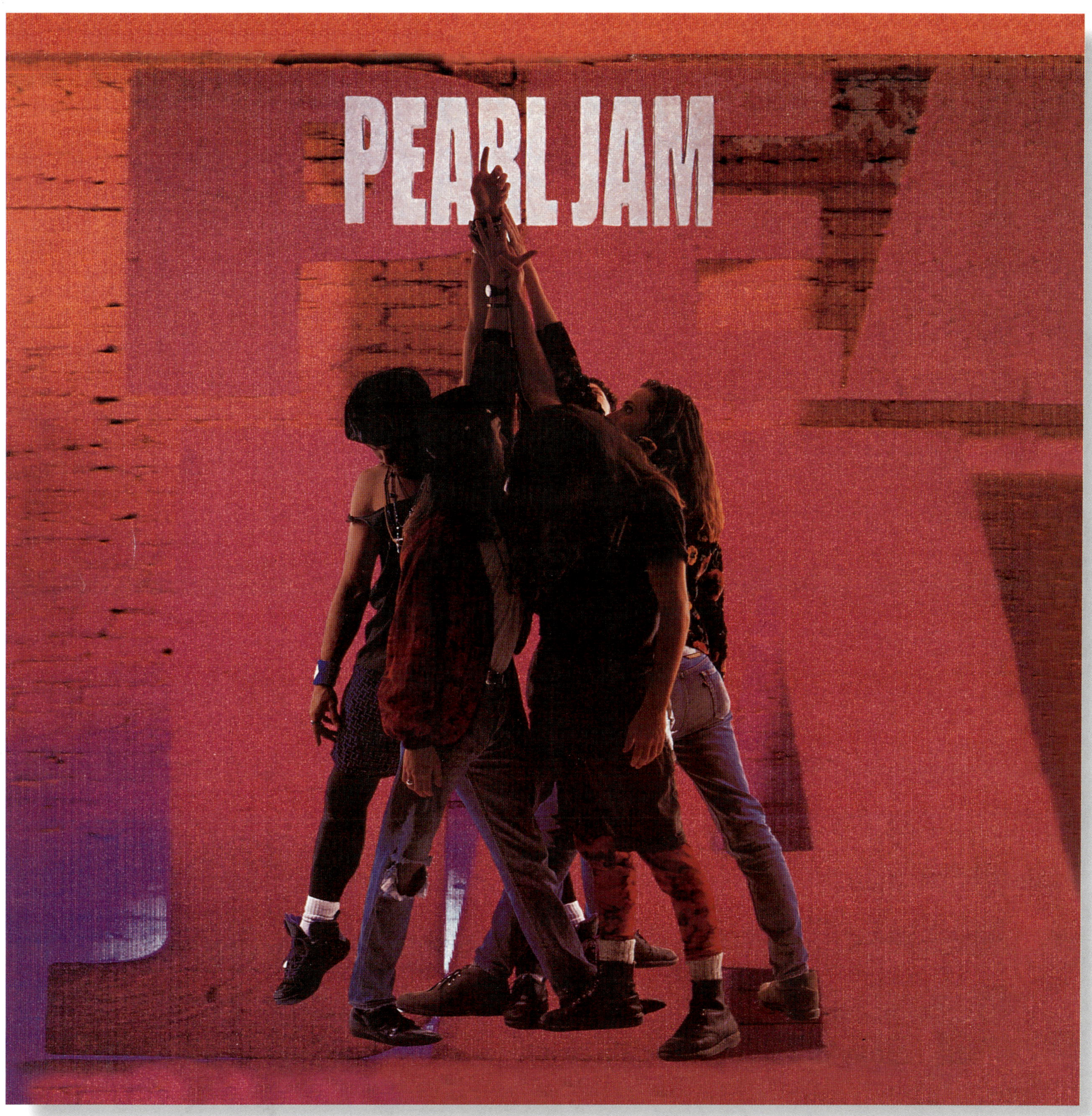

Sleeve artwork by Jeff Ament, Lisa Sparagano and Lance Mercer

1990s
12

Millennium

| • **Album sales:** 13,400,000 | • **Release date:** May 1999 |

It's impossible to look at the album *Millennium* without acknowledging the phenomenal success Stateside of the band's 1997 predecessor, *Backstreet Boys*. Brought together by Swedish svengali and songwriter Max Martin, the Backstreet Boys had been Euro-pop sensations for a couple of years before this US debut – an amalgam of the best of what they had so far achieved – rocketed them to stardom in America. More than 10,000,000 albums later, the *Backstreet Boys* was still in the Top 40 when their follow-up *Millennium* was released.

How could they follow this success? More of the same was the order of the day with the Backstreet Boys sticking to the tried-and-tested formula that had powered them to global success. Pop harmonies, irresistible dance grooves and some high-quality balladry were more than enough to keep fans happy, as the single 'I Want It That Way' amply demonstrates.

The album was nominated for the 1999 Grammy award for Album of the Year and for Best Pop Vocal Album. 'I Want It That Way' was up for Record of the Year and Song of the Year, and 'Show Me the Meaning of Being Lonely' was nominated for the 2000 Grammy award for Best Pop Performance.

Number One singles: None

Grammy awards: None

Label: US & UK: Jive

Recorded in: Various locations

Personnel:
Kevin Richardson
Howard Dorough
Alexander James McLean
Brian Littrell
Nick Carter

Producers:
Kristian Lundin
Max Martin
Rami
Robert John 'Mutt' Lange
Stephen Lipson

BOY BANDS

The term 'boy band' has had a fairly strict usage since the 1990s, referring to a prefabricated group of young men, four–six in number (five being most common), all in frontman roles as singers/dancers, and rarely playing their own instruments. Strictly speaking, versions of boy bands have been a feature of pop since the 1960s – The Monkees and The Jackson 5 fit almost all the criteria for a boy band. However, it was in the 1990s that boy bands truly took shape, from the Backstreet Boys and *NSYNC in the US to Take That in the UK. Boy bands are a commercial product, with every aspect of their sound and 'branding' controlled, and consequently the individual members can struggle to succeed when the band falls apart, notable exceptions being Justin Timberlake, Robbie Williams and Michael Jackson.

▲ **BACK COVER**

1 **Larger than Life (3:52)**
2 **I Want It That Way (3:33)**
3 **Show Me the Meaning of Being Lonely (3:54)**
4 **It's Gotta Be You (2:55)**
5 **I Need You Tonight (4:25)**
6 **Don't Want You Back (3:25)**
7 **Don't Wanna Lose You Now (3:54)**
8 **The One (3:46)**
9 **Back to Your Heart (4:21)**
10 **Spanish Eyes (3:53)**
11 **No One Else Comes Close (3:42)**

Total album length: 46 minutes

MILLENNIUM

1990s
11

...Baby One More Time

| • **Album sales:** 14,100,000 | • **Release date:** January 1999 |

Britney Spears has Mickey Mouse partly to thank for her rise to stardom, as her first spell in the limelight was on the Disney's *New Mickey Mouse Club*. This exposure paved the way for her debut album, ...*Baby One More Time*, which established Spears as a top teen-pop singer in the tradition of Debbie Gibson and Tiffany.

Already a mature adolescent, Spears peddled her nouveau bubblegum pop with confidence and style, blending the traditional with occasional modern rap and dance inflections. Euro producer Max Martin, a guiding force behind the Backstreet Boys, made sure Spears had her share of hooky choruses and persuasive melodies, as featured in the title track, and the other hits 'Sometimes' and '(You Drive Me) Crazy'.

Her ambiguous image – part female teenage role model, part coquettish tease – was reflected by her performance in school uniform on the video for the title track. During much of the 1990s, teen pop had been eclipsed by more sassy, streetwise sounds but with Britney Spears bubblegum was back with a vengeance.

Number One singles: US & UK: ...Baby One More Time; UK: Born to Make You Happy

Grammy awards: None

Label: US & UK: Jive

Recorded in: Stockholm, Sweden; New York, USA

Personnel:
Britney Spears
Mickie Bassie
Don Philip
Esbjorn Ohrwall
Dan Petty
Eric Foster White
Johan Carlberg
Andrew McIntyre
Max Martin
Per Magnusson
David Kreuger
Kristian Lundin
Doug Petty
Tomas Lindberg
Various other personnel

Producer:
Eric Foster White
Kristian Lundin
Per Magnusson
David Kreuger
Max Martin

STARS OF THE MICKEY MOUSE CLUB

The Mickey Mouse Club first aired in the 1950s, and soon became one of the most popular children's television programmes in the United States. It began in a basic variety show format, with music, dance and sketches being performed by the Club's team of child 'Mouseketeers'. The show went through two subsequent revivals, one in the 1970s and the other from 1989. In its third incarnation, the show represented much more modern, independent teen sensibilities. It also featured some precocious talent destined for greater things. Britney Spears joined the show in 1993, alongside Christina Aguilera, Justin Timberlake and Joshua 'J.C.' Chavez. All four made major pop careers after the MMC, the show providing contacts, some fame and professionalism.

1. ...Baby One More Time 3:30
2. (You Drive Me) Crazy 3:17
3. Sometimes 4:05
4. Soda Pop 3:20
5. Born To Make You Happy 4:03
6. From The Bottom Of My Broken Heart 5:11
7. I Will Be There 3:53
8. I Will Still Love You (Duet With Don Philip) 4:02
9. Deep In My Heart 3:34
10. Thinkin' About You 3:35
11. E-Mail My Heart 3:41
12. The Beat Goes On 3:43

▲ **BACK COVER**

1 ...Baby One More Time (3:30)
2 (You Drive Me) Crazy (3:17)
3 Sometimes (4:05)
4 Soda Pop (3:20)
5 Born To Make You Happy (4:03)
6 From The Bottom Of My Broken Heart (5:11)
7 I Will Be There (3:53)
8 I Will Still Love You (4:02)
9 Deep in My Heart (3:34)
10 Thinkin' About You (3:35)
11 E-Mail My Heart (3:41)
12 The Beat Goes On (3:43)

Total album length: 42 minutes

Britney Spears
...baby one more time

1990s
10

Ropin' The Wind

| • **Album sales:** 14,100,000 | • **Release date:** September 1991 |

Garth Brooks was an great admirer of Billy Joel. The inclusion of one of Joel's songs, 'Shameless', on *Ropin' The Wind* illuminates the links between the two artists' brand of blue-collar balladry, as well as illustrating Brooks' easy ability to straddle the country-pop divide.

The country star's comfort with rock forms is evident throughout the album, from the grand sweep of 'The River', to the honky-tonk excitement of 'The Rodeo', or the epic storytelling of 'In Lonesome Dove'. However, Brooks' strength is that he never turns his back on country – *Ropin' The Wind* attracted hordes of new admirers without ever disenfranchising his country audience.

The result speaks for itself: it was the first country album to enter at the top spot of the Billboard Top 200.

Even with the crossover factor, the subject matter remains unswervingly country, as Brooks journeys effortlessly through a world of truckers, jail, drinking, family, love and the Western mythology. Brooks' second album *No Fences* was the release that had broken him into the mainstream. This follow-up established him as an enduring force in popular music.

Number One singles: None

Grammy awards: None

Label: US & UK: Capitol

Recorded in: Nashville, Tennessee

Personnel:
Garth Brooks
Mark Casstevens
Chris Leuzinger
Bruce Bouton
Jerry Douglas
Sam Bush
Rob Hajacos
Bobby Wood
Edgar Meyer
Mike Chapman
Milton Sledge
Trisha Yearwood
Carl Jackson
Larry Cordle
Susan Ashton

Producer:
Allen Reynolds

PIRATED MUSIC

Although Brooks' album sales have been enormous, the true popularity of his music is obscured by the proliferation of pirated CDs. The easy availability of CD copying software from the early 2000s pushed music piracy to previously unimaginable levels. Today it's illegal downloading that is the problem. In 2010, 370 million digital tracks were legally sold in the UK and there are 67 legal music services available online. However, there were an estimated 1.2 billion music tracks illegally downloaded in the UK that year.

▲ **BACK COVER**

1. **Against The Grain (2:22)**
2. **Rodeo (3:53)**
3. **What She's Doing Now (3:26)**
4. **Burning Bridges (3:34)**
5. **Papa Loved Mama (4:48)**
6. **Shameless (2:51)**
7. **Cold Shoulder (4:20)**
8. **We Bury the Hatchet (3:55)**
9. **In Lonesome Dove (3:05)**
10. **The River (4:28)**

Total album length: 36 minutes

GARTH
BROOKS
ROPIN' THE WIND
ONE VOICE • ONE DECADE • ONE HUNDRED MILLION •

1990s

1990s
9

Backstreet Boys

| • **Album sales:** 14,200,000 | • **Release date:** December 1997 |

Although they formed in Orlando, Florida, it was in Europe – Germany to be precise – that the Backstreet Boys had their first taste of the big time. As a result, it was almost a year later that their eponymous US debut album, a collection of tracks taken from their two European offerings, was released. The delay certainly did them no harm, as it became the third best-selling album of 1998. By then, with the charts peppered with frothy pop from the likes of The Spice Girls and a host of easy listening boy bands, the group slotted neatly into the prevailing scene.

Like their other boy band contemporaries, the Backstreet Boys served up a menu of fashionably crafted tunes embracing the full gamut from lively dance numbers to languorous ballads, and garnished with a spot of rapping and some *à la mode* hip-hop splashes. Despite the hint of menace in their name, the Backstreet Boys were parent-friendly and made music for teenagers to swoon to.

'Get Down (You're The One For Me)', the track that got them started in Europe, was joined on *Backstreet Boys* by a host of radio-friendly smash hits that had already proved their worth on the other side of the Atlantic.

Number One singles: None

Grammy awards: None

Label: US & UK: Jive

Recorded in: Stockholm, Sweden; Orlando & New York, USA

Personnel:
Nick Carter
Brian 'B-Rok' Littrell
Kevin Richardson
Howard Dorough
Alexander James McLean

Producers:
Bulent Aris
Denniz Pop
Larry 'Rock' Campbell
Max Martin
Mookie
P M Dawn
Robert John 'Mutt' Lange
Toni Cottura
Veit Renn

RAP

The use of rap by the Backstreet Boys shows how mainstream the musical style became in the 1990s. Rap's origins reach back to the early 1970s, when traditional forms of African-American toasting were blended into a musical fusion of reggae and funk. Rap singles began to appear around 1978–79, but the rap genre exploded onto the musical, and political, scene during the 1980s. Rap's press was often poor during the 1980s and 1990s, with groups such as Public Enemy, NWA and Ice-T pushing lyrics with explicit comment on murder, criminality and sex. However, rap was also steadily appropriated into innocuous pop, starting with Blondie's rap in 'Rapture' in 1981. Rap's fashionability has continued, with artists including Dr Dre, Snoop Dog and Eminem achieving a powerful hold within the mainstream music charts, the audience being far less shockable than those of the early 1980s.

▲ **BACK COVER**

1 **We've Got It Goin' On (3:39)**
2 **Quit Playing Games (With My Heart) (3:52)**
3 **As Long As You Love Me (3:40)**
4 **Everybody (Backstreet's Back) (4:38)**
5 **All I Have To Give (4:36)**
6 **Anywhere For You (4:40)**
7 **Hey, Mr DJ (Keep Playin' This Song) (4:42)**
8 **I'll Never Break Your Heart (4:48)**
9 **Darlin' (5:31)**
10 **Get Down (You're The One For Me) (3:50)**
11 **Set Adrift On Memory Bliss (3:30)**
12 **If You Want It To Be Good Girl (4:49)**

Total album length: 49 minutes

1990s

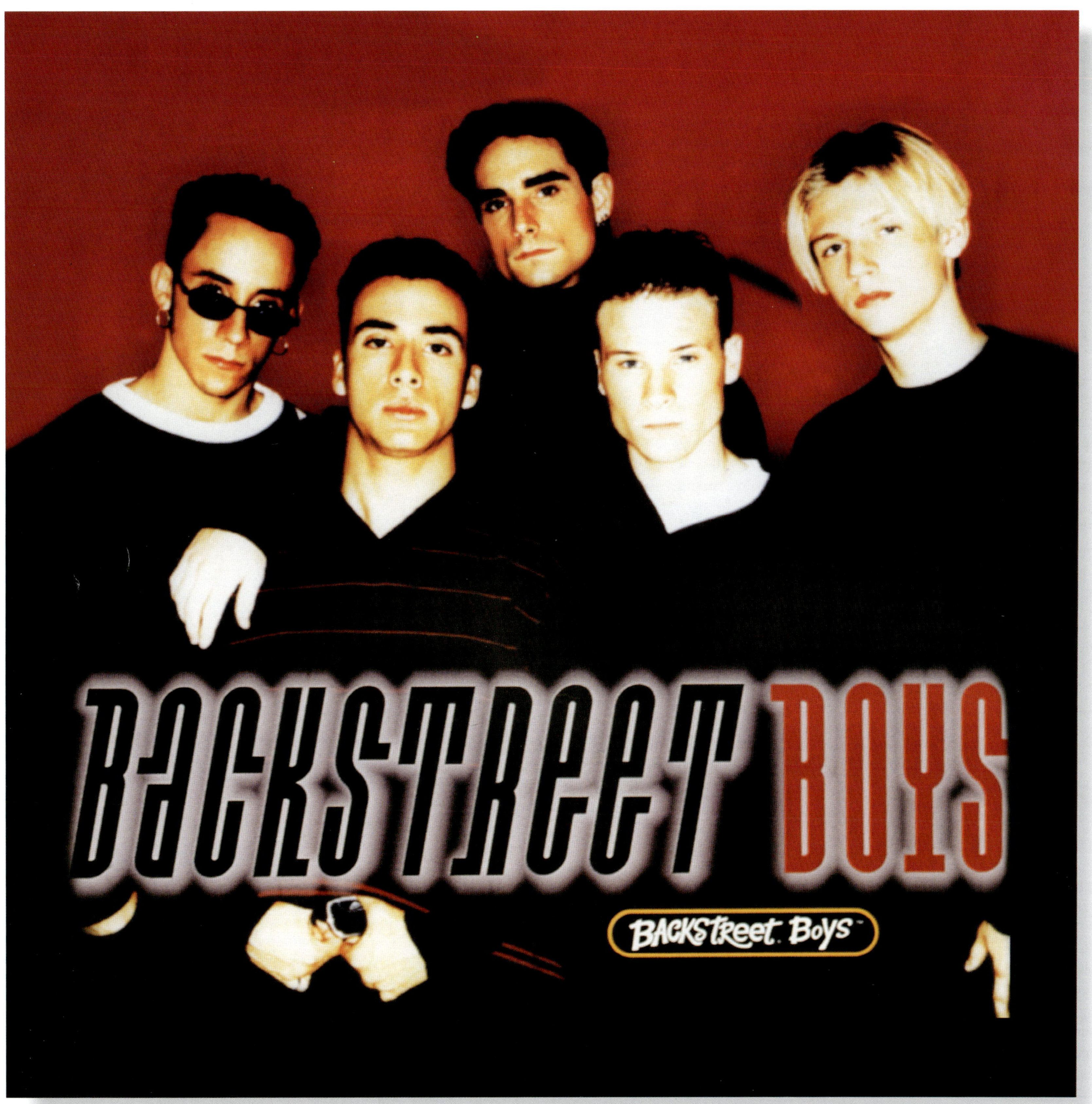

1990s
8

Double Live

| • **Album sales:** 15,000,000 | • **Release date:** November 1998 |

Garth Brooks was 10 albums into his career before his first live album was released. To keep his fans happy, each of the 25 cuts on the album was recorded at a different gig, ensuring that the souvenir hunters would be first in line.

The album does not disappoint, delivering crisp renditions of all Brooks' favourites. Although he stays pretty faithful to the studio originals, the audience does get a look-in on many tracks, notably 'Unanswered Prayers', 'The Dance', 'Shameless' and 'That Summer', all of which are lifted above their original versions by audience participation. Those who want something more than a 'best of' package are not disappointed, either. Not only does he add extra verses to 'Friends in Low Places' and 'The Thunder Rolls', there are also three previously unreleased numbers, including 'It's Your Song', 'Wild As The Wind,' and 'Tearin' It Up (and Burnin' It Down)'.

Number One singles: None

Grammy awards: None

Label: US & UK: Capitol

Recorded in: Various locations, USA

Personnel:
Garth Brooks
Trisha Yearwood
Charles Cochran
Jimmy Mattingly
Debbie Nims
Steve Wariner
Stephanie Davis
Mark Casstevens
Ty England
James Garver
Steve McClure
Chris Leuzinger
Gordon Kennedy
John Kinsch
Keith Urban
Bruce Bouton
Various other personnel

Producers:
Allen Reynolds
Carlton Davis

GARTH BROOKS

Garth Brooks is a renowned live performer, not only for the quality of his concerts, but also for his incredible crowd-pulling power. In 1994, a concert in the Hollywood Bowl, a venue with an 18,000 seating capacity, sold out in just 21 minutes. A tour between 1996 and 1998 involving 350 shows saw ticket sales of 5.3 million. His treatment of the fans is also impressive. At a fan event in Nashville in 1996, he once signed autographs for over 23 hours straight, and those who buy a millionth ticket in a tour are treated to lavish gifts from the singer, including all-expenses Florida holidays and Chevrolet cars.

▲ **BACK COVER**

1 Callin' Baton Rouge (2:58)
2 Two of A Kind, Workin' On A Full House (2:44)
3 Shameless (3:55)
4 Papa Loved Mama (2:51)
5 The Thunder Rolls (4:48)
6 We Shall Be Free (4:43)
7 Unanswered Prayers (3:41)
8 Standing Outside The Fire (3:43)
9 Longneck Bottle (2:42)
10 It's Your Song (4:18)
11 Much Too Young (To Feel This Damn Old) (3:12)
12 The River (3:48)
13 Tearin' It Up (And Burnin' It Down) (3:56)
14 Ain't Goin' Down ('Til The Sun Comes Up) (4:45)
15 Rodeo (3:44)
16 The Beaches Of Cheyenne (3:51)
17 Two Pina Coladas (4:38)
18 Wild As The Wind (4:10)
19 To Make You Feel My Love (3:17)
20 That Summer (4:42)
21 American Honky-Tonk Bar Association (4:05)
22 If Tomorrow Never Comes (3:44)
23 The Fever (3:40)
24 Friends In Low Places (8:56)
25 The Dance (3:56)

Total album length: 101 minutes

Sleeve artwork by Chris Ferrara and Henry Diltz

1990s
7

Supernatural

| • **Album sales:** 15,100,000 | • **Release date:** June 1999 |

A highly respected guitarist since the 1960s with a supple latin/jazz style, Carlos Santana's career continued to flourish in the 1990s, although mainly on stage. *Supernatural*, his debut album for Arista, marked a successful return to the chart mainstream.

Santana's reputation secured the participation of performers as diverse as Eric Clapton, The Dust Brothers, Everlast, Lauryn Hill and Eagle-Eye Cherry. The result was an eclectic mix of styles and genres, underlined by Santana's Latin roots and scintillating guitar work.

The album reached Number One in 23 countries and gave Santana two US Number One singles, 'Maria, Maria' and 'Smooth' (which reached Number Six and Number 75, respectively, in the UK). Santana also swept the board at that year's Grammys, winning three awards for *Supernatural* as an album and another five for individual songs from it.

Number One singles: US: Smooth; Maria Maria

Grammy awards: Record of the year; Album of the year; Best rock album; Best rock performance by a duo or group with vocal; Best pop performance by a duo or group with vocal; Best pop collaboration with vocals; Best rock instrumental performance; Best pop instrumental performance

Label: US & UK: Arista

Recorded in: Various locations, USA

Personnel:
Carlos Santana
Dave Matthews
Lauryn Hill
Eagle-Eye Cherry
Eric Clapton
Francis Dunnery
Al Anderson
Sergio Vallin
J.B. Eckl
Danny Wolinski
Mic Gillette
Jose Abel Figueroa
Various other personnel

Producers:
Carlos Santana
Steve Harris
Wyclef Jean
Jerry 'Wonder' Duplessis
K.C. Porter

LATIN-AMERICAN MUSIC IN THE 1990s

Latin-American music underwent a distinct renaissance in the 1990s, especially in the United States. The new popularity was aided by the growth of Spanish-speaking populations in the US, which in turn led to increased numbers of Spanish-language radio stations. Latin music of the 1990s was experimental as well as traditional, with acts such as Barrio Boyz fusing pop and rap with Latin-American rhythms, while mainstream act Gloria Estefan released a Spanish-language album to appeal to listeners with her native tongue. At the end of the decade, Ricky Martin and Jennifer Lopez pushed the Latin genre even further through stunning looks and skilful pop packaging.

▲ **BACK COVER**

1 **(Da Le) Yalleo (5:51)**
2 **Love Of My Life (5:48)**
3 **Put Your Lights On (4:47)**
4 **Africa Bamba (4:40)**
5 **Smooth (4:56)**
6 **Do You Like The Way (5:52)**
7 **Maria, Maria (4:21)**
8 **Migra (5:24)**
9 **Corazon Espinado (4:32)**
10 **Wishing It Was (4:59)**
11 **El Farol (4:49)**
12 **Primavera (5:17)**
13 **The Calling (7:48)**

Total album length: 69 minutes

SUPERNATURAL
THE WORLDWIDE PHENOMENON
Over 13 million copies sold
9 GRAMMY AWARDS
including
ALBUM OF THE YEAR
Includes the singles
"SMOOTH"
(Song of the Year &
Record of the Year)
plus "Maria Maria".
Santana
180g
audiofile vinyl
special limited
edition

1990s
6

Metallica

| • **Album sales:** 15,700,000 | • **Release date:** July 1991 |

Metallica's 1988 album *And Justice for All…* perhaps best exemplified the band's progressive hard metal sound, but for their 1991 follow-up the group decided to explore previously uncharted territory – the mainstream.

An expertly crafted marriage of production and musicianship, *Metallica* (also known as 'The Black Album') was, as its title was intended to suggest, something of a renaissance for a group who had developed an enviable reputation largely without the benefit of airplay. The name was also a signal for listeners to concentrate on the stripped-down songs, rather than the packaging. For the first time Metallica recruited the services of an outside producer, Bob Rock, who was brought in on the strength of his work on Mötley Crüe's *Dr Feelgood* album. Rock's task was to give the new recording a deliberately 'bigger', more listener-friendly sound.

The songs were written during a two-month period in the summer of 1990. However, it would take 10 months in the studio – at a cost of around a million dollars – and a certain degree of tension between producer and band members, before the album was completed. The final product was debuted at a free party in New York's Madison Square Gardens, where it received an enthusiastic response from fans.

Number One singles:
None

Grammy awards:
Best metal performance with vocal

Label: US: Elektra; UK: Phonogram

Recorded in: Los Angeles, USA

Personnel:
James Hetfield
Kirk Hammett
Jason Newstead
Lars Ulrich

Producers:
Bob Rock
James Hetfield
Lars Ulrich

METAL SATANISM

Like some revisitation of the Middle Ages, the 1980s saw a new wave of panic sweep the United States as the Christian right once again raised cries of 'satanism'. Some lurid proclamations from religious groups estimated that up to *two million* children a year were being sacrificed in satanic rituals. Heavy metal was naturally targeted, the rise of extreme forms, such as Death Metal, indeed seeing a proliferation of openly satanic lyrics. Yet bands with no genuine satanic undercurrents, such as Metallica and Judas Priest, were also accused. In 1985, two teenage boys shot themselves in the US after drinking, taking drugs and listening to Judas Priest's track, 'Better By You Better Than Me'. In 1990 the parents of the boys claimed that subliminal messages implanted on the track, urging the boys to 'do it', contributed to the suicide. The accusations were shown to be groundless, and the band was acquitted, but the case was indicative of the moral cloud under which metal hung in the 1980s and early 1990s.

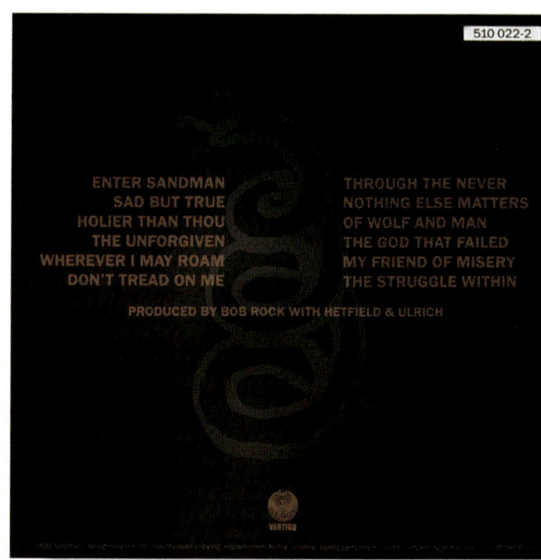

▲ **BACK COVER**

1 **Enter Sandman (5:29)**
2 **Sad But True (5:24)**
3 **Holier Than Thou (3:47)**
4 **The Unforgiven (6:26)**
5 **Wherever I May Roam (6:42)**
6 **Don't Tread On Me (3:59)**
7 **Through The Never (4:01)**
8 **Nothing Else Matters (6:29)**
9 **Of Wolf And Man (4:16)**
10 **The God That Failed (5:05)**
11 **My Friend Of Misery (6:47)**
12 **The Struggle Within (3:51)**

Total album length: 62 minutes

1990s
5

No Fences

| • **Album sales:** 16,200,000 | • **Release date:** August 1990 |

Seen by many as the saviour of country music, Garth Brooks took traditional country idioms and reinterpreted them using pop hooks and rock 'n' roll attitude. His second major release, *No Fences*, saw him grow more confident in his role as the aspirant new king of country. As with his female counterpart, Shania Twain, his success relied on his skilful blend of old and new, creating music that would appeal to listeners across a wide spectrum.

Brooks is in particularly fine form on the album's ballads, where soft folk tones and tougher rock arrangements are used to striking effect. His blue-collar credentials are carefully maintained on the likes of the honky-tonk-ish 'Friends In Low Places', one of the album's five hit singles. The other four singles, 'The Thunder Rolls', 'Two Of A Kind, 'Workin' On A Full House' and 'Unanswered Prayers', helped extend the album's shelf life and notch up impressive sales.

No Fences as a whole is of a consistently high quality, with the moving 'New Way To Fly' and the infectious 'Mr Blue' showing him at ease with both heartbreak and humour. With cowboy hat already in place, *No Fences* set the standard by which Brooks meant to continue.

Number One singles: None

Grammy awards: None

Label: US & UK: Capitol

Recorded in: Nashville, USA

Personnel:
Garth Brooks
Chris Leuzinger
Pat Alger
Johnny Christopher
Mark Casstevens
Bruce Bouton
Rob Hajacos
Bobby Wood
Edgar Meyer
Milton Sledge
Mike Chapman

Producer:
Allen Reynolds

MAKING GARTH BROOKS

The road to success was paved with initial disappointment for the young Garth Brooks. In 1984, having just left college with a degree in advertising, Brooks went to Nashville in the hope of selling his musical talent. Disillusioned in less than 24 hours, he went home to Oklahoma, where he was a popular club act. It would be three years before he returned to Nashville to try to make the big time again (this time with his wife, Sandy Mahl). He began performing, but no label showed an interest for over a year. Then a Capitol A&R man caught a Brooks show, and he recommended that Capitol sign Brooks up, despite having rejected him on previous occasions. The Capitol executives agreed, and Brooks released his first album in 1989.

▲ **BACK COVER**

1. **The Thunder Rolls (3:42)**
2. **New Way To Fly (3:54)**
3. **Two Of A Kind, Workin' On A Full House (2:31)**
4. **Victim Of The Game (2:17)**
5. **Friends In Low Places (4:18)**
6. **Wild Horses (3:08)**
7. **Unanswered Prayers (3:23)**
8. **Same Old Story (2:52)**
9. **Mr Blue (3:16)**
10. **Wolves (4:08)**

Total album length: 33 minutes

garth brooks
NO FENCES
ONE VOICE
ONE HUNDRED MILLION

1990s
4

Cracked Rear View

| • **Album sales:** 16,300,000 | • **Release date:** December 1994 |

To sell more than 16 million copies of your first major album (an earlier indie release, *Koochypop*, had come out in 1993) is no mean feat, but that was exactly what Hootie & the Blowfish managed with *Cracked Rear View*. It certainly helped that the album was an extremely confident and mature entré, packed to the rafters with harmonies and hooks. Clearly their early years as a standard rock covers band had honed their skills and allowed them to develop the songwriting that bloomed here, with a host of tunes penned by the band.

Hootie and Co. were hardly charting new or unmapped territory, they simply delivered up straight-down-the-line, soft-to-firm rock in an extremely palatable form. Tracks like 'Hold My Hand' and 'Let Her Cry', which earned them a Best Pop Performance Grammy, bear an easy-rock hallmark similar to predecessors as diverse as The Allman Brothers and REM.

Completing the picture is the distinctive baritone vocal style of Darius Rucker, whose delivery lends an authority to Hootie & The Blowfish material that may have been lacking with a weaker singer. This may have been their major-label debut, but the band found the right formula and stuck to it.

Number One singles: None

Grammy awards: Best new artist; Best pop performance by a duo or group with vocal

Label: US & UK: Atlantic

Recorded in: North Hollywood, USA

Personnel:
Mark Bryan
Darius Rucker
Dean Felber
Jim 'Soni' Sonefeld

Producer:
Don Gehman

NEW FORMS OF ROCK

By the 1990s, rock music had fragmented into a bewildering variety of styles. At the gentle end of the scale was classic stadium rock, this blending likeable pop riffs with epic guitar melodies and chords (Bon Jovi is an example). At the exact opposite end were the many varieties of 'Death Metal', frenzied, chaotic thrash music from the like of Sepultura and Slayer, with sub-variants including 'Progressive', 'Gothenburg Metal' and 'Doom Metal'. During the 1990s, bands such as Metallica occupied the popular centre ground of metal, while many of the other forms became nihilistic underground movements.

▲ **BACK COVER**

1. **Hannah Jane (3:33)**
2. **Hold My Hand (4:15)**
3. **Let Her Cry (5:08)**
4. **Only Wanna Be With You (3:46)**
5. **Running From An Angel (3:37)**
6. **I'm Goin' Home (4:10)**
7. **Drowning (5:01)**
8. **Time (4:53)**
9. **Look Away (2:38)**
10. **Not Even The Trees (4:37)**
11. **Goodbye (4:05)**
12. **Untitled (3:33)**

Total album length: 43 minutes

HOOTIE & THE BLOWFISH
cracked rear view

1990s
3

The Bodyguard

| • **Album sales:** 19,400,000 | • **Release date:** November 1992 |

Country chanteuse Dolly Parton is probably as much responsible for the success of this collection as Whitney Houston herself. It was Parton's 1974 ballad, 'I Will Always Love You', that propelled *The Bodyguard* into the record books. 'I Will Always Love You' gave Houston the room to emote massively, helping secure the song an astonishing 14-week run at the top of the Billboard singles chart.

This is one of those rare examples where the music from a film – assisted by Houston's performance of it – outshines the movie and propels the film to greater heights than it might have enjoyed otherwise. *The Bodyguard* was by no means a one song album. Houston provided another seven tracks, including 'Run To You' and 'I'm Every Woman', and other artists, including Kenny G, Joe Cocker and Aaron Neville, also contribute. A stand-out track in an album comprised of strong writing and performances is Curtis Stigers' rendition of Nick Lowe's '(What's So Funny 'Bout) Peace, Love And Understanding'.

Number One singles: US & UK: I Will Always Love You

Grammy awards: Album of the Year

Label: US & UK: Arista

Recorded in: Various locations

Personnel:
Whitney Houston (d. 2012)
Aaron Neville
Curtis Stigers
Joe Cocker
Kenny G
Lisa Stansfield
Various other personnel

Producers:
Narada Michael Walden
L.A. Reid
Ian Devaney
Jazz Summers
Clive Davis
BeBe Winans
Babyface
Various other producers

SOUNDTRACKS

***The Bodyguard* album was a milestone in soundtrack recordings. Whereas a soundtrack such as *Oklahoma!* sold around three million copies in the 1950s, Whitney Houston's classic album sold over 19 million units. *The Bodyguard*'s success was part of a growing trend from the 1970s onwards for films to fuel high-level sales of music. Sometimes the soundtrack could simply be a case of repackaging old hits and infusing them with the post-cinema emotion of the film. The soundtrack to *Forrest Gump* (1994), for example, went platinum 12 times, despite being little more than a compilation of famous tracks from the 1960s to 1980s. More original material, such as the *Titanic* soundtrack, sold nearly 12 million copies, mostly on the strength of Celine Dion's love theme, 'My Heart Will Go On'.**

▲ **BACK COVER**

1. **I Will Always Love You (Whitney Houston) (4:31)**
2. **I Have Nothing (Whitney Houston) (4:48)**
3. **I'm Every Woman (Whitney Houston) (4:45)**
4. **Run To You (Whitney Houston) (4:22)**
5. **Queen Of The Night (Whitney Houston) (3:08)**
6. **Jesus Loves Me (Whitney Houston) (5:11)**
7. **Even If My Heart Would Break (Aaron Neville) (4:58)**
8. **Someday (I'm Coming Back) (Lisa Stansfield) (4:57)**
9. **It's Gonna Be A Lovely Day (S.O.U.L. S.Y.S.T.E.M.) (4:47)**
10. **(What's So Funny 'Bout) Peace, Love And Understanding (Curtis Stigers) (4:04)**
11. **Waiting For You (Kenny G) (2:43)**
12. **Trust In Me (Joe Cocker) (4:12)**
13. **Theme From The Bodyguard (2:40)**

Total album length: 75 minutes

KEVIN COSTNER
WHITNEY HOUSTON
THE BODYGUARD
ORIGINAL MOTION PICTURE SOUNDTRACK

1990s
2

Jagged Little Pill

| • **Album sales:** 19,700,000 | • **Release date:** June 1995 |

Rarely has 'angry' been so popular as on this angst-ridden Alanis Morissette album. 'Hell hath no fury like a woman scorned' is writ large as the mantra for this collection of embittered love songs, sung, yelled and shouted by the 19-year-old Canadian. Her painful encounters with love, and their public exorcism, struck a chord and in the process redirected the singer from campus leftfield to full-on mainstream.

Fortunately for Morissette, her bitter pill was made more palatable by a gloss provided by the pop sensibilities of her musical collaborator Glen Ballard, with whom she co-wrote the album. Yet it was her in-your-face rants that engaged listeners and landed her two Grammy awards.

A combination of traditional techniques such as power chords and acoustic guitar embellishments, combined with of-the-moment touches, created a soundscape that seemed both familiar and immediate.

Although she had enjoyed a couple of releases in Canada before *Jagged Little Pill*, this was her first proper release in the US and the rest of the world – and what an entrance it was!

Number One singles:
None

Grammy awards:
Album of the year; Best rock album; Best rock song – You Oughta Know; Best female rock vocal performance – You Oughta Know

Label: US & UK: Maverick

Recorded in: Hollywood, USA

Personnel:
Alanis Morissette
Glen Ballard
Basil Fung
Joel Shearer
Michael Landau
Dave Navarro
Benmont Tench
Lance Morrison
Flea
Rob Ladd
Matt Laug
Gota Yashiki

Producer:
Glen Ballard

GIRL POWER

The 1990s were the decade of 'girl power'. The phrase is popularly credited to the Spice Girls, but they took it over secondhand from the 'riot girl' (or 'grrrl') movement of the United States. Riot girls had a vigorous manifesto of female assertion, and began with the Washington State feminist rock band Bikini Kill and its lead singer Kathleen Hanna. Riot girl attitudes were aggressive and politically charged, but the Spice Girls borrowed the girl power concept and turned it into something palatable to a mainstream audience. The OED defined girl power as 'a self-reliant attitude among girls and young women manifested in ambition, assertiveness and individualism', but the Spice Girls' embodiment of this movement disintegrated with the falling apart of the band in the early 2000s.

▲ **BACK COVER**

1 **All I Really Want (4:44)**
2 **You Oughta Know (4:09)**
3 **Perfect (3:07)**
4 **Hand In My Pocket (3:41)**
5 **Right Through You (2:55)**
6 **Forgiven (5:00)**
7 **You Learn (3:59)**
8 **Head Over Feet (4:27)**
9 **Mary Jane (4:40)**
10 **Ironic (3:49)**
11 **Not The Doctor (3:47)**
12 **Wake Up (4:53)**
13 **You Oughta Know (8:12)**

Total album length: 54 minutes

1990s

1990s
1

Come On Over

| • **Album sales:** 23,000,000 | • **Release date:** November 1997 |

Country singer Shania Twain's third album, *Come On Over*, her second with husband and producer 'Mutt' Lange, consolidated the twosome's reputation as a self-contained hit factory. All 16 cuts on the album were written by the husband-and-wife team – and the hits and awards were plentiful.

Sales were supported by an ambitious tour and four Grammys, including Best Female Country Vocal Performance for 'Man! I Feel Like a Woman!' and Best Country Song for 'Come On Over'. Another song from the album, 'You're Still the One', had won the same two awards at the previous year's awards ceremony.

The couple's pop sensibility was now clearly defined, dressing up country idioms in fashionable rock clothes. *Come On Over* went on to gain 22 platinum awards.

Number One singles: None

Grammy awards: Best female country vocal performance – Man! I Feel Like A Woman!, You're Still The One; Best country song – Come On Over, You're Still The One

Label: US & UK: Mercury

Recorded in: Nashville, USA

Personnel:
Shania Twain
Brian White
Joe Chemay
Bruce Bouton
Larry Byrom
Stuart Duncan
Larry Franklin
Paul Franklin
Rob Hajacos
John Hobbs
Dann Huff
John Hughey (d. 2007)
John Jarvis
Robert John 'Mutt Lange
Paul Leim
Carl Marsh
Brent Mason
Glenn Meadows
Joey Miskulin
Michael Omartian
Olle Romo
Eric Silver
Various other personnel

Producer:
Robert John 'Mutt' Lange

THE SHANIA CONTROVERSY

Shania Twain's remarkable global success has not been accomplished without generating controversy. When Twain launched her second album, *The Woman In Me,* in 1995, the country music community had fairly rigid expectations of how a country singer should make it big. The traditional process involved being signed up in Nashville, projecting a fairly clean and recognizable image to the country community, and then promoting the music through touring. Shania, teaming up with her husband/producer 'Mutt' Lange, instead packaged herself with a pop-sexy flesh-baring image, and sold herself straight to a large audience through music videos. While many country critics objected to this tactic, and to Shania's more poppy sound, the strategy turned her into one of the best-selling female artists of all time.

▲ **BACK COVER**

International version (1998):

1 **You're Still The One (3:33)**
2 **When (3:38)**
3 **From This Moment On (4:52)**
4 **Black Eyes, Blue Tears (3:37)**
5 **I Won't Leave You Lonely (4:07)**
6 **I'm Holdin' On To Love (To Save My Life) (3:27)**
7 **Come On Over (2:54)**
8 **You've Got A Way (Notting Hill Remix) (3:25)**
9 **Whatever You Do! Don't! (3:49)**
10 **Man! I Feel Like A Woman! (3:54)**
11 **Love Gets Me Every Time (3:33)**
12 **Don't Be Stupid (You Know I Love You) (3:34)**
13 **That Don't Impress Me Much (3:59)**
14 **Honey, I'm Home (3:34)**
15 **If You Wanna Touch Her, Ask! (4:14)**
16 **Rock This Country! (4:26)**

Total album length: 60 minutes

SHANIA TWAIN
COME ON OVER

Norah Jones
come away with me
Shania Twain
UP!
NSYNC
NO STRINGS ATTACHED
OUTKAST
Speakerboxxx/The Love Bel

The Best-Selling Albums of the 2000s

As the new decade – the new millennium – began, music was dominated largely by commercial pop. The boy band phenomenon was reaching its peak with the likes of the Backstreet Boys and *NSYNC breaking sales records every time an album of theirs hit the record stores.

Yet despite pop's seeming stranglehold on the hearts and minds of music fans around the world, another genre was making its presence felt: youngsters were embracing rap and hip-hop on a scale never seen before. No longer the preserve of the street or the ghetto, rap finally became the mainstream on both side of the Atlantic at the start of the 2000s.

One artist who played a significant part in the growth of rap's popularity, particularly amongst white kids in the US and Europe, was Eminem, aka Marshall Mathers, whose first two albums sold nearly 25 million copies combined. Both his material and his delivery are punctuated with indignation, anger and sometimes pure, plain bile, and it was this disregard for sentiment in a world they perceived as being harsh and cruel that found empathy among many young disaffected music fans.

While black R&B artists, rappers and hip-hop merchants such as Nelly and Usher were becoming established and selling significant numbers of records, Eminem opened up rap to an audience that would possibly have shown less interest had he not been white.

More recently rap and hip-hop have both been given a unique twist by the duo of Andre Benjamin and Antwan Patton, otherwise known as Outkast. Theirs is a combination of traditional rap and hip-hop methods combined with a quirkier, tighter sound, whose roots lie in the direction of 70s funk legends such as Parliament, Funkadelic and Sly & The Family Stone.

Rap was also being taken to the heart of a strand within parts of the rock community, notably by the likes of Rage Against The Machine, Limp Bizkit and later by Linkin Park, whose debut album, *Hybrid Theory*, was a cauldron of styles and a musical approach that genuinely broke the mould.

The loud and raucous have not had it all their way in the 2000s, however. The surprising success of Norah Jones took many by surprise, her *Come Away With Me* album being a collection of smooth jazzy, country-styled self-penned songs and covers, delivered in a soft, laid back way that had non-traditional music buyers flocking to their local record stores.

Similarly many fans of country/pop diva Shania Twain, 34,000,000 of them already being in possession of her *Come On Over* album, went out and bought the follow up record to that success story, *Up!*. Acknowledging the power wielded by her country critics, Twain recorded all of the album's material twice; once in a pop style, the other with a distinctly country feel. While not repeating the staggering feat of its predecessor, the record has gone on to sell more than 11 million copies.

2000s
20

A Day Without Rain

| • **Album sales:** 7,500,000 | • **Release date:** November 2000 |

After a five year absence, Enya (Eithne Patricia Ní Bhraonáin) returned with her first album of new material in 2000. Since she'd left Clannad in the 1980s, the Irish composer and vocalist had set the bar for ethereal New Age music – her soothing multi-tracked vocals and layered synths became the chosen chill-out music for millions.

The visual feel of Enya's music and Roma Ryan's lyrics mean they have long been used in film and TV soundtracks – her initial solo credits were for the 1984 movie *The Frog Prince* and subsequent tracks found their way into Martin Scorsese's *The Age Of Innocence* and the Tom Cruise and Nicole Kidman yarn *Far and Away*. *A Day Without Rain* was no exception: the album's first single featured in the film *Sweet November* while 'Only Time' was used to trail the new TV season of *Friends*.

Although criticised for its simplistic style, the cathedral tone proved to be a balm for those in need of calming easy listening, and the album went on to sell seven million copies in America – massively more than any other territory.

Number One singles:
Only Time, Wild Child

Personnel:
Enya

Grammy awards:
Best New Age Album

Producer:
Nicky Ryan

Label:
US: Reprise, Warner Bros;
UK: WEA, Warner Music

Recorded in:
Dublin, Ireland

SOUNDTRACK TO A TRAGEDY

Sometimes music transcends being just music and becomes something much bigger. Such was the case with a track from Enya's *A Day Without Rain* album. In the immediate aftermath of the 11 September 2001 terrorist attacks, 'Only Time' was used by American TV news networks as a soundtrack to their news reports. The song was released as a single with profits going to help victims of the tragedy.

▲ **BACK COVER**

1 **A Day Without Rain (2:38)**
2 **Wild Child (3:47)**
3 **Only Time (3:38)**
4 **Tempus Vernum (2:24)**
5 **Deora Ar Mo Chroí (2:48)**
6 **Flora's Secret (4:07)**
7 **Fallen Embers (2:31)**
8 **Silver Inches (1:37)**
9 **Pilgrim (3:12)**
10 **One by One (3:56)**
11 **The First of Autumn (3:10)**
12 **Lazy Days (3:42)**
13 **Isobella (4:29)**

Total album length: 42 minutes

enya
a day without rain

2000s
19

Chocolate Starfish and the Hot Dog Flavored Water

I • **Album sales:** 7,500,000 I • **Release date:** October 2000 I

That the album featured a track commissioned by the World Wrestling Foundation as theme music for *Wrestlemania X-Seven* and another that became entrance music for wrestler The Undertaker is a good fit. *Chocolate Starfish and the Hot Dog Flavored Water*, Limp Bizkit's third studio album, is loaded with Wes Borland's muscular riffing and knuckle-headed raps from the out of control ego that was Fred Durst that slammed the listener into submission.

Although they quickly became relics of the shortlived rap-rock era, the album was a huge phenomenon at the start of the 21st century when Durst – who'd been blamed by some for inciting the riots at the 1999 Woodstock Festival – became an anti-hero much admired for his gonzo attitude. Among the album's home-runs were the powerful 'My Generation' and the low-rider groove of 'Rollin' (Air Raid Vehicle)', both of which helped the album to sales that totalled 12 million worldwide.

Despite rave reviews at the time of the release, the album now regularly features on 'Worst Album of All Time' lists – which is unfair, really. Durst made a great job of annoying everyone, including his own fans, but *Chocolate Starfish* remains nu metal's creative highpoint.

Number One singles:
UK: Rollin' (Air Raid Vehicle)

Grammy awards:
None

Label: Interscope

Recorded in:
California, USA

Personnel:
DJ Lethal
Wes Borland
John Otto
Tom Rivers
Fred Durst

Producers:
DJ Lethal
Fred Durst
Josh Abraham
Scott Weiland
Swizz Beatz
Terry Date

FEUD FOR THOUGHT

Whether onstage or off of it, Limp Bizkit front man Fred Durst seemed to spend a large amount of time upsetting people. At one point around the time of *Chocolate Starfish and the Hot Dog Flavored Water* he was in dispute with Eminem, Slipknot, Britney Spears and Christina Aguilera – the latter he claimed to have performed with in order to get some 'nookie'. The pop star denied Durst's claim and issued a brief statement that read 'He got no nookie'.

▲ **BACK COVER**

1 **Intro (1:18)**
2 **Hot Dog (3:50)**
3 **My Generation (3:41)**
4 **Full Nelson (4:07)**
5 **My Way (4:33)**
6 **Rollin' (Air Raid Vehicle) (3:34)**
7 **Livin' It Up (4:24)**
8 **The One (3:42)**
9 **Getcha Groove On (4:29)**
10 **Take a Look Around (5:18)**
11 **It'll Be OK (5:06)**
12 **Boiler (5:47)**
13 **Hold On (5:47)**
14 **Rollin' (Urban Assault Vehicle) (6:23)**
15 **Outro (2:01)**

Total album length: 75 minutes

limp bizkit
presents
PARENTAL
ADVISORY
EXPLICIT CONTENT
chocolate st★rfish and the hot dog flavored water

2000s
18

Breakaway

| • **Album sales:** 7,600,000 | • **Release date:** November 2004 |

The most successful *American Idol* contestant to date, Kelly Clarkson won the inaugural season of the TV talent show in 2002. At her audition in Dallas she impressed judges not only with her vocal style but also her sense of humour – forcing Randy Jackson to swap places and audition for her – and the nation was similarly smitten. Her debut album came out in the afterglow of *American Idol* and Clarkson took more control over the second, co-writing four of the tracks including one, 'Because of You', with former Evanescence guitarist and songwriter Ben Moody.

Although varied in styles, *Breakaway* featured a handful of fun rock songs that pitched Clarkson closer to the punk-pop of P!nk and Avril Lavigne (whose name appears in the credits of the title track), particularly the spiky 'Since U Been Gone', which demonstrated an edgier side to the girl nextdoor.

Released in November 2004, the album was a huge critical and commercial success, selling in excess of five million copies (the third biggest selling of the year) and earning Clarkson Best Female Pop Vocal and Best Pop Vocal Album at the Grammy Awards in early 2006. Most winners struggled to escape the shadow of American Idol, but with *Breakaway* Clarkson became a star across the world.

Number One singles:
US: Breakaway,
Since U Been Gone,
Because of You

Grammy awards:
Best female pop vocal performance- Since U Been Gone; Best pop vocal album

Label:
US: RCA Records
UK: Sony BMG

Recorded in: California and New York, USA; Stockholm, Sweden

Personnel:
Kelly Clarkson

Producers:
Clive Davis (exec.)
Kara DioGuardi
Lukasz Gottwald
David Hodges
Chantal Kreviazuk
Clif Magness
Raine Maida
Max Martin
Ben Moody

AMERICAN IDOL WINNERS

In terms of award victories, Season Four winner Carrie Underwood is the hottest act to emerge from *American Idol*, having racked up five Grammy Awards compared to Kelly Clarkson's two and Fantasia Barrino's one. But in sales terms, no champ in TV talent show history comes close to Kelly Clarkson, whose sales peaked with her second album, *Breakaway* – bucking the trend of all other Idol winners, who peaked with their debuts.

▲ **BACK COVER**

1 **Breakaway (3:57)**
2 **Since U Been Gone (3:09)**
3 **Behind These Hazel Eyes (3:19)**
4 **Because of You (3:39)**
5 **Gone (3:26)**
6 **Addicted (3:56)**
7 **Where Is Your Heart (4:38)**
8 **Walk Away (3:08)**
9 **You Found Me (3:39)**
10 **I Hate Myself for Losing You (3:20)**
11 **Hear Me (3:54)**
12 **Beautiful Disaster (Live) (4:35)**
Bonus tracks:
13 **Miss Independence (3:35)**
14 **Low (3:28)**

Total album length: 45 minutes

KELLY CLARKSON
BREAKAWAY

2000s
17

Hot Shot

| • **Album sales:** 7,700,000 | • **Release date:** October 2000 |

Hits 'Oh Carolina' and 'Mr Boombastic' had made Shaggy a huge worldwide star in the mid 90s and made his rich Jamaican baritone one of the most recognisable in pop. However, his fourth album, *Midnite Lover*, flopped badly and failed to chart anywhere. Shaggy slipped off the radar.

In 2000, with the release of *Hot Shot* (reissued in extended form in 2001) he made a huge comeback on the back of two massive hits. 'It Wasn't Me' featured a man (Rik Rok) asking his friend (Shaggy) what he should do after his girlfriend caught him in bed with a neighbour. Shaggy's advice is to deny everything and say 'It wasn't me' despite the fact that he'd been caught 'butt naked banging on the bathroom floor' and in various other compromising positions. The album's other major hit, 'Angel', played more earnestly on Shaggy's romantic capabilities, borrowing from 'Angel of the Morning' and Steve Miller's 'The Joker', as he paid tribute to the girl who stood by him "in spite of my behaviour".

The album shipped six million copies in the US and just under a million in the UK, a phenomenal success, but one he has failed to follow up, despite collaborations with Akon and Pitbull.

Number One singles:
Angel
It Wasn't Me

Grammy awards: None

Label: MCA Records

Recorded in: New York City, USA

Personnel:
Shaggy
Ricardo 'Rikrok' Ducent
Samantha Cole
Janet Jackson
Pee Wee

Producers:
Robert Livingston

DANCEHALL STARS

Jamaica-born New Yorker Shaggy made his name with a dancehall version of the Folkes Brothers' ska classic, 'Oh Carolina' in 1993. Dancehall – a DJ rapping over a reggae rhythm – first started crossing over into mainstream pop in the 1990s with songs such as 'Chaka Demus' and Pliers's 'Murder She Wrote'. In recent time Sean Paul has become the first global dancehall star, recording duets with Beyonce and Rihanna.

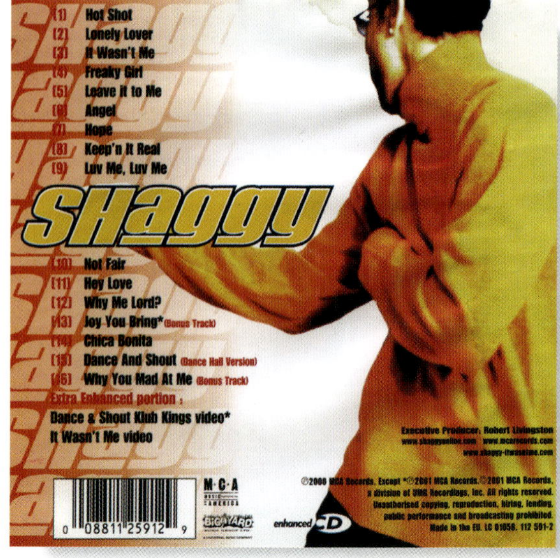

▲ **BACK COVER**

1 **Hot Shot (3:49)**
2 **Lonely Lover (3:47)**
3 **It Wasn't Me (3:47)**
4 **Freaky Girl (featuring The Kraft) (3:44)**
5 **Leave It To Me (featuring Brian and Tony Gold) (3:37)**
6 **Angel (featuring Rayvon) (3:55)**
7 **Hope (featuring Mister Mydas) (3:47)**
8 **Keep'n It Real (3:55)**
9 **Luv Me, Luv Me (featuring Janet Jackson) (3:17)**
10 **Not Fair (featuring RUDE) (3:47)**
11 **Hey Love (4:01)**
12 **Why Me Lord? (3:34)**
13 **Joy You Bring (3:28)**
14 **Chica Bonita (featuring Ricardo 'RikRok' Ducent) (4:01)**
15 **Dance & Shout (Original Version) (4:22)**
16 **Why You Mad At Me (3:12)**

Total album length: 54 minutes

SHAGGY
HOT SHOT

2000s
16

O Brother, Where Art Thou?

| • **Album sales:** 7,900,000 | • **Release date:** September 2000 |

The Coen Brothers' movie followed the jailbreak and misadventures of three convicts during the depression era, who amongst other scrapes stumble upon the birth of radio. Tempted by financial reward, the trio find themselves at a backwater radio station and record a song which ends up becoming an unlikely hit. That song, 'I Am a Man Of Constant Sorrow', features here alongside bluegrass, country, gospel and folk music of the period. Harry McClintock's 1928 recording of 'Big Rock Candy Mountain' aside, most of the 18 tracks were new recordings.

Unusually, the soundtrack found an audience beyond those who had actually seen the film and became an important country album in its own right, acting as a catalyst for a bluegrass revival. It was awarded Album of the Year at the 2002 Grammy Awards while Dan Tyminski, who'd overdubbed George Clooney's vocals, won Best Male Country Vocal Performance.

In an era when country music was becoming increasingly distant from its roots, *O Brother, Where Art Thou?* became a totem for a past that had been largely forgotten – and one that turned out to be both charming and compelling. The soundtrack's success led to tours, a documentary and several follow-up compilations.

Number One singles:
None

Grammy awards:
Album of the year,
Best compilation soundtrack album for a motion picture, television or other visual media

Label: Mercury Records

Recorded in: Los Angeles, USA

Personnel:
Alison Krauss
Emmylou Harris
The Stanley Brothers
The Fairfield Four
The Cox Family
Dan Tyminski
Gillian Welch
David Rawlings
Norman Blake
John Hartford

Producers:
T-Bone Burnett

HIT SOUNDTRACKS

Three soundtrack albums sold in such huge numbers in the 1960s that they topped sales charts in the USA for six consecutive years before Herb Alpert & The Tijuana Brass bucked the trend. Since then only *Saturday Night Fever* in 1978 has had such a huge cultural effect. The soundtrack to *O Brother, Where Art Thou?* didn't sell in such vast numbers (although its 7.9 million total makes it the 11th best selling soundtrack of the last 35 years – a list topped by *The Bodyguard*), but it completely eclipsed the movie and also helped to revitalise traditional American music.

▲ **BACK COVER**

1 **Po' Lazarus (4:31)**
2 **Big Rock Candy Mountain (2:16)**
3 **You Are My Sunshine (4:26)**
4 **Down to the River to Pray (2:55)**
5 **I am a Man of Constant Sorrow (radio station version) (3:10)**
6 **Hard Time Killing Floor Blues (2:42)**
7 **I am a Man Of Constant Sorrow (instrumental) (4:28)**
8 **Keep On the Sunny Side (3:33)**
9 **I'll Fly Away (3:57)**
10 **Didn't Leave Nobody but the Baby (1:57)**
11 **In the Highways (1:35)**
12 **I Am Weary, Let Me Rest (3:13)**
13 **I Am a Man of Constant Sorrow (instrumental) (2:34)**
14 **O Death (3:19)**
15 **In the Jailhouse Now (3:34)**
16 **I Am a Man of Constant Sorrow (4:16)**
17 **Indian War Whoop (instrumental) (1:30)**
18 **Lonesome Valley (4:07)**
19 **Angel Band (2:15)**

Total album length: 61 minutes

MUSIC FROM THE MOTION PICTURE
O BROTHER,
WHERE ART THOU?

2000s
15

American Idiot

| • **Album sales:** 8,100,000 | • **Release date:** September 2004 |

Long ago, every other album was a rock opera with the tracks and artwork linked by some unifying theme or storyline. Such an approach has been pretty much ridiculed as pretentious since the late 1970s, but the format saw an unlikely revival in 2004 by Green Day, whose *American Idiot* articulated the anxiety of a nation on the verge of war and saw the band reborn as protest rockers.

The album's central character is the Jesus of Suburbia, an anti-hero who leaves the hometown he's grown to loathe and is reborn as punk rock freedom fighter, St. Jimmy. Although the story itself – which subsequently became a Broadway musical – baffled some, there was no denying the group's bold ambition or the strength of many of the tracks: the title track, 'Boulevard Of Broken Dreams' and 'Wake Me Up When September Ends' ranking as the greatest of their career. The set was also performed with conviction and there was none of the irony or toilet humour that marked out their early years. Green Day were suddenly major rock stars.

In 2005, *American Idiot* won a Grammy for Best Rock Album, while its reputation held through to the end of the noughties when *Rolling Stone* magazine voted it the Greatest Album of the Decade.

Number One singles:
US: American Idiot, Holiday, Boulevard of Broken Dreams

Grammy awards:
Best rock album

Label: Reprise

Recorded in: California & Hollywood, USA

Personnel:
Billie Joe Armstrong
Mike Dirnt
Tré Cool
Rob Cavallo
Jason Freese
Kathleen Hanna

Producers:
Rob Cavallo
Green Day

ON BROADWAY

Queen, Abba and Buddy Holly have all enjoyed later success in stage musicals but in 2011, the most talked about Broadway musical was inspired by a band who were still very much together. Conceived as a story album about three teenagers escaping suburbia, Green Day's *American Idiot* album could have been made into a movie (like The Who's concept albums *Tommy* and *Quadrophenia*), but instead found itself on the Broadway stage. Plenty thought it would fail – due to the songs' less than traditional tone and the high cost of the production – but its 12 month run grossed US$36 million and had won numerous awards. Next, just as a band would, the musical announced details of a national tour.

▲ **BACK COVER**

1 American Idiot (2:54)
2 Jesus of Suburbia (9:08)
I. Jesus of Suburbia
II. City of the Damned
III. I Don't Care
IV. Dearly Beloved
V. Tales of Another Broken Home
3 Holiday (3:52)
4 Boulevard Of Broken Dreams (4:20)
5 Are We the Waiting (2:42)
6 St. Jimmy (2:55)
7 Give Me Novacaine (3:25)
8 She's a Rebel (2:00)
9 Extraordinary Girl (3:33)
10 Letterbomb (4:06)
11 Wake Me Up When September Ends (4:45)
12 Homecoming (9.18)
I. The Death of St. Jimmy
II. East 12th St.
III. Nobody Likes You
IV. Rock and Roll Girlfriend
V. We're Coming Home Again
13 Whatsername (4:14)

Total album length: 57 minutes

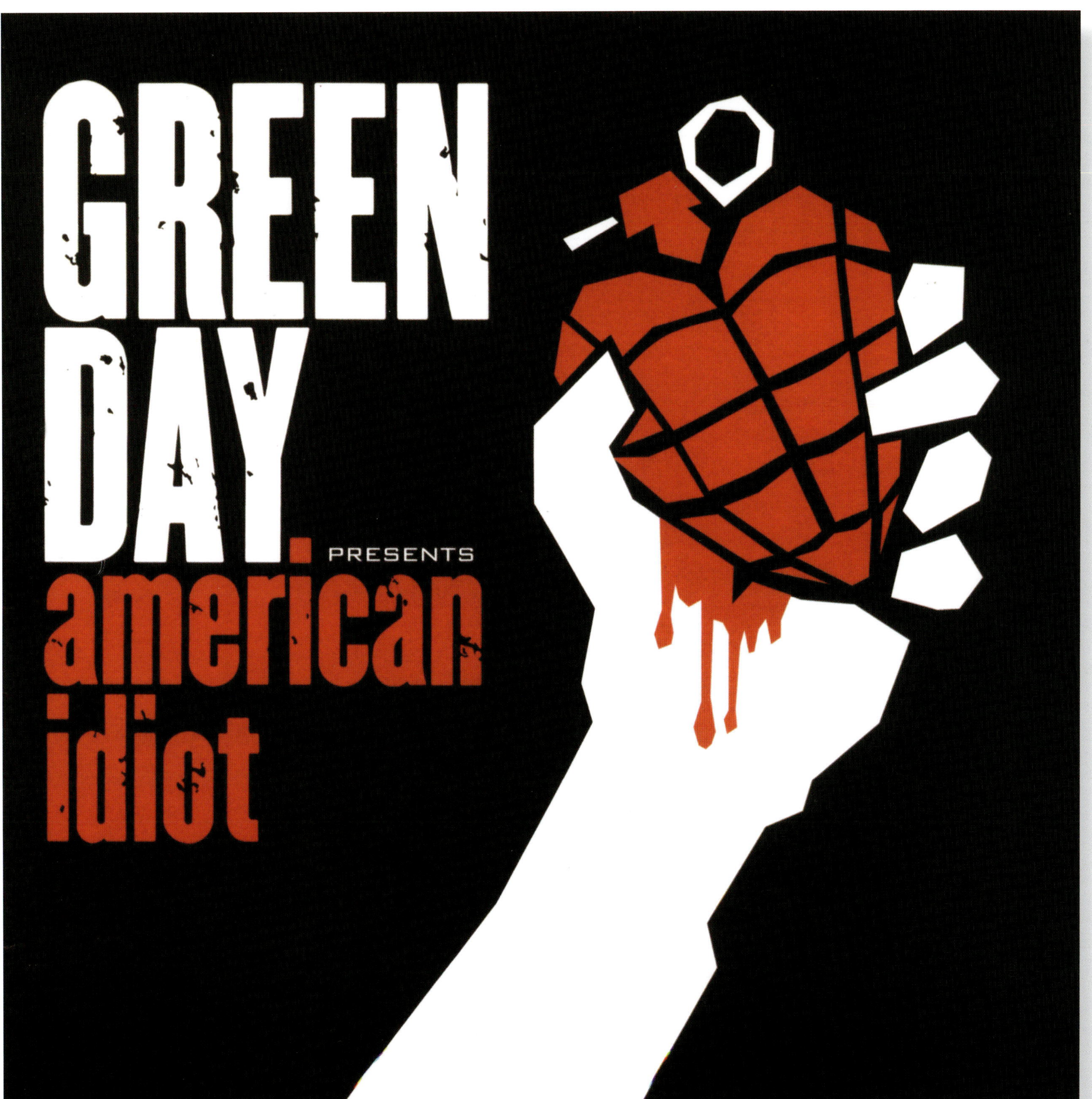
GREEN DAY.
PRESENTS
american idiot

2000s
14

Let Go

| • **Album sales:** 8,500,000 | • **Release date:** June 2002 |

In 1998 a 14-year-old Canadian girl won a radio contest to perform with Shania Twain in front of an audience of 20,000. After singing 'What Made You Say That', the teenager told Twain that she was going to be 'a famous singer'. The claim was no fairytale and just two years later Avril Lavigne had signed a US$1.25 million recording contract on the back of a 15 minute audition.

What the head of Arista Records saw was a teen singer who had her own style and wasn't trying to be a Britney clone, and who wrote her own songs – but it wasn't until he teamed her up with production team The Matrix that her music came together. Featured on the TV show *Dawson's Creek*, first single 'Complicated' was an immediate hit. Second single 'Sk8er Boi', which retold *Romeo and Juliet* as a star-crossed punk and a ballerina, cemented her reputation, and by the time *Let Go* was released, she was the most famous teenager in the world.

The album went on to sell over 17 million copies worldwide.

Number One singles:
US: Complicated, Sk8er Boi, I'm With You

Grammy awards:
None

Label: Arista

Recorded in:
Los Angeles, USA

Personnel:
Avril Lavigne
Sabelle Breer
The Matrix
Clif Magness
Jeff Allen
Suzie Katayama
Joe Bonadio
Josh Freese
Alex Elena
Curt Frasca
Gerry Leonard
Peter Zizzo
Corky James

Producers:
Antonio 'LA' Reid
The Matrix
Clif Magness
Curt Frasca
Peter Zizzo

IF THE SHIRT FITS

As well as a successful career in music and film, Avril Lavigne also has her own hit clothing brand – Abbey Dawn (her childhood nickname), which draws on her own punky style. Since 2008, the line has expanded from teen wear to include clothes for men and women, as well as jewelry and watches. Other musicians with their own clothing brands include Blink 182's Travis Barker (Famous Stars and Straps), Maroon 5's Adam Levine (222), former Oasis frontman Liam Gallagher (Pretty Green) and Tennessee rockers Kings of Leon (Surface to Air).

▲ **BACK COVER**

1. **Losing Grip (3:53)**
2. **Complicated (4:05)**
3. **Sk8er Boi (3:23)**
4. **I'm With You (3:44)**
5. **Mobile (3:31)**
6. **Unwanted (3:40)**
7. **Tomorrow (3:48)**
8. **Anything But Ordinary (4:12)**
9. **Things I'll Never Say (3:44)**
10. **My World (3:27)**
11. **Nobody's Fool (3:57)**
12. **Too Much To Ask (3:46)**
13. **Naked (3:27)**

Total album length: 49 minutes

Avril Lavigne . Let Go

2000s
13

All The Right Reasons

| • **Album sales:** 8,600,000 | • **Release date:** November 2006 |

Few albums have ever had such extended life spans as *All The Right Reasons*. The Canadian rockers' fifth studio album was released on 4 October 2005 and could still be found in the top 10 of the Billboard 200 chart 100 weeks later. Away from America, the album's chart runs were equally unusual. In the UK, it charted at Number 13 in the week it was released, before disappearing. Over two years later 'Rockstar' – which poked fun at the rockstar lifestyle – became a huge hit, peaking at Number Two and remaining in the Top 40 for a staggering 35 weeks. The turnaround in fortune relaunched the album, which ended up selling half-a-million copies, and climbed to Number Two in the album chart.

Nickelback were the kind of band it wasn't cool to admit liking – they were seen by many as pale imitations of Nirvana, thanks to their quiet-loud song structures, plodding riffs and Chad Kroeger's strained vocal style, and were criticised for their overblown production.

The facts, however, speak for themselves and for the two years following *All The Right Reasons* release no other artist sold as many albums as Nickelback.

Number One singles:
US: Photograph, Animals
UK: Photograph, Rockstar

Grammy awards: None

Label: Roadrunner

Recorded in: British Columbia, Canada

Personnel:
Chad Kroeger
Ryan Peake
Mike Kroeger
Daniel Adair
Billy Gibbons
Timmy Dawson
Brian Larson
Dimebag Darrell
Chris Gestrin

Producers:
Nickelback
Joey Moi
Tom Cruise

SOFA SO GOOD

Nickelback turned up in Britain to promote their forthcoming tour thinking they'd be discussing their music; instead the most common thing everyone wanted to talk to them about were sofas. The licensing of 'Rockstar' to budget sofa chain DFS meant the track was on constant rotation on UK TV (where a selection of everyday folk mimed to it, while modelling the delights of bargain furniture). Not cool, but it undoubtedly helped the band sell a few more copies.

▲ **BACK COVER**

1 Follow You Home (4:20)
2 Fight For All the Wrong Reasons (3:34)
3 Photograph (4:19)
4 Animals (3:06)
5 Savin' Me (3:39)
6 Far Away (3:58)
7 Next Contestant (3:35)
8 Side Of A Bullet (3:00)
9 If Everyone Cared (3:38)
10 Someone That You're With (4:01)
11 Rockstar (4:14)

Total album length: 42 minutes

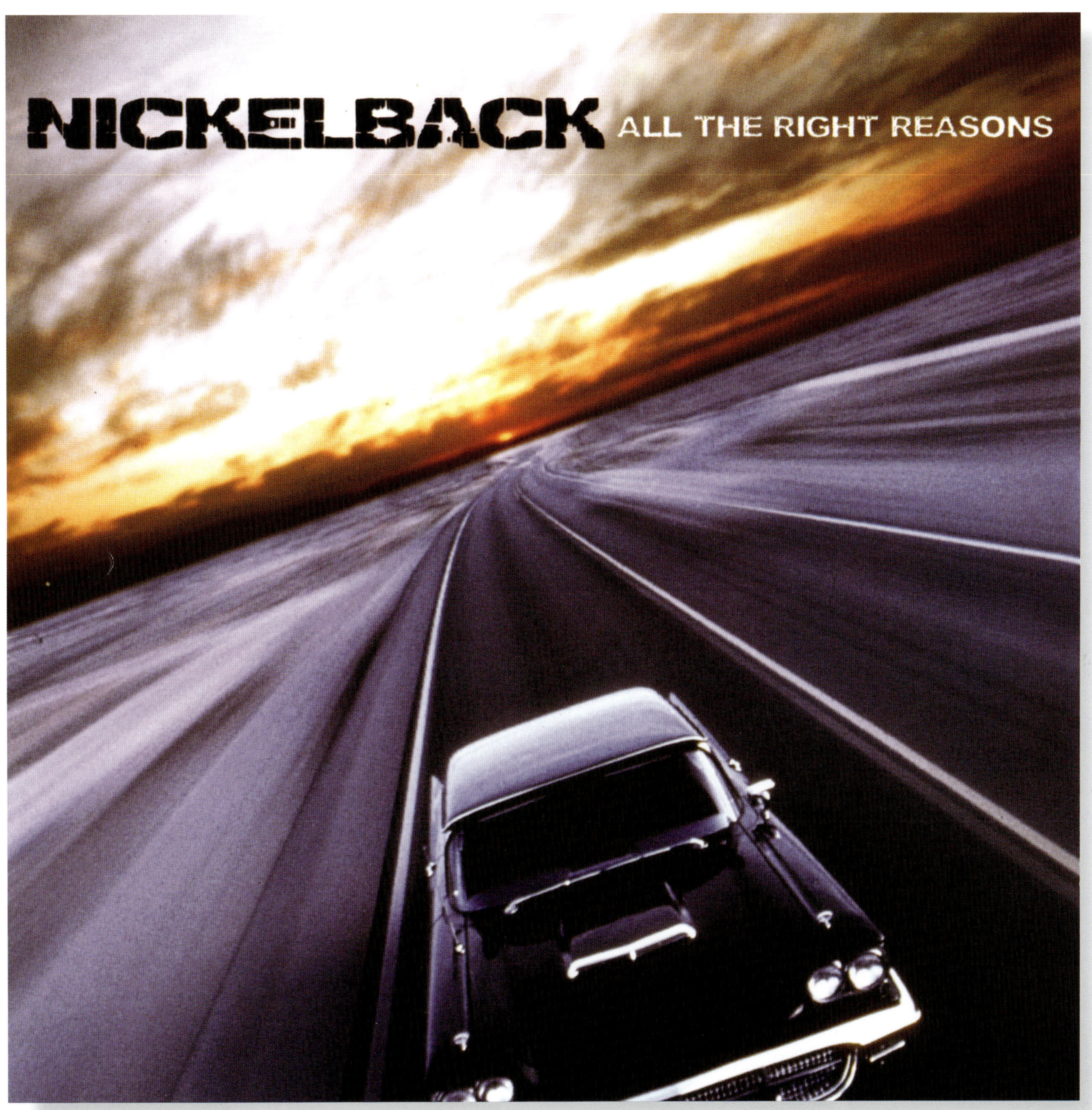
NICKELBACK
ALL THE RIGHT REASONS

2000s
12

Fallen

| • **Album sales:** 8,800,000 | • **Release date:** April 2003 |

This Arkansas five-piece made it to the top of the album charts in 2003 with their debut album. Singer/pianist Amy Lee met guitarist/songwriter Ben Moody at a Christian youth camp, and although they initially released an EP as a duo, their dramatic sound, which mixed the rap-rock of groups like Linkin Park and Korn with Lee's gothic Tori Amos-style poetics, only came together when they became a band.

Their debut single, the epic 'Bring Me To Life', which featured guest vocals from Paul McCoy of 12 Stones, made it to Number Five in the US and Number One in the UK singles charts. The song was helped by its inclusion in the soundtrack to the film *Daredevil* and a video that cast Lee as a tragic, sleepwalking heroine falling to her death from a windowledge (don't worry, it was all a dream).

Managing to please both Christian and mainstream rock fans, *Fallen* majored in a similarly theatrical mood throughout and proved a massive hit, remaining in the US Top 10 for 43 weeks and selling 15 million copies worldwide.

Sadly, it was a success Evanescence were never to repeat. Moody left during their European tour, citing creative differences, and the remaining members have only managed to make two albums (2006's *Open Door* and 2011's *Evanescence*) ever since.

Number One singles:
Bring Me To Life

Grammy awards:
Best new artist;
Album of the year;
Best hard rock perfomance

Label: US: Wind-Up
UK: EMI

Recorded in: California, USA

Personnel:
David Hodges
Amy Lee
Ben Moody
Rocky Gray
John LeCompt
Josh Freese

Producers:
Dave Fortman
Ben Moody

I DON'T BELIEVE IT

Something that Evanescence have never been able to escape is whether they are or are not a Christian rock band. When *Fallen* was first released the band were heavily promoted on Christian rock radio stations and stores, due to the band members' religious backgrounds. But when songwriter Ben Moody questioned their inclusion in the genre they found themselves removed from the Christian charts. The issue, though, continued to follow them. During an interview with Billboard in 2006, singer Amy Lee drew a line under the debate saying, "I'm so over it. It's the lamest thing. I fought that from the beginning; I never wanted to be associated with it."

▲ **BACK COVER**

1. **Going Under (3:35)**
2. **Bring Me to Life (featuring Paul McCoy) (3:58)**
3. **Everybody's Fool (3:16)**
4. **My Immortal (4:24)**
5. **Haunted (3:06)**
6. **Tourniquet (4:38)**
7. **Imaginary (4:17)**
8. **Taking Over Me (3:50)**
9. **Hello (3:40)**
10. **My Last Breath (4:08)**
11. **Whisper (5:27)**
12. **My Immortal (4:33)**

Total album length: 49 minutes

EVANESCENCE
FALLEN

2000s
11

Country Grammar

| • **Album sales:** 8,800,000 | • **Release date:** June 2000 |

The son of a member of the US Air Force, Nelly – aka Cornell Haynes Jr – led a nomadic childhood before settling down with his parents in St Louis, Missouri.

While at school, Nelly started a group with a bunch of friends called the St. Lunatics. In 1996 they released a single, 'Gimme What You Got' – the record sold nearly 10,000 copies in the St Louis area and was a local airwave hit.

Then came success on a national scale with his first album, *Country Grammar,* which sold more than 250,000 copies in its first week and spent an impressive seven weeks at the top of the chart. Aided by further hits 'E.I.' and 'Ride Wit Me', *Country Grammar* has gone on to sell more than nine million copies worldwide since its release.

It wasn't just Nelly's near-instant success upon his arrival on the rap scene that made him stand out; he was the first of the rap stars who played on his good looks. As he asks on *Country Grammar:* 'Who said pretty boys can't be niggers?'

The album's slick production, together with the brutal street imagery, announced its hit potential and, sure enough, the single made Number One in the US.

ST. LOUIS SLANG

The title track's sentiment is clear, as Nelly explained to *Rolling Stone* magazine: "My whole purpose was to make people who speak country grammar not ashamed of how they talk, and turn it into the hot slang. *Country Grammar* is a celebration of having a national album come out of St. Louis. We're on a whole other level now, so let's kick it. And in St. Louis, we kick it."

Number One singles: US: Country Grammar (Hot...)

Grammy awards: None

Label: Universal Records

Recorded in: New York City, USA

Personnel:
Nelly
Ali
Kewjaun
Murphy Lee
City Spud

Producers:
Jason "Jay E" Epperson
City Spud

▲ **BACK COVER**

1 **St. Louie (4:27)**
2 **Greed, Hate, Envy (4:15)**
3 **Country Grammar (Hot...) (4:47)**
4 **Steal The Show (5:27)**
5 **Ride Wit Me (4:51)**
6 **E.I. (4:45)**
7 **Thicky Thick Girl (4:34)**
8 **For My (4:08)**
9 **Utha Side (4:33)**
10 **Tho Dem Wrappas (4:08)**
11 **Wrap Sumden (4:15)**
12 **Batter Up (5:27)**
13 **Never Let 'Em C U Sweat (4:14)**
14 **Luven Me (4:07)**

Total album length: 66 minutes

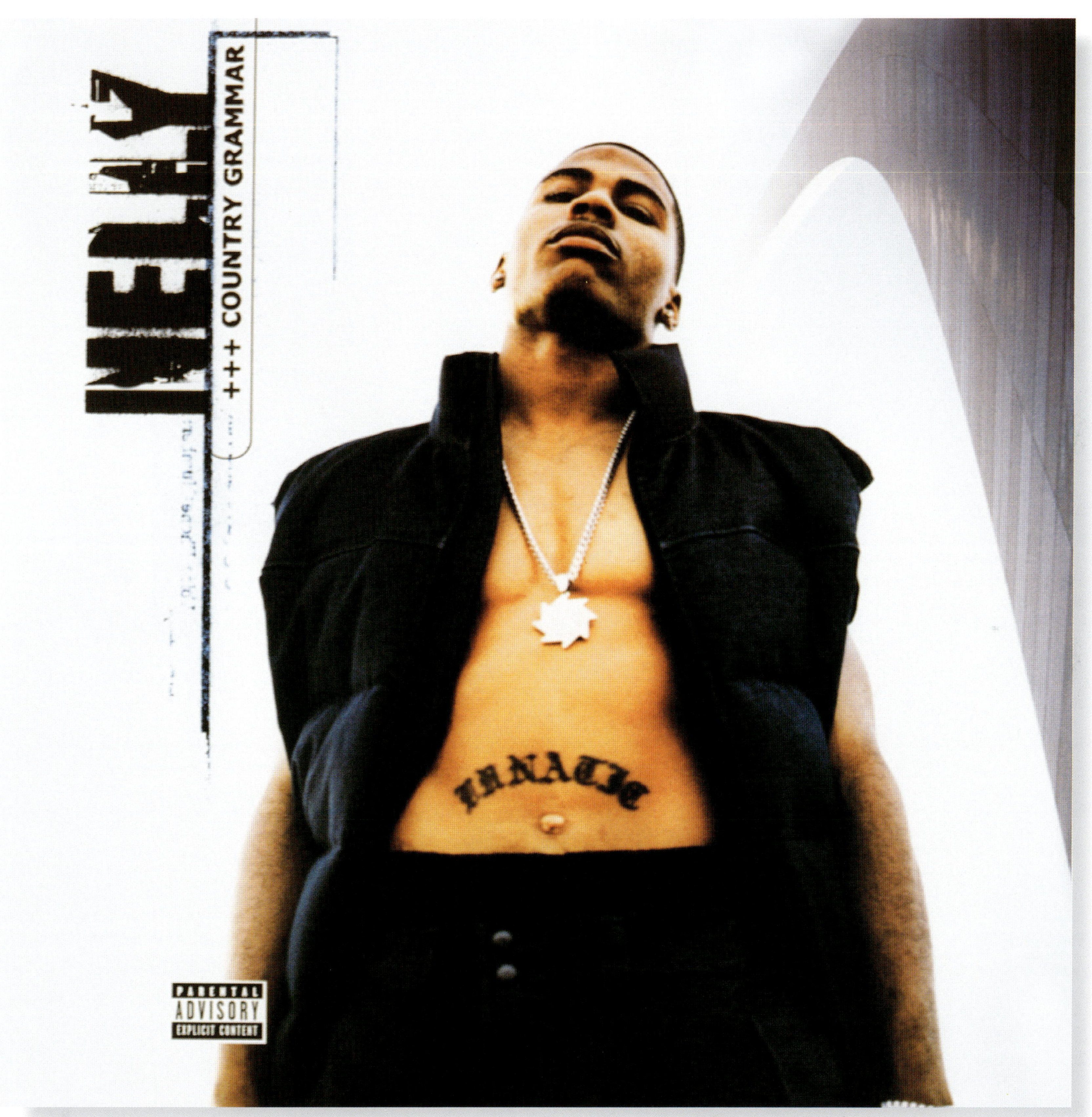
NELLY
+++ COUNTRY GRAMMAR
PARENTAL ADVISORY
EXPLICIT CONTENT

2000s
10

Get Rich Or Die Tryin'

| • **Album sales:** 9,000,000 | • **Release date:** February 2003 |

Curtis '50 Cent' Jackson's past as a drug dealer and survivor of a shooting incident gave him an immediate street credibility and invincibility. His street-hustling youth and survival tale were constant themes throughout his debut album, which featured him on the sleeve posing like a boxer, six-pack gleaming. It was as though 50 Cent's lyrical style and muscle, rather than his back story, which made *Get Rich Or Die Tryin'* so appealing and overnight breathed new life into the tired gangsta-rap genre.

Dark and synthy with sparse handclaps and the occasional guitar riff, the album had a funky bounce that matched the hydraulic pump of a customised low rider; 50 ('Fiddy' to his friends) complemented the groove with a laid-back, clipped rap flow and an unsophisticated tenor croon. Lead single 'In Da Club' lived up to the hype that surrounded the album's release, and by the time it finally came out it was already the most talked about hip-hop album in decades.

Feuds and fall-outs followed and 50's reign as the world's most famous rapper continued over the next couple of albums, until he made the switch to acting, appearing in the semi-autobiographical film *Get Rich Or Die Tryin'* (2005).

Number One singles:
US: In Da Club, P.I.M.P., 21 Questions

Grammy awards: None

Label:
US: Interscope
UK: Polydor

Personnel:
50 Cent
Justin Bendo
Sean Blaze
Darrell Branch
Tom Coster
Terence Dudley
Mike Elizondo
Eminem
Ron Feemster
John 'J. Praize' Freeman
Marcus Heisser
Steven King
Tracy McNew
Megahertz
Red Spyda
Luis Resto
Ruben Rivera
Rockwilder
Tom Rounds
Sha Money XL
Tracie Spencer
Rob Tewlow
Patrick Viala
Sacha Waldman
Ted Wohlsen
Carlisle Young

Producers:
Sean Blaze, Darrell Branch, Dirty Swift, DJ Rad, Dr. Dre, Terence Dudley, Mike Elizondo, Eminem, John 'J-Praize' Freeman, Megahertz, Denaun Porter, Red Spyda, Reef, Rockwilder, Sha Money XL

BORN SURVIVOR

The shooting incident that inspired *Get Rich Or Die Tryin'* happened on 24 May 2000, when Curtis '50 Cent' Jackson was hit nine times outside his grandmother's house in South Jamaica, Queens, New York. The bullets struck his right hand, arm, hip, both legs, chest and left cheek. The facial wound resulted in the loss of a wisdom tooth, as well as the swollen tongue which caused his slurred voice.

▲ **BACK COVER**

1 Intro (0:06)
2 What Up Gangsta (2:59)
3 Patiently Waiting (featuring Eminem) (4:48)
4 Many Men (Wish Death) (4:16)
5 In Da Club (3:13)
6 High All The Time (4:29)
7 Heat (4:14)
8 If I Can't (3:16)
9 Blood Hound (featuring Young Buck) (4:00)
10 Back Down (4:03)
11 P.I.M.P. (4:09)
12 Like My Style (featuring Tony Yayo) (3:13)
13 Poor Lil Rich (3:19)
14 21 Questions (featuring Nate Dogg) (3:44)
15 Don't Push Me (featuring Lloyd Banks & Eminem) (4:08)
16 Gotta Make It To Heaven (4:01)

Total album length: 70 minutes

Get Rich Or Die Tryin'
50
CENT
PARENTAL
ADVISORY
EXPLICIT CONTENT

2000s
9

Speakerboxxx/ The Love Below

• Album sales: 11,000,000 **• Release date:** September 2003

Celebrating more than 10 years on the music scene, the success of duo André Benjamin (Andre '3000') and Antwan Patton (Big Boi), aka Outkast, had gone from that of respected hit-makers, with tunes such as 'Player's Ball' and their first Number One pop single 'Ms Jackson', to world chart-dominating superstars, thanks to their fifth studio longplayer, *Speakerboxxx/The Love Below,* and hits from it such as 'Hey Ya!', 'Way You Move' and 'Ghetto Musick'.

While some of the songs exhibit the traditional strong language and violent imagery of their peers, many are laced with humour, notably on *The Love Below* set, such as 'Where Are My Panties?' and 'Hey Ya!' There is even room for some ironic lounge jazz, as on 'Love Below (Intro)' and 'Love Hater'.

Speakerboxxx, on the other hand, is a far darker, bleaker set, featuring songs about war – as on the bluntly titled 'War' – and street and domestic violence. Throughout the album there are musical nods to the 1970s' funk of the likes of Parliament and Sly & The Family Stone, while maintaining the rap/hip-hop groove.

There is no slacking on the music with Outkast: the songs, dark or light, are well constructed and performed, as one would come to expect with an executive producer like Antonio 'LA' Reid at the helm alongside Outkast themselves.

Number One singles: US: Hey Ya!; The Way You Move

Grammy awards: Album of the Year; Best urban/alternative performance; Best rap album

Label: Arista

Recorded in: Los Angeles, USA; Atlanta, USA

Personnel:
Andre Benjamin
Antwan 'Big Boi' Patton

Producers:
André '3000'
Mr. DJ
Big Boi
Carl Mo
Dojo 5

COMBINED TALENT

Blessed by the opportunity to combine their enormous talents, Outkast's biggest-selling album may never have seen the light of day. Duo Dre and Big Boi were on the verge of parting company when Arista finally released *Speakerboxxx/The Love Below*. Indeed, the original intention was that both records should be put out as solo efforts. Taking hip-hop to another level, it is ironic therefore to find that *Speakerboxxx/The Love Below* is Outkast at the height of their creative, if controversial, powers – liberally covered with stickers warning of strong language together with sexual and violent material. A 'clean' version was released for those of a more sensitive disposition.

▲ **BACK COVER**

Speakerboxxx:
1 Intro (1:29)
2 Ghetto Musick (3:56)
3 Unhappy (3:19)
4 Bowtie (3:56)
5 Way You Move (3:54)
6 Rooster (3:57)
7 Bust (3:08)
8 War (2:43)
9 Church (3:27)
10 Bamboo (Interlude) (2:09)
11 Tomb Of The Boom (4:46)
12 E-Mac (Interlude) (0:24)
13 Knowing (3:32)
14 Flip Flop Rock (4:35)
15 Interlude (1:15)
16 Reset (4:35)
17 D-Boi (Interlude) (0:40)
18 Last Call (3:57)
19 Bowtie (Postlude) (0:34)

The Love Below:
20 Love Below (Intro) (1:27)
21 Love Hater (2:49)
22 God (Interlude) (2:20)
23 Happy Valentine's Day (5:23)
24 Spread (3:51)
25 Where Are My Panties? (1:54)
26 Prototype (5:26)
27 She Lives In My Lap (4:27)
28 Hey Ya! (3:55)
29 Roses (6:09)
30 Good Day, Good Sir (1:24)
31 Behold A Lady (4:37)
32 Pink & Blue (5:04)
33 Love In War (3:25)
34 She's Alive (4:06)
35 Dracula's Wedding (2:32)
36 My Favorite Things (5:13)
37 Take Off Your Cool (2:38)
38 Vibrate (6:33)
39 A Life In The Day Of Benjamin André (Incomplete) (5:11)

Total album length: 134 minutes

OUT
KAST
Speakerboxxx / The Love Below

2000s
8

Oops!... I Did It Again

| • **Album sales:** 11,300,000 | • **Release date:** May 2000 |

Following a 26 million selling debut album is no easy feat, especially when you consider that Britney Spears was just 18 years old at the time, but *Oops!... I Did It Again* was a confident step forward for the former Mouseketeer. The title track and lead single may have seemed similar to *...Baby One More Time* – and sold in equally huge numbers – but it portrayed a singer who was growing up fast and eager to present a more mature, sexier style than the innocent teen grinning from the covers of her first releases.

There was still plenty of the girl next door about Britney, though, as demonstrated on a slowed down arrangement of The Rolling Stones' '(I Can't Get No) Satisfaction'. The original may have been about the unquenchable sexual appetite of Mick Jagger, but here, beginning with a sassy phone call between Spears and a girlfriend, the dissatisfaction stems from an innocent desire for a proper relationship. Elsewhere the album majors in slickly crafted dance-pop that echoes the signature synth stabs of *...Baby One More Time* ('What U See (Is What You Get)'), cute bubblegum pop ('One Kiss From You') and sultry ballads ('When Your Eyes Say It').

Oops! was never going to match her debut – although it still sold 20 million copies worldwide – but it set the tone for the more daring albums and provocative image that followed.

Number One singles:
Oops!... I Did it Again

Grammy awards: None

Label:
US: Jive; UK: RCA

Recorded in: Stockholm, Sweden; Orlando and New York City, USA

Personnel:
Britney Spears
Jeanne LeBlanc
Jesse Levy
Kermit Moore
Larry 'Rock' Campbell
Marji Danilow
Judith Sugarman
Thomas Lindberg
Per Magnusson
Kristian Lundin
Rami
David Kreuger

Producers:
Max Martin
Larry 'Rock' Campbell
Barry Eastmond
Jake Robert
Jazayeri Darkchild
Robert Lange
David Kreuger
Kristian Lundin
Steve Lunt
Per Magnusson
Timmy Allen

DISNEY PRESENTS...

A revival of a hit 1950s family TV show, *The All-New Mickey Mouse Club* featured an all-singing, all-dancing cast of Mouseketeers performing comic skits and musical numbers. Although it was cancelled in 1994, the final year of the Disney show produced an incredible number of future pop stars, including Christina Aguilera, Justin Timberlake and, of course, Britney Spears. Britney's angelic appearance as a Mouseketeer meant many Americans felt uncomfortable with her sexual image in years to come.

▲ **BACK COVER**

1 **Oops!... I Did It Again (3:31)**
2 **Stronger (3:23)**
3 **Don't Go Knockin' On My Door (3:14)**
4 **(I Can't Get No) Satisfaction (4:28)**
5 **Don't Let Me Be The Last To Know (3:50)**
6 **What U See (Is What U Get) (3:16)**
7 **Lucky (3:25)**
8 **One Kiss From You (3:23)**
9 **Where Are You Now (4:39)**
10 **Can't Make You Love Me (3:16)**
11 **When Your Eyes Say It (4:06)**
12 **Girl In The Mirror (3:36)**
13 **Dear Diary (2:46)**

Total album length: 45 minutes

britney spears
oops!...I did it again

2000s
7

Confessions

| • **Album sales:** 11,500,000 | • **Release date:** March 2004 |

In a break with the more pop-oriented R&B grooves that had weaved throughout Usher's previous work, *Confessions* is a markedly deeper record from the Atlanta singer. Indeed many have observed that it is a coming-of-age album, pinpointing the time and place where boy became man.

There are upbeat songs, such as 'Yeah!' and there are tunes that are designed, if not to break the listener's heart, then to at least give it a good shake, such as 'Burn'.

While its maturity may have unsettled those Usher fans more comfortable with his lighter offerings, *Confessions* had no problems in breaking a number of records on its own road to success, including surpassing Norah Jones' claim to the highest overall chart debut of 2004 with *Feels Like Home*, and the highest overall R&B (non hip-hop) debut in the Soundscan era, surpassing Destiny's Child's *Survivor* in May 2001. The album also gave Usher his first Number One album and his first simultaneous pop and R&B chart Number One, while the record won Grammys for R&B performance by a Duo or Group With Vocals for 'My Boo' with Alicia Keys, which features on the *Confessions* Special Edition release, as well as Contemporary R&B Album*;* and Rap/Sung Collaboration for 'Yeah!' with Ludacris and Lil Jon.

Number One singles:
US: Yeah!

Grammy awards: None

Label: Arista Records

Recorded in: New York City, Atlanta, Los Angeles & Santa Monica, USA

Personnel:
Usher Raymond
Ludacris

Producers:
Usher Raymond
Antonio 'L.A.' Reid
Sean Garrett
Jermaine Dupri
Rich Harrison
Andre Harris
Vidal Davis

MULTI-TALENTED STARS

One of a long line of urban music stars who have moved between music and other forms of creativity – notably Will Smith – the transition has seen Usher juggle several roles as well as that of a superstar singer; he finds time to be a vocalist, a composer, producer, film and television actor, businessman and philanthropist.

When it comes to *Confessions*, the title says it all. Known, typecast even, as a powerful balladeer, Usher bares his soul with this, his fifth album, listing affairs, infidelities, hopes, fears and dreams and the consequences of his failed relationship with TLC member Chili Thomas.

▲ **BACK COVER**

1 **Intro (0:46)**
2 **Yeah! (4:10)**
3 **Throwback (4:01)**
4 **Confessions (Interlude) (1:15)**
5 **Confessions Part II (3:49)**
6 **Burn (4:15)**
7 **Caught Up (3:44)**
8 **Superstar (Interlude) (1:04)**
9 **Superstar (3:28)**
10 **Truth Hurts (3:51)**
11 **Bad Girl (4:22)**
12 **Simple Things (4:57)**
13 **That's What It's Made For (4:37)**
14 **Can U Handle It? (5:44)**
15 **Do It To Me (3:54)**
16 **Take Your Hand (3:03)**
17 **Follow Me (3:31)**

Total album length: 61 minutes

USHER
CONFESSIONS

2000s
6

Hybrid Theory

| • **Album sales:** 11,700,000 | • **Release date:** October 2000 |

Encapsulating the band's penchant for mixing up metal licks, break beats and energetic rapping, *Hybrid Theory,* Linkin Park's debut set produced by Don Gilmore (whose credits include Pearl Jam and Eve 6) hit the ground running in 2001, entering the US album charts at Number 16. It went on to become the country's best-selling album of the year, spawning three hit singles, including 'In The End' and 'One Step Closer'. The album earned the band a Grammy for Best Hard Rock Performance for the song 'Crawling', while there were Grammy nominations for Best Rock Album and Best New Artist.

Part of the then-trend for nu-metal acts, Linkin Park split opinions amongst people who liked either hip-hop or rock. Some felt the experiment, which continued with their later material, worked. Others believed it was like pouring port over stilton cheese. Two things enjoyable on their own become a mess when combined in such a way.

Interestingly for a band playing a raucous blend of rap 'n' roll, *Hybrid Theory* does not bear a 'Parental Advisory' sticker, devoid as it is of strong language and violent imagery.

Number One singles: None

Grammy awards: Best hard rock performance – Crawling

Label: Warner Bros.

Recorded in: North Hollywood, USA

Personnel:
Chester Bennington
Rob Bourdon
Brad Delson
Joseph Hahn
Mike Shinoda

Producer:
Don Gilmore

HYBRID GENRES

As rap began to dominate the musical tastes of a whole new generation of young consumers, it was inevitable that it would find a meeting point with rock. With both fans and performers of both genres equally regarded as potential threats to society, rappers and rockers had things in common from the outset. Rap, in the right hands, injected a fresh vitality into rock, tapping into its street fashion, language and imagery. Bands such as Rage Against The Machine harnessed rap to their agitprop wagon of thundering rock riffs to great effect, and while Limp Bizkit might have lacked the critical credibility of RATM, they still made rap 'n' roll commercially viable.

▲ **BACK COVER**

1 **Papercut (3:05)**
2 **One Step Closer (2:35)**
3 **With You (3:23)**
4 **Points Of Authority (3:20)**
5 **Crawling (3:29)**
6 **Runaway (3:03)**
7 **By Myself (3:09)**
8 **In The End (3:36)**
9 **A Place For My Head (3:04)**
10 **Forgotten (3:14)**
11 **Cure For The Itch (2:37)**
12 **Pushing Me Away (3:11)**
13 **My December (4:16)**

Total album length: 42:02 minutes

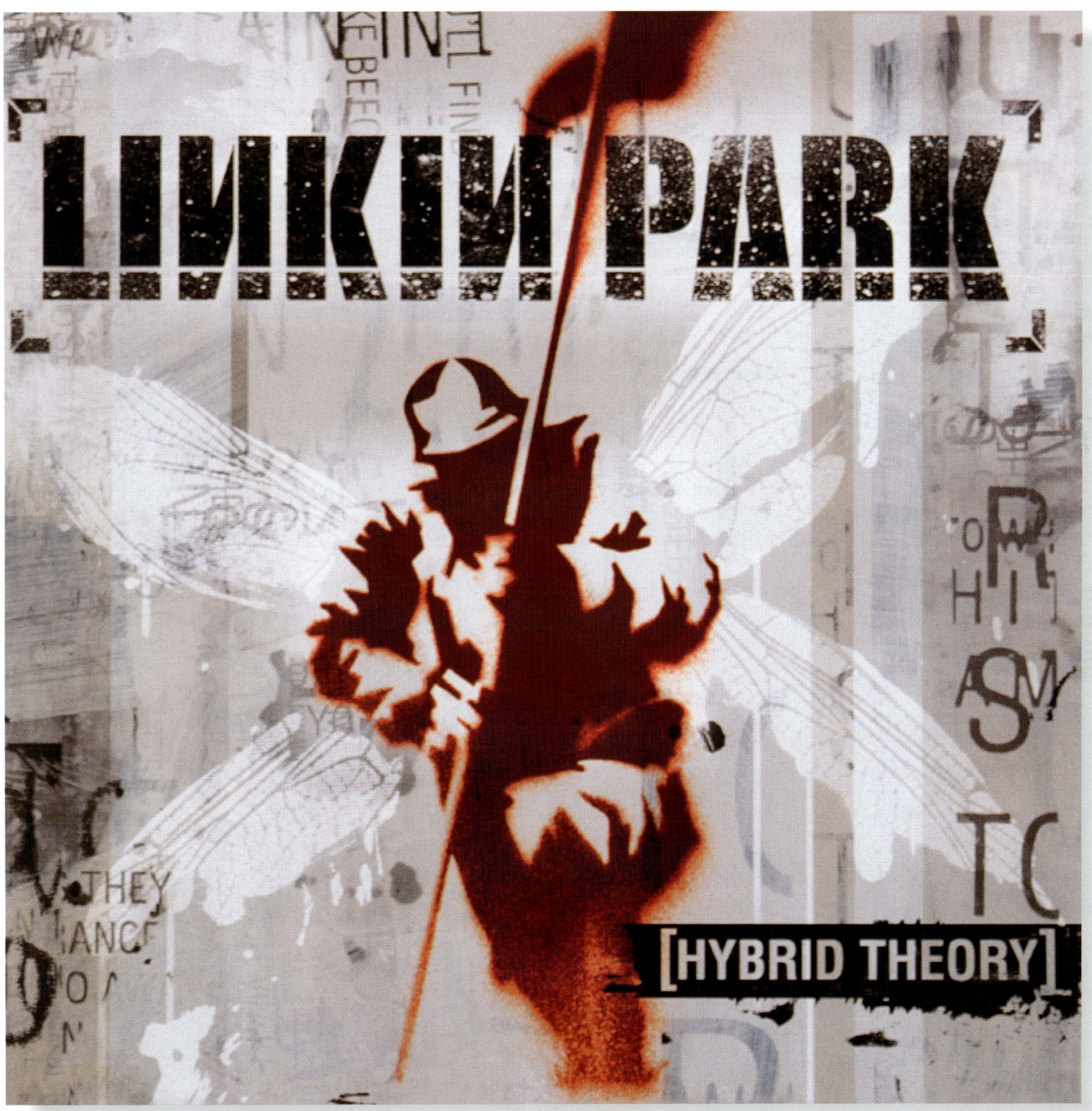
LINKIN PARK
[HYBRID THEORY]

2000s
5

The Eminem Show

| • **Album sales:** 11,800,000 | • **Release date:** May 2002 |

Any Eminem fans fearing a change of artistic direction with the rapper's 2002 album *The Eminem Show* would have nothing to worry about, while those who regarded his material as an affront to all things decent and upstanding would have had a field day.

A concept album of sorts, *The Eminem Show* bites hard from the first track, 'White America', in which Eminem lambasts what he sees as the hypocrisy of politicians and others who claim to hold up the value of the freedom of speech while all the time making every effort possible to prevent him from saying the things he wants to say. 'Cleanin' Out My Closet' is another deeply personal song in which he revisits his turbulent family life, while his anarchic humour – and ironic lack of self deprecation – is clearly in evidence on 'Without Me', where he puts it to the listening public that their lives are empty without Eminem to liven things up. Released as a single, the video for 'Without Me' attracted predictable controversy, thanks to a less-than-flattering swipe at electronic artist Moby, with whom Eminem had had an ongoing feud, and a scene depicting the rapper dressed up as Osama bin Laden dancing to his record in a cave.

Number One singles: UK: Without Me

Grammy awards: Best rap album; Best music video, short form

Label: Aftermath Records

Recorded in: Detroit, USA

Personnel:
Eminem
Nate Dogg (d. 2011)
Dr. Dre
Obie Trice
Hailie Jade
D-12
Dina Rae

Producer:
Dr. Dre

RAP AND POLITICS

Rap has long been used to communicate a political message and Eminem, together with other rap artists such as Public Enemy and NWA, uses his music to blaze home his point. Such language of the street is in many ways simply an extension of the protest/observational songs of the likes of Bob Dylan and Crosby, Stills, Nash & Young, who took up public causes in their music and highlighted serious political and social issues. The intriguing aspect about Eminem is that he manages to annoy both sides of the political spectrum, left and right, liberal and conservative. Which probably means he is hitting the right buttons every time.

▲ **BACK COVER**

1 Curtains Up (Skit) (0:29)
2 White America (5:24)
3 Business (4:11)
4 Cleanin' Out My Closet (4:57)
5 Square Dance (5:23)
6 Kiss (Skit) (1:15)
7 Soldier (3:46)
8 Say Goodbye Hollywood (4:32)
9 Drips (4:45)
10 Without Me (4:50)
11 Paul Rosenberg (Skit) (0:22)
12 Sing For The Moment (5:39)
13 Superman (5:50)
14 Hailie's Song (5:20)
15 Steve Berman (Skit) (0:33)
16 When The Music Stops (4:29)
17 Say What You Say (5:09)
18 'Till I Collapse (4:57)
19 My Dad's Gone Crazy (4:27)
20 Curtains Close (Skit) (1:01)

Total album length: 77 minutes

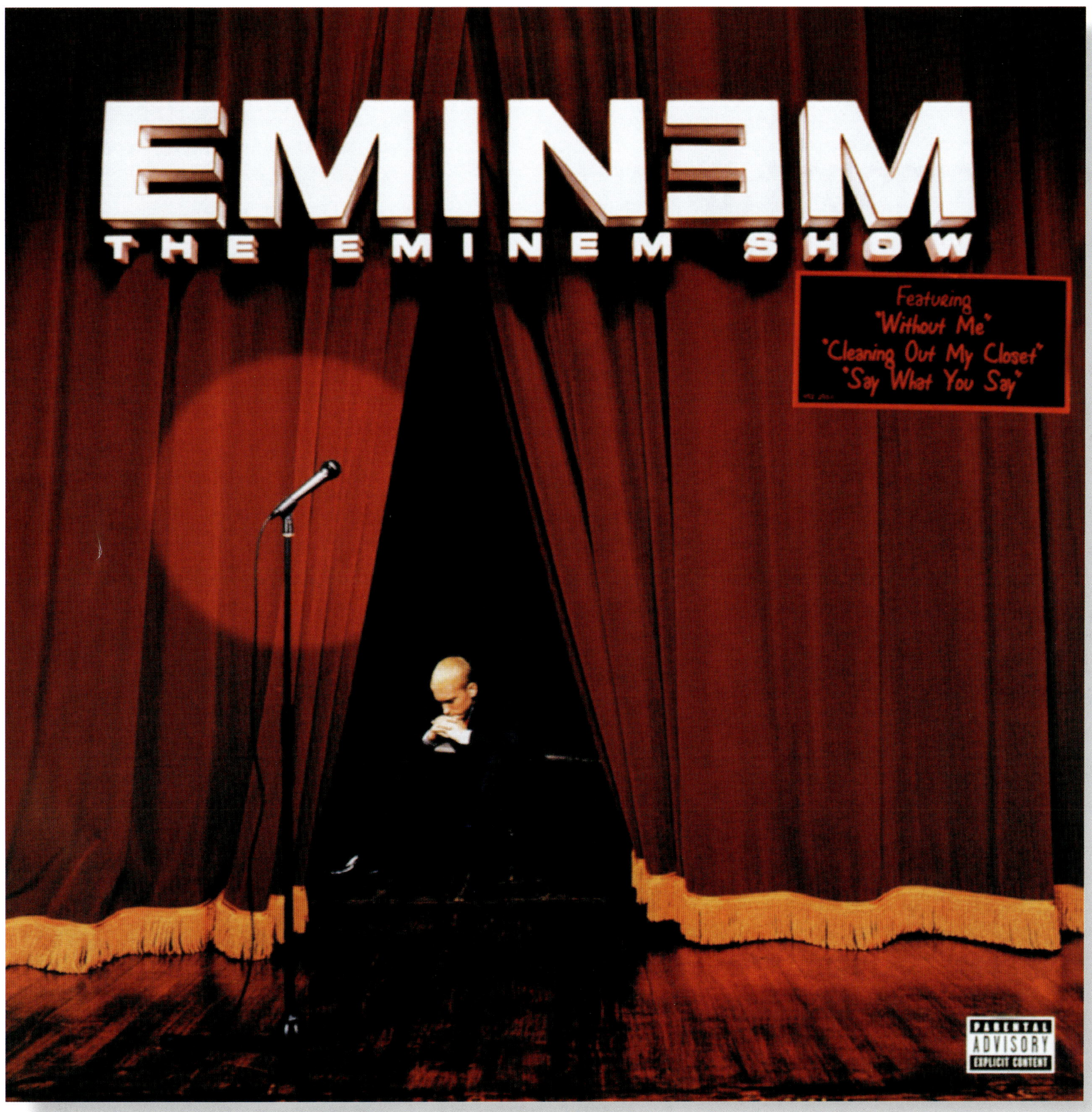
EMINƎM
THE EMINEM SHOW
Featuring
"Without Me"
"Cleaning Out My Closet"
"Say What You Say"
PARENTAL ADVISORY
EXPLICIT CONTENT

2000s
4

No Strings Attached

| • **Album sales:** 13,000,000 | • **Release date:** March 2000 |

By the time *No Strings Attached,* *NSYNC's fifth official album release, was ready to be unleashed onto an unsuspecting public, they were one of the hottest acts on the planet.

Initial sales of the record, particularly in the US, reflected the fevered interest. *No Strings Attached* sold more than a million copies on the first day of its release in March 2000 and nearly two-and-a-half million in its first week alone, spawning hits such as 'Bye Bye Bye' and 'It's Gonna Be You'. The album was supported by a record-breaking arena tour of the US later that year.

The success of the album must have come as a welcome relief to the band, who had gone into the studio to record on the back of a bitter dispute with their management, during which they clawed back, among other things, their name and a significant amount of money. They had also fought to leave their record label, RCA, and move to Jive Records, home to the likes of Britney Spears. Ironic it must have seemed to many when a couple of years later RCA owners Bertelsmann bought Jive as part of an earlier deal agreement.

Number One singles:
US: It's Gonna Be Me

Grammy awards: None

Label: Jive

Recorded in: Stockholm, Sweden; Orlando, Virginia Beach, & New York City, USA

Personnel:
Justin Timberlake
JC Chasez
Chris Kirkpatrick
Lance Bass
Joey Fatone

Producers:
Kristian Lundin
Rami
Teddy Riley
Riprock 'n' Alex G.
Veit Renn
Guy Roche
Gary Carolla
Robin Wiley

CONTINENTAL SUCCESS

While the USA is the acknowledged home of rap and R&B, Europe has long been the starting point for a number of American boy bands, including *NSYNC. In addition to the diverse populations and cultures throughout the continent, the region's long and successful pop heritage also meant that it was more receptive to newer forms of the genre, as managers of boy bands certainly recognized. Countries like Sweden – where the hits for the likes of Britney Spears, the Backstreet Boys and *NSYNC were written and recorded – Germany and the UK all acted as career launchpads for those keen to conquer the world with catchy, polished pop.

▲ **BACK COVER**

1 **Bye Bye Bye (3:20)**
2 **It's Gonna Be Me (3:11)**
3 **Space Cowboy (Yippie-Yi-Yay) (4:21)**
4 **Just Got Paid (4:08)**
5 **It Makes Me Ill (3:26)**
6 **This I Promise You (4:44)**
7 **No Strings Attached (3:50)**
8 **Digital Get Down (4:23)**
9 **Bringin' Da Noise (3:30)**
10 **That's When I'll Stop Loving You (4:50)**
11 **I'll Be Good For You (3:56)**
12 **I Thought She Knew (3:21)**

Total album length: 47 minutes

NSYNC
NO STRINGS ATTACHED

2000s
3

Up!

| • **Album sales:** 13,000,000 | • **Release date:** November 2002 |

How to follow up a multi-million selling album is a question that has been posed to many artists down the years, but few have had the task of chasing a target of almost 23 million sales achieved by their previous record.

Such a 'fate' befell Canadian pop/country singer Shania Twain in late 2002 when she released her fourth studio album, *Up!* Few people, least of all Twain herself, expected the new record to do as well as its illustrious predecessor, *Come On Over,* which after a sluggish start has at the time of writing sold a staggering 35 million copies worldwide – boosted by the release of an international version two years after its original release in 1997. Yet *Up!* has still managed to notch up 13 million sales since its release in November 2002.

In an attempt to satisfy both her pop fans and her country critics, *Up!* came with two discs: a red one with the songs in a pop style, a blue one with the same tunes sung in a more traditional country style.

The album has its fair share of pop standards, such as 'I'm Gonna Getcha Good!', but Twain also dabbles with political themes on 'Ka-Ching!' – about the 'evils' of consumerism – and on 'What A Way To Wanna Be!', on which Twain decries the diet and fashion industries for making women feel inadequate about the way they look and their weight.

Number One singles: None

Grammy awards: None

Label: Mercury Records

Recorded in: Dublin, Ireland; Milan, Italy; Nassau, The Bahamas

Personnel:
Shania Twain
RJ Lange
Brian Masterson
Bob Bullock
Mike Shipley

Producer:
Robert John 'Mutt' Lange

COUNTRY CROSSOVERS

Prior to Shania Twain's career taking off in the late 1990s, country music and pop were poor bedfellows. True, there were crossover hits in the Seventies by the likes of Dolly Parton – 'Jolene' – and Tammy Wynette – 'Stand By Your Man' and 'D.I.V.O.R.C.E.' – but these were rare. Twain's arrival changed all that, as she served up a musical style that blended the sassiness of country with the beat and melodic feel of pop. While this strategy certainly has its critics, many acknowledge that not following directly in the footsteps of Parton and Wynette has enabled Twain to connect with an audience previously averse to country music, thereby gaining potential exposure for a raft of other country artists.

▲ **BACK COVER**

1 **Up!** (2:53)
2 **I'm Gonna Getcha Good!** (4:29)
3 **She's Not Just A Pretty Face** (3:49)
4 **Juanita** (3:50)
5 **Forever And For Always** (4:43)
6 **Ain't No Particular Way** (4:24)
7 **It Only Hurts When I'm Breathing** (3:19)
8 **Nah!** (4:08)
9 **(Wanna Get To Know You) That Good!** (4:33)
10 **C'est La Vie** (3:42)
11 **I'm Jealous** (4:05)
12 **Ka-Ching!** (3:20)
13 **Thank You Baby! (For Makin' Someday Come So Soon)** (4:00)
14 **Waiter! Bring Me Water!** (3:19)
15 **What A Way To Wanna Be!** (3:36)
16 **I Ain't Goin' Down** (3:57)
17 **I'm Not In The Mood (To Say No)!** (3:25)
18 **In My Car (I'll Be The Driver)** (3:16)
19 **When You Kiss Me** (4:08)

Total album length: 73 minutes

Shania Twain
ÜP!

2000s
2

The Marshall Mathers LP

| • **Album sales:** 13,300,000 | • **Release date:** May 2000 |

In a country where rap music was previously the preserve of black performers, Eminem bucked racial stereotypes and quickly showed there was more to him than simply a re-working of Caucasian rap in the style of predecessors such as Vanilla Ice.

Mentored by eminent rap producer Dr. Dre, Eminem's debut album is a groundbreaker: he settles domestic scores in visceral fashion, with targets including his on/off wife Kim, and his mother – notably on 'Kill You' – while his contempt for those people who either wouldn't give him airtime or who just wrote him off without a hearing is eloquently channelled on 'The Way I Am'. Several songs from the album went on to be hit singles on both sides of the Atlantic.

It is a highly personal record and not without moments of dark insight, as on 'Stan' – which sampled a song by UK singer Dido and rocketed her to stardom in the process – which told an unnerving tale about an obsessive Eminem fan, or on 'Marshall Mathers,' where he ironically questions his new-found popularity when set against earlier rejection by the masses and the record industry.

The content of the album prompted accusations of misogyny and homophobia, and while Eminem refuted such claims, many of his songs are imbued with such vitriol that it makes such accusations easy to understand, if not necessarily agree with.

Number One singles: UK: The Real Slim Shady; Stan

Grammy awards: Best rap solo performance; Best rap album

Label: Interscope Records

Recorded in: Detroit, USA

Personnel:
Eminem
Snoop Dogg
Xzibit
Nate Dogg (d. 2011)
Sticky Fingaz
Dido

Producers:
Dr. Dre
Eminem
Jeff Bass

WHITE RAPPERS

Looking back to rap's emergence as a musical force, the history of white rappers is a fairly limited one and, until Eminem came along, one largely devoid of any credibility. It is hard to believe today that Vanilla Ice was taken seriously by music fans some 25 years ago, but for many he was as hip as it was possible to get. Eminem's success illustrates that race is still an issue for music fans around the world and particularly in the United States. No doubt talented, many observers have suggested that his material would not have had the level of success it has had at home and abroad if he had been a black performer.

▲ **BACK COVER**

1 **Public Service Announcement (0:25)**
2 **Kill You (4:24)**
3 **Stan (6:43)**
4 **Paul (Skit) (0:10)**
5 **Who Knew (3:47)**
6 **Steve Berman (0:53)**
7 **The Way I Am (4:44)**
8 **Real Slim Shady (4:50)**
9 **Remember Me? (3:38)**
10 **I'm Back (5:10)**
11 **Marshall Mathers (5:20)**
12 **Ken Kaniff (Skit) (1:01)**
13 **Drug Ballad (5:00)**
14 **Amityville (4:14)**
15 **B**** Please II (4:48)**
16 **Kim (6:17)**
17 **Under The Influence (5:22)**
18 **Criminal (5:19)**

Total album length: 72 minutes

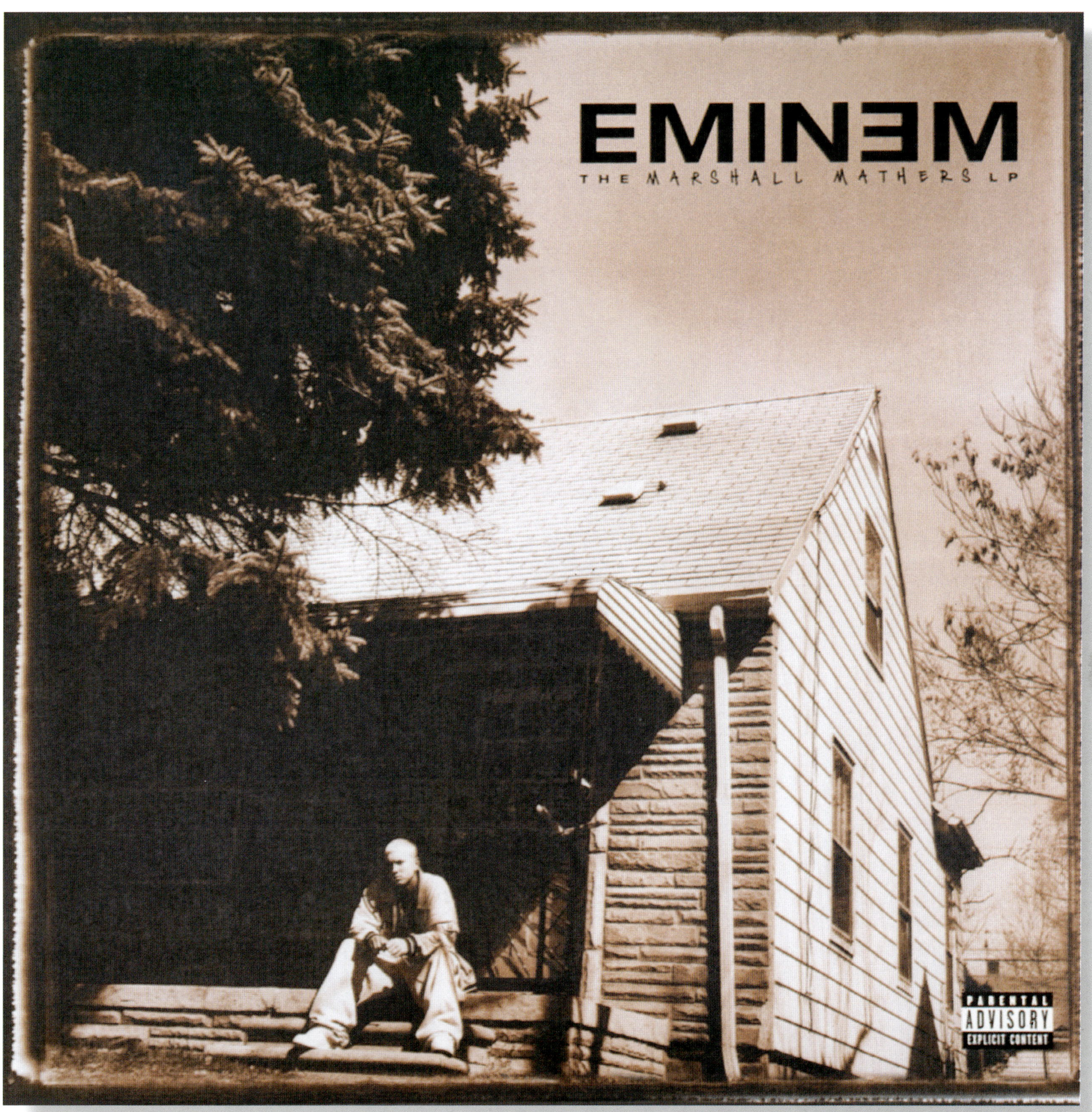
EMINEM
THE MARSHALL MATHERS LP
PARENTAL
ADVISORY
EXPLICIT CONTENT

2000s
1

Come Away With Me

| • **Album sales:** 13,400,000 | • **Release date:** February 2002 |

Norah Jones' debut album was a classic example of the slow-burner. Released to considerable critical acclaim, commercial success was slow in coming, but come it did, in spectacular fashion. Produced in part by legendary deskman Arif Mardin – who worked with the likes of Aretha Franklin, Willie Nelson and Roberta Flack – it showcased perfectly Jones' vocal style: at once husky, coy and silky, yet hugely melodic throughout.

Her approach throughout the record is overtly jazz-like – she covers Hoagy Carmichael's 'The Nearness Of You' – yet there is much more to her performance than just jazz. She plays the blues, as on her rendition of JD Loudermilk's 'Turn Me On', where she sounds like a smooth Janis Joplin, while her version of Hank Williams' classic 'Cold Cold Heart' suffuses her own style with the sensibilities of Williams' lilting country sound.

The self-penned title track is a heart-rending ballad, and 'Nightingale', another Jones composition, is the perfect example of her ability to meld jazz, country music and Americana; the finessed duelling of Jones' piano and Adam Levy's guitar is breathtakingly simple yet central to the song's power.

Number One singles: None

Grammy awards: Album of the year; Record of the Year; Song of the year; Best female pop vocal performance; Best pop vocal album; Producer of the year

Label: Blue Note Records

Recorded in: New York City and Shokan, USA

Personnel:
Norah Jones
Lee Alexander
Brian Blade
Kevin Breit
Rob Burger
Bill Frisell
Jesse Harris
Dan Rieser
Adam Rogers
Jenny Scheinman

Producers:
Arif Mardin (d. 2006)
Craig Street
Jay Newland

FEMALE SINGER/SONGWRITERS

Norah Jones' arrival on the music scene marked her out as the latest in a distinguished line of female singer-songwriters whose music has connected with the hearts of millions. Women have achieved commercial success by picking up a guitar or sitting at a piano and singing self-penned material – whether it be protest songs or poignant love ballads – for the past 40 years or so. From the emergence of adult-oriented rock in the 1960s and singers such as Joan Baez, Joni Mitchell and Carole King, through to country artists such as Emmylou Harris and Bonnie Raitt, right up to more contemporary proponents of the female singer-songwriter genre: Tori Amos, Suzanne Vega and Alanis Morrisette. Jones' commercial and critical success simply confirmed that the listening public still had time for this very personal style of music.

▲ **BACK COVER**

1 **Don't Know Why (3:06)**
2 **Seven Years (2:25)**
3 **Cold Cold Heart (3:38)**
4 **Feelin' The Same Way (2:57)**
5 **Come Away With Me (3:18)**
6 **Shoot The Moon (3:56)**
7 **Turn Me On (2:34)**
8 **Lonestar (3:06)**
9 **I've Got To See You Again (4:13)**
10 **Painter Song (2:42)**
11 **One Flight Down (3:05)**
12 **Nightingale (4:12)**
13 **The Long Day Is Over (2:44)**
14 **The Nearness Of You (3:07)**

Total album length: 45 minutes

Norah Jones
come away with me

ORIGINAL SONGS BY KRISTEN ANDERSON-LOPEZ AND ROBERT LOPEZ
ORIGINAL SCORE BY CHRISTOPHE BECK
Disney
FROZEN

RECOVER

ADELE 21

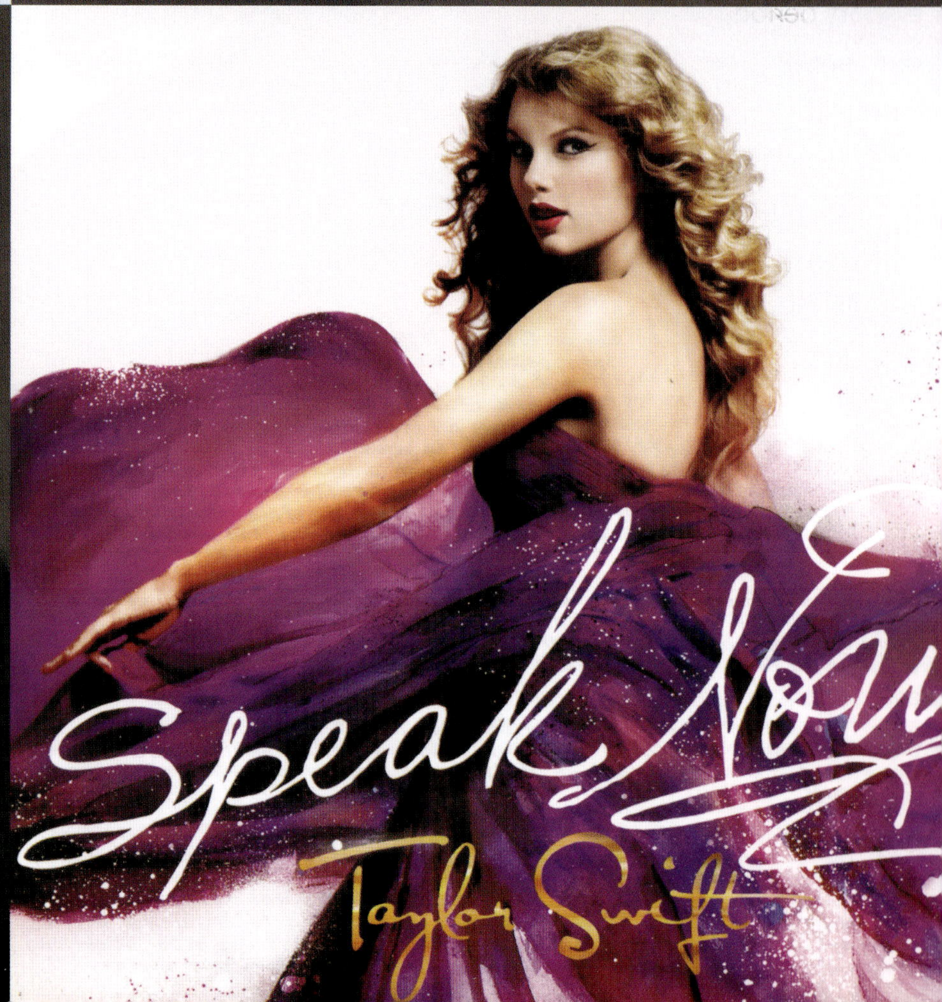
Speak Now
Taylor Swift

The Best-Selling Albums of the 2010s

In the second decade of the twenty-first century, the album itself has been under attack. As if declining sales due to illegal downloading wasn't challenging enough for the format, some commentators and artists were calling time on the album as a thing in itself. Thanks to the rise of streaming services like Spotify, music listening now was about playlists; for artists, their releases were 'projects' and 'campaigns'. For a short period at the turn of the decade some acts toyed with different approaches: UK indie band Ash, bored of the tour–album–tour sequence, released a single every fortnight for a year; Blur frontman Damon Albarn branched out into operas and collaborative field recordings.

However, for all the bold talk and acknowledgement that people do consume music differently, no one has come up with a better or more satisfying way to deliver a bunch of new tracks than an album. In December 2013, the most highly regarded pop artist of the decade, Beyoncé, didn't release a series of videos – she could have done, as she'd made a separate film for each song – she released an album. Attempting to rescue a sense of event for the occasion of her fifth solo album, the former Destiny's Child frontwoman released it without any prior announcement or publicity.

In truth, the decline of the album has been hugely exaggerated. The reality is that more albums were made in the 2010s than ever before. Without the limitations of manufacturing, anyone could release an album and, if they strayed from the record company business model, record them with complete creative freedom – something never enjoyed by artists from other eras. In the 2010s, the biggest barrier to someone making themselves heard is sheer volume of competitors – which does not signal an industry in decline.

For all the debate, the thing that halted all talk of the album's demise was the staggering sales of Adele's *21*, which would have been a phenomenon in any decade. Music fans no longer needed to purchase an album to enjoy it, but sometimes people feel they have to own the physical object. The other important factor in *21*'s success was that it appealed to an older age group, a demographic still loyal to buying physical music. Acknowledging this, the music industry promoted artists who previously might have been regarded as too mature, such as British talent-show discovery Susan Boyle, or too middle of the road to be worth developing – Michael Bublé is one of many artists who previous generations would have dismissed as a 'housewives' choice'.

On a lower scale in terms of sales but similarly bucking the trend, the early 2010s also saw a resurgence of sales and interest in a format digital music had supposedly destroyed forever – vinyl. In 2014, Jack White sold 60,000 copies of his album *Lazeretto* on vinyl, the highest figures for 20 years.

Playlists may satisfy the fast-food needs of some, but for people who still love music the message was clear – the album lives on.

2010s

5

Speak Now

| • **Album sales:** 4,500,000 | • **Release date:** October 2010 |

In 2009 financial magazine *Forbes* ranked Taylor Swift as the 69th most powerful celebrity with earnings of US$18 million. A year later and she had leapt to 12th, while her earnings had swollen to US$45 million. In January of 2010, Nielsen Soundscan listed her as the most successful country artist in history, with over 33 million digital tracks sold. All this was before the release of *Speak Now* that October. Swift's third album sold an incredible one million copies in America in the first week, clocking up over five million worldwide sales over the following few months.

Written while on tour and without any co-writers – a unique situation in mainstream pop – *Speak Now* shifts Swift slightly apart from her country roots and further into the pop field, but lyrically it's also a lot more grown-up than her previous two albums. Ridiculously catchy and enjoyable throughout (Swift's recipe is not a complicated one), the stand-outs are story songs 'Mine' – an immediate echo to the star-crossed lovers of her breakthrough single 'Love Story' – and 'Speak Now', about breaking up a wedding, both of which could be storylines to Hollywood teen movies. On the wistful 'Innocent' she even addresses Kanye West's infamous interruption of her MTV Award in 2009 by empathizing that he was "32 and still growing up". Nothing can stop her – not even Kanye.

Number One singles: None

Grammy awards: None

Label: Big Machine Records

Recorded in: Nashville, USA

Personnel:
Taylor Swift
Nathan Chapman
Tommy Sims
Bryan Sutton
Nick Buda
Paul Buckmaster

Producers:
Nathan Chapman
Taylor Swift

THE EX LIST

Date Taylor Swift and chances are that someday you'll find yourself featuring in one of her songs. "If you listen to my albums, it's like reading my diary," she told the *New York Times*, revealing that she uses people's real names in her songs. "There was this guy who opened a couple of shows for me on tour and I talked to him a couple of times, but he never knew that I liked him. So I wrote this song called 'Hey Stephen', and when my album came out, I sent him a text message: 'Hey, Track 5'."

▲ **BACK COVER**

1 Mine (3:51)
2 Sparks Fly (4:21)
3 Back To December (4:54)
4 Speak Now (4:02)
5 Dear John (6:44)
6 Mean (3:58)
7 The Story of Us (4:27)
8 Never Grow Up (4:50)
9 Enchanted (5:52)
10 Better Than Revenge (3:37)
11 Innocent (5:02)
12 Haunted (4:02)
13 Last Kiss (6:07)
14 Long Live (5:17)

Total album length: 67 minutes

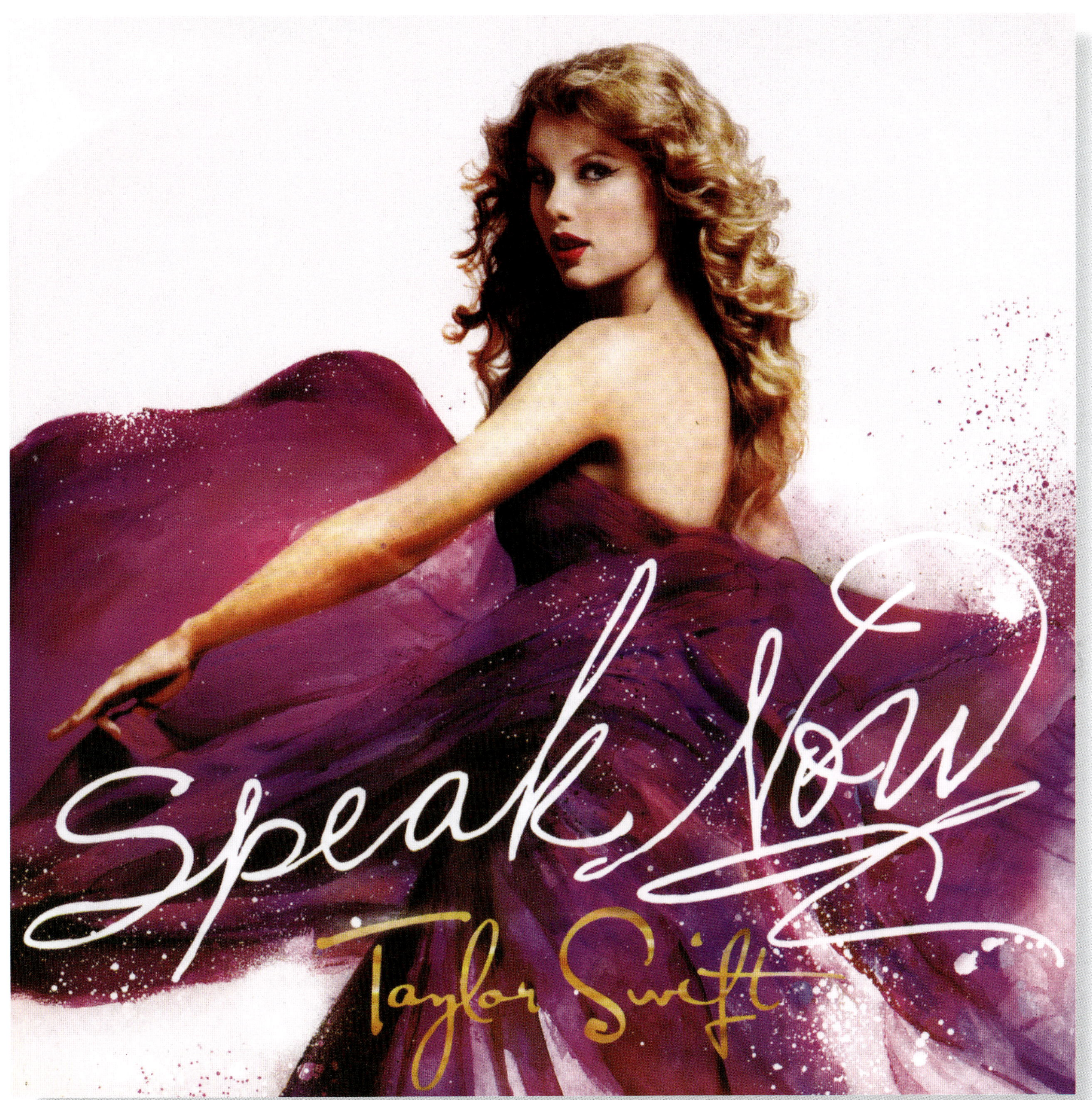

Speak Now
Taylor Swift

2010s
4

Frozen (Soundtrack)

| • **Album sales:** 4,900,000 | • **Release date:** November 2013 |

Loosely based on Hans Christian Andersen's 'The Snow Queen', Disney's animated movie *Frozen* told the story of a fearless princess's epic journey to rescue her sister. While the animated film proved an immediate hit, racking up over US$1 billion in box office takings, the soundtrack was slower to lift off. However, once it made the top of the Billboard charts in January 2014 it stayed there for 13 weeks.

Unlike other Disney films, the *Frozen* soundtrack took its inspiration from classic storytelling musicals and merged them with the current trend for feel-good pop ballads as made popular by the hit TV show *Glee*. Both of *Frozen*'s key vocalists, Idina Menzel and Jonathan Groff, were members of rival choir Vocal Adrenaline in the Fox series.

Although the approach was classic and winningly designed to appeal to both parents and pre-teens, *Frozen*'s songs were also funnier and sharper than similar musicals. The outrageously catchy 'For The First Time In Forever' included the self-deprecating line 'Don't know if I'm elated or gassy'. You'd never catch Belle from *Beauty And The Beast* being so sassy.

For all its wit, it was the wholesomeness of *Frozen* that really helped it succeed. In an era when even the most mainstream of pop princesses toyed with violent sexual imagery, *Frozen* offered a pure alternative that was as easy for parents to embrace as it was for their children to become obsessed with.

Number One singles: None

Grammy awards: Best compilation soundtrack for visual media; Best song written for visual media

Label: Walt Disney

Recorded in: Capitol Studios, Los Angeles, USA

Personnel:
Idina Menzel
Jonathan Groff
Kristen Bell
Christophe Beck

Producers:
Kristen Anderson-Lopez
Robert Lopez
Christophe Beck
Chris Montan
Tom MacDougall

YOUTUBE POWER

Even if you have never seen the movie, you will probably be familiar with at least one of *Frozen*'s songs. The official video for 'Let It Go' has been viewed over 400 million times on YouTube, but more impressive still is the fact that fans have posted over 30,000 different versions of the song. Alongside karaoke videos by everyone from toddlers to grandfathers, there are also countless parodies, including one rewritten version of the song by a father who has endured the track one too many times and is at breaking point. It ends with the kicker line, 'The Olaf song is better anyway'.

▲ **BACK COVER**

1 Frozen Heart (Cast (Frozen)) (1:45)
2 Do You Want To Build A Snowman? (Kristen Bell, Agatha LeeMonn and Katie Lopez) (3:27)
3 For The First Time In Forever (Kristen Bell and Idina Menzel) (3:45)
4 Love Is An Open Door (Kristen Bell and Santino Fontana) (2:07)
5 Let It Go (Idina Menzel) (3:44)
6 Reindeer(s) Are Better Than People (Jonathan Groff) (0:50)
7 In Summer (Josh Gad) (1:54)
8 For The First Time In Forever (Reprise) (Kristen Bell and Idina Menzel) (2:30)
9 Fixer Upper (Cast – Frozen and Maia Wilson) (3:02)
10 Let It Go (Demi Lovato) (3:47)
11 Vuelie (feat. Cantus) (Christophe Beck) (1:36)
12 Elsa and Anna (Christophe Beck) (2:43)
13 The Trolls (Christophe Beck) (1:48)
14 Coronation Day (Christophe Beck) (1:14)
15 Heimr Arnadalr (Christophe Beck) (1:25)
16 Winter's Waltz (Christophe Beck) (1:00)
17 Sorcery (Christophe Beck) (3:17)
18 Royal Pursuit (Christophe Beck) (1:02)
19 Onward and Upward (Christophe Beck) (1:54)
20 Wolves (Christophe Beck) (1:44)
21 The North Mountain (Christophe Beck) (1:34)
22 We Were So Close (Christophe Beck) (1:53)
23 Marshmallow Attack! (Christophe Beck) (1:43)
24 Conceal, Don't Feel (Christophe Beck) (1:07)
25 Only An Act of True Love (Christophe Beck) (1:07)
26 Summit Siege (Christophe Beck) (2:32)
27 Return to Arendelle (Christophe Beck) (1:38)
28 Treason (Christophe Beck) (1:36)
29 Some People Are Worth Melting For (Christophe Beck) (2:06)
30 Whiteout (Christophe Beck) (4:17)
31 The Great Thaw (Vuelie Reprise) (Christophe Beck and Frode Fjellheim) (2:29)
32 Epilogue (Christophe Beck) (3:04)

Total album length: 70 minutes

ORIGINAL SONGS BY KRISTEN ANDERSON-LOPEZ AND ROBERT LOPEZ
ORIGINAL SCORE BY CHRISTOPHE BECK
DISNEY
FROZEN

2010s
3

Recovery

| • **Album sales:** 5,400,000 | • **Release date:** June 2010 |

His 2009 comeback album *Relapse* was originally going to be followed by a sequel tackling similar themes, but during the recording of *Relapse 2* Eminem had a rethink, ditched his Slim Shady persona and returned as plain old Eminem. Exposing his weaknesses and apologising for past failures, *Recovery* was Eminem's attempt to find his hunger again. As he puts it on the album's confessional second track, 'Talkin' 2 Myself': "It's different, them last two albums don't count/*Encore* I was on drugs, *Relapse* I was flushing them out."

Although *Recovery* lacks the anarchic humour and comic skits that first made him a star, Eminem's redemption makes for compelling listening, with many tracks up there with the best of his career – defiant heavy metal pounder 'Won't Back Down' is the perfect companion to 'Lose Yourself'; the Rihanna duet 'Love The Way You Lie' his most melodic track since 'Stan'. The album does, though, find Eminem returning to the fast-spitting style of his past, with guest rapper Lil Wayne struggling to keep up on 'No Love'.

CD sales didn't match the astonishing figures of his early albums, but *Recovery* was still the best-selling album of 2010 in the US, where it also holds the title of the most downloaded album of all time.

Number One singles:
US: Not Afraid; Love The Way You Lie

Grammy awards:
Best rap solo performance; Best rap album

Label: Aftermath Records

Recorded in:
Various locations

Personnel:
Eminem
Rihanna
Lil Wayne
P!nk
Kobe
And other artists

Producers:
Alex da Kid
Boi-1da
Dr. Dre
Emile Haynie
Eminem
DJ Khalil
Jim Jonsin
Just Blaze
Mr. Porter
Supa Dups

SEQUEL ALBUMS

Eminem had a change of mind about calling his seventh album *Relapse 2* – a wise decision, as nearly every sequel album, from Meat Loaf's *Bat Out Of Hell II* (and *III*) to Neil Young's *Harvest Moon*, has been overshadowed by the original. The phenomenon is particularly common in rap, where Jay-Z leads the way with his trilogy of Blueprint albums (which also includes a re-cut version of the second album called *The Blueprint 2.1*). Eminem does things differently and all his albums come in twins: *The Eminem Show* and *Encore*, *The Slim Shady LP* and *The Marshall Mathers LP*, and now *Relapse* and *Recovery*. Calling the album *Relapse 2* would have messed with the sequence.

▲ **BACK COVER**

1 Cold Wind Blows (5:04)
2 Talkin' 2 Myself (5:00)
3 On Fire (3:34)
4 Won't Back Down (4:26)
5 W.T.P. (3:58)
6 Going Through Changes (4:59)
7 Not Afraid (4:08)
8 Seduction (4:35)
9 No Love (5:25)
10 Space Bound (4:39)
11 Cinderella Man (4:39)
12 25 To Life (4:02)
13 So Bad (5:25)
14 Almost Famous (4:53)
15 Love The Way You Lie (4:23)
16 You're Never Over (5:06)
17 Untitled (hidden track) (3:14)

Total album length: 77 minutes

2000s

2010s

2

Christmas

| • **Album sales:** 6,200,000 | • **Release date:** October 2011 |

Few artists are more perfectly suited to making a Christmas album than Michael Bublé. With his smooth vocals and easy-going charm, he slipped easily into the space at the back of the sleigh that had been vacant since Elvis, Nat 'King' Cole, Bing Crosby, Frank Sinatra and the golden era of crooners set the tone for the perfect holiday soundtrack in the 1950s. The suave Canadian could have taken the easy road and merely performed a dozen straight festive favourites, accompanied by lush strings and the occasional angelic choir, but there is a surprising amount of risky experimentation on *Christmas* – as well as three of his own compositions, respectfully tucked away towards the end of the CD.

Taking on Mariah Carey's 'All I Want For Christmas Is You', he slows down the Motown tempo and fools around with auto-tune; 'White Christmas' is given a doo-wop twist and some added country glitter from Shania Twain; 'Jingle Bells' casts The Puppini Sisters as latter-day successors to The Andrews Sisters. None of the japery is needed, of course, and these three tracks aside, *Christmas* could have been recorded in 1958, with all the lush trimmings you'd expect. The album was an immediate hit: released in October and backed by two TV specials (one in the US, another in the UK), it served as the reliable soundtrack to millions of family gatherings.

Number One singles:
None

Grammy awards:
None

Label: 143, Reprise

Recorded in: Capitol Studios, Los Angeles, USA

Personnel:
Michael Bublé
David Foster
Graham Dechter
The Puppini Sisters
Greg Fields
Alan Pasqua
Craig Polasko
Chuck Berghofer
Alan Chang
Shania Twain
Thalia

Producers:
David Foster
Bob Rock
Humberto Gatica

MERRY BEST

Christmas albums seem such a banker of an idea that it's a puzzle why more artists don't make them. The truth is they do, we just don't notice most of them. Michael Bublé's smooth crooning was a perfect fit, but he has a long way to go to equal pop's most famous Christmas album. Released in 1957, *Elvis' Christmas Album* has sold 16 million copies in the US alone, making it the biggest-selling Christmas album of all time.

▲ **BACK COVER**

1. **It's Beginning To Look A Lot Like Christmas (3:27)**
2. **Santa Claus Is Coming To Town (2:52)**
3. **Jingle Bells (featuring the Puppini Sisters) (2:41)**
4. **White Christmas (with Shania Twain) (3:37)**
5. **All I Want For Christmas Is You (2:52)**
6. **Holly Jolly Christmas (2:01)**
7. **Santa Baby (3:53)**
8. **Have Yourself A Merry Little Christmas (3:52)**
9. **Christmas (Baby Please Come Home) (3:09)**
10. **Silent Night (3:49)**
11. **Blue Christmas (3:43)**
12. **Cold December Night (3:18)**
13. **I'll Be Home For Christmas (4:27)**
14. **Ave Maria (4:02)**
15. **Mis Deseos/Feliz Navidad (with Thalia) (4:25)**
16. **Michael's Christmas Greeting (0:05)**

Total album length: 51 minutes

michael
bublé
christmas

2010s
1

21

| • **Album sales:** 14,800,000 | • **Release date:** January 2011 |

Second albums are supposed to be tougher. All your years of toil and setbacks, all the songs you've been saving and honing, they all go in to the debut. The second album is where you have to prove you're in it for the long haul.

Following up the popular *19* album initially proved troublesome for London singer-songwriter Adele Adkins. Having made a down-tempo debut majoring in ballads, she initially wanted to record a more upbeat set of songs, but unhappy with these first sessions, she ditched the material. Then, after traumatically ending a long-term relationship, she returned to the studio and poured her heart out into her songwriting. The results were staggering.

Although the album was already Number One around the world, one performance sealed *21*'s position as a classic. On a February evening in 2011 at the Brit Awards at London's O2 Arena, Adele sang the album's emotive closing track 'Someone Like You' with just piano accompaniment. It was an entrancing performance that, thanks to millions of shares on YouTube, rocketed her to even greater stardom.

Fortunately the album's other ten tracks – a stylishly produced mix of pop, jazz and soul in the tradition of Dusty Springfield and Carole King – were the equal of its killer closer. *21* spawned five global radio hits, and in an era when people were supposedly not buying records anymore, became one of the biggest-selling releases of all time, surpassing the likes of The Beatles' *Abbey Road*.

Number One singles: UK and US – Someone Like You; US – Rolling In The Deep, Set Fire To The Rain

Grammy awards: 2012: Album of the year; Best pop vocal; Record of the year; Song of the year; Short form music video; Best pop solo performance; 2013: Best pop solo performance

Label: XL

Recorded in: London, UK; Los Angeles & Denver, USA

Personnel:
Adele Adkins
And various artists

Producers:
Paul Epworth
Rick Rubin
Fraser T Smith
Ryan Tedder
Dan Wilson
Adele
Jim Abbiss

THE BRITS ARE COMING

Inspired by the film *Fame* about New York's High School of Performing Arts, and funded initially by the British music industry, the BRIT School in South London has an astonishing array of stars amongst its alumni. Adele famously studied here, but so, too, did Amy Winehouse, Ella Eyre, Leona Lewis and Jessie J – the latter two were both classmates of Adele's. In an era where middle-class people noticeably dominate popular British culture, the school is one of very few places offering opportunities to people from more modest backgrounds to take their first steps in the arts.

▲ **BACK COVER**

1 **Rolling In The Deep (3:48)**
2 **Rumour Has It (3:43)**
3 **Turning Tables (4:10)**
4 **Don't You Remember (4:03)**
5 **Set Fire To The Rain (4:02)**
6 **He Won't Go (4:38)**
7 **Take It All (3:48)**
8 **I'll Be Waiting (4:01)**
9 **One And Only (5:48)**
10 **Lovesong (5:16)**
11 **Someone Like You (4:45)**

Total album length: 48 minutes

ADELE 21

Statistics

Grammy Awards for Best Album, 1958–2014

1958	*The Music From Peter Gunn*	Henry Mancini
1959	*Come Dance With Me*	Frank Sinatra
1960	*Button Down Mind*	Bob Newhart
1961	*Judy at Carnegie Hall*	Judy Garland
1962	*The First Family*	First Family
1963	*The Barbra Streisand Album*	Barbra Streisand
1964	*Getz/Gilberto*	Stan Getz, Astrud Gilberto
1965	*September of My Years*	Frank Sinatra
1966	*A Man and His Music*	Frank Sinatra
1967	*Sgt. Pepper's Lonely Hearts Club Band*	The Beatles
1968	*By the Time I Get to Phoenix*	Glen Campbell
1969	*Blood, Sweat and Tears*	Blood, Sweat & Tears
1970	*Bridge Over Troubled Water*	Simon & Garfunkel
1971	*Tapestry*	Carole King
1972	*The Concert for Bangladesh*	George Harrison and Friends
1973	*Innervisions*	Stevie Wonder
1974	*Fulfillingness' First Finale*	Stevie Wonder
1975	*Still Crazy After All These Years*	Paul Simon
1976	*Songs in the Key of Life*	Stevie Wonder
1977	*Rumours*	Fleetwood Mac
1978	*Saturday Night Fever (soundtrack)*	Bee Gees
1979	*52nd Street*	Billy Joel
1980	*Christopher Cross*	Christopher Cross
1981	*Double Fantasy*	John Lennon
1982	*Toto IV*	Toto
1983	*Thriller*	Michael Jackson
1984	*Can't Slow Down*	Lionel Richie
1985	*No Jacket Required*	Phil Collins
1986	*Graceland*	Paul Simon
1987	*The Joshua Tree*	U2
1988	*Faith*	George Michael
1989	*Nick of Time*	Bonnie Raitt
1990	*Back on the Block*	Quincy Jones
1991	*Unforgettable*	Natalie Cole
1992	*Unplugged*	Eric Clapton
1993	*The Bodyguard (soundtrack)*	Whitney Houston
1994	*MTV Unplugged*	Tony Bennett
1995	*Jagged Little Pill*	Alanis Morissette
1996	*Falling Into You*	Celine Dion
1997	*Time Out of Mind*	Bob Dylan
1998	*The Miseducation of Lauryn Hill*	Lauryn Hill
1999	*Supernatural*	Santana
2000	*Two Against Nature*	Steely Dan
2001	*O Brother Where Art Thou? (soundtrack)*	Various Artists
2002	*Come Away With Me*	Norah Jones
2003	*Speakerboxxx/The Love Below*	OutKast
2004	*Genius Loves Company*	Ray Charles & Various Artists
2005	*How to Dismantle An Atomic Bomb*	U2
2006	*Taking the Long Way*	Dixie Chicks
2007	*River: The Joni Letters*	Herbie Hancock
2008	*Raising Sand*	Alison Krauss & Robert Plant
2009	*Fearless*	Taylor Swift
2010	*The Suburbs*	Arcade Fire
2011	*21*	Adele
2012	*Babel*	Mumford & Sons
2013	*Random Access Memories*	Daft Punk
2014	*Morning Phase*	Beck

Featured Albums with Multiple Number One singles (US and UK)

Original Soundtrack	*Saturday Night Fever*	7
Michael Jackson	*Bad*	5
Whitney Houston	*Whitney*	4
George Michael	*Faith*	4
Whitney Houston	*Whitney Houston*	3
The Beatles	*Help!*	2
The Beatles	*A Hard Day's Night*	2
The Beatles	*Magical Mystery Tour*	2
Michael Jackson	*Off the Wall*	2
Original Soundtrack	*Grease*	2
Stevie Wonder	*Songs in the Key of Life*	2
Carole King	*Tapestry*	2
Eagles	*Hotel California*	2
Prince	*Purple Rain*	2
Phil Collins	*No Jacket Required*	2
Michael Jackson	*Thriller*	2
Boyz II Men	*II*	2
Britney Spears	*…Baby One More Time*	2
Eminem	*The Marshall Mathers LP*	2

Top 20 All-Time Bestselling Film Soundtracks

1.	Whitney Houston	*The Bodyguard*	19,400,000
2.	Bee Gees (and others)	*Saturday Night Fever*	15,450,000
3.	Prince	*Purple Rain*	13,600,000
4.	Original Soundtrack	*Dirty Dancing*	13,550,000
5.	Original Soundtrack	*Forrest Gump*	12,250,000
6.	Original Soundtrack	*Titanic*	12,000,000
7.	Original Soundtrack	*Top Gun*	10,300,000
8.	Original Soundtrack	*Lion King*	10,300,000
9.	Original Soundtrack	*Grease*	9,400,000
10.	Original Soundtrack	*Footloose*	9,100,000
11.	Original Soundtrack	*O Brother, Where Art Thou?*	7,650,000
12.	Original Soundtrack	*Waiting to Exhale*	7,000,000
13.	The Beatles	*Magical Mystery Tour*	6,650,000
14.	Soundtrack	*Flashdance*	6,100,000
15.	Eminem (and others)	*8 Mile*	5,400,000
16.	Original Soundtrack	*Frozen*	4,900,000
17.	The Beatles	*A Hard Day's Night*	4,550,000
18.	LeAnn Rimes	*Coyote Ugly*	4,300,000
19.	Barbra Streisand	*A Star is Born*	4,000,000
20.	Miley Cyrus (and others)	*Hannah Montana*	3,900,000

The Best-Selling 100 Albums of All Time

	Artist	Album	Sales
1.	Michael Jackson	*Thriller*	31,100,000
2.	Led Zeppelin	*Led Zeppelin IV* (Four Symbols)	24,450,000
3.	Pink Floyd	*The Wall*	24,300,000
4.	Shania Twain	*Come On Over*	22,950,000
5.	AC/DC	*Back In Black*	22,050,000
6.	The Beatles	*The Beatles* (The White Album)	20,250,000
7.	Alanis Morissette	*Jagged Little Pill*	19,750,000
8.	Fleetwood Mac	*Rumours*	19,700,000
9.	Whitney Houston	*The Bodyguard*	19,400,000
10.	Pink Floyd	*Dark Side Of The Moon*	18,500,000
11.	Eagles	*Hotel California*	17,900,000
12.	Boston	*Boston*	17,600,000
13.	Guns N' Roses	*Appetite For Destruction*	17,100,000
14.	Bruce Springsteen	*Born In The U.S.A.*	16,500,000
15.	Hootie & the Blowfish	*Cracked Rear View*	16,300,000
16.	Garth Brooks	*No Fences*	16,200,000
17.	Metallica	*Metallica*	15,700,000
18.	Led Zeppelin	*Physical Graffiti*	15,600,000
19.	Original Soundtrack	*Saturday Night Fever*	15,450,000
20.	Santana	*Supernatural*	15,150,000
21.	Garth Brooks	*Double Live*	15,050,000
22.	Meatloaf	*Bat Out Of Hell*	15,000,000
23.	Adele	*21*	14,800,000
24.	Prince and the Revolution	*Purple Rain*	14,400,000
25.	Whitney Houston	*Whitney Houston*	14,350,000
26.	Backstreet Boys	*Backstreet Boys*	14,200,000
27.	Bon Jovi	*Slippery When Wet*	14,150,000
28.	Garth Brooks	*Ropin' The Wind*	14,150,000
29.	Britney Spears	*...Baby One More Time*	14,100,000
30.	Phil Collins	*No Jacket Required*	13,950,000
31.	The Beatles	*Abbey Road*	13,750,000
32.	Original Soundtrack	*Dirty Dancing*	13,550,000
33.	Dire Straits	*Brothers In Arms*	13,500,000
34.	Backstreet Boys	*Millennium*	13,400,000
35.	Bruce Springsteen & The E Street Band	*Live/1975–85*	13,250,000
36.	Pearl Jam	*Ten*	13,250,000
37.	Celine Dion	*Falling Into You*	13,200,000
38.	Def Leppard	*Hysteria*	13,050,000
39.	Michael Jackson	*Bad*	12,950,000
40.	The Beatles	*Sgt. Pepper's Lonely Hearts Club Band*	12,750,000
41.	U2	*The Joshua Tree*	12,750,000
42.	Dixie Chicks	*Wide Open Spaces*	12,750,000
43.	Norah Jones	*Come Away With Me*	12,700,000
44.	Led Zeppelin	*Led Zeppelin II*	12,700,000
45.	Matchbox 20	*Yourself Or Someone Like You*	12,400,000
46.	Shania Twain	*The Woman In Me*	12,350,000
47.	Kenny G	*Breathless*	12,250,000
48.	Original Soundtrack	*Forrest Gump*	12,250,000
49.	Kid Rock	*Devil Without A Cause*	12,100,000
50.	Eminem	*The Marshall Mathers LP*	12,050,000
51.	Boyz II Men	*II*	12,050,000
52.	Celine Dion	*Let's Talk About Love*	12,050,000
53.	Nirvana	*Nevermind*	12,000,000
54.	Shania Twain	*Up!*	11,750,000
55.	Mariah Carey	*Music Box*	11,650,000
56.	Green Day	*Dookie*	11,600,000
57.	Led Zeppelin	*Houses Of The Holy*	11,500,000
58.	TLC	*CrazySexyCool*	11,500,000
59.	George Michael	*Faith*	11,450,000
60.	Eric Clapton	*Unplugged*	11,450,000
61.	Jewel	*Pieces Of You*	11,300,000
62.	*NSYNC	*No Strings Attached*	11,220,000
63.	Eminem	*The Eminem Show*	11,050,000
64.	Madonna	*Like A Virgin*	11,050,000
65.	Carole King	*Tapestry*	11,000,000
66.	Lionel Richie	*Can't Slow Down*	11,000,000
67.	Usher	*Confessions*	10,950,000
68.	Linkin Park	*Hybrid Theory*	10,900,000
69.	Mariah Carey	*Daydream*	10,700,000
70.	The Notorius B.I.G.	*Life After Death*	10,700,000
71.	Original Soundtrack	*The Lion King*	10,650,000
72.	MC Hammer	*Please Hammer, Don't Hurt 'Em*	10,650,000
73.	No Doubt	*Tragic Kingdom*	10,600,000
74.	Van Halen	*Van Halen*	10,550,000
75.	Led Zeppelin	*Led Zeppelin*	10,500,000
76.	Whitney Houston	*Whitney*	10,500,000
77.	Van Halen	*1984*	10,500,000
78.	Dixie Chicks	*Fly*	10,450,000
79.	Creed	*Human Clay*	10,400,000
80.	Billy Joel	*The Stranger*	10,350,000
81.	Original Soundtrack	*Top Gun*	10,300,000
82.	The Spice Girls	*Spice*	10,150,000
83.	Britney Spears	*Oops!... I Did It Again*	10,100,000
84.	Will Smith	*Big Willie Style*	9,650,000
85.	The Smashing Pumpkins	*Mellon Collie And The Infinite Sadness*	9,600,000
86.	Michael Jackson	*Dangerous*	9,550,000
87.	U2	*Achtung Baby*	9,500,000
88.	Lauryn Hill	*The Miseducation Of Lauryn Hill*	9,500,000
89.	Original Soundtrack	*Grease*	9,400,000
90.	Mariah Carey	*Mariah Carey*	9,350,000
91.	Stevie Wonder	*Songs In The Key Of Life*	9,300,000
92.	Michael Bolton	*Time, Love & Tenderness*	9,250,000
93.	Original Soundtrack	*Footloose*	9,200,000
94.	Madonna	*True Blue*	9,200,000
95.	Billy Ray Cyrus	*Some Gave All*	9,200,000
96.	Destiny's Child	*The Writing's On The Wall*	9,200,000
97.	REO Speedwagon	*Hi Infidelity*	9,150,000
98.	Def Leppard	*Pyromania*	9,150,000
99.	Ace Of Base	*The Sign*	9,150,000
100.	Boyz II Men	*Cooleyhighharmony*	9,150,000